International Standard Book Number: 0-226-72167-1
Library of Congress Catalog Number: 57-6271

THE UNIVERSITY OF CHICAGO PRESS, CHICAGO 60637
Cambridge University Press, London, N.W. 1, England
The University of Chicago Press, Ltd., London

DEVELOPING PERMANENT INTEREST IN READING

Proceedings of the Annual Conference on Reading
Held at the University of Chicago, 1956
Volume XVIII

Compiled and Edited by

HELEN M. ROBINSON

THE UNIVERSITY OF CHICAGO PRESS

Supplementary Educational Monographs

PUBLISHED IN CONJUNCTION WITH *The School Review*
AND *The Elementary School Journal*

NUMBER 84 · DECEMBER 1956

154661

PREFACE

*

THE Nineteenth Annual Reading Conference focused on various aspects of the challenging topic, "Developing Permanent Interest in Reading." It is true that this topic has received some consideration during the preceding eighteen conferences, but this year it was the central theme.

Each paper presented at the general sessions was designed to set forth basic principles and to provide information. The papers at the sectional meetings, at levels from kindergarten through junior college, were prepared by teachers who could share their practical experiences with conferees. Furthermore, each sectional meeting served as a forum, at which teachers raised questions and discussed procedures and materials. A special section for administrators and supervisors considered means for improving staff competence in promoting reading interests.

The proceedings of seventeen conferences have been published under the following titles:

I wish to express my sincere appreciation to the scores of persons who assisted in planning the program, in preparing and presenting papers, and in numerous other ways. My special gratitude goes to the members of the conference advisory committee and especially to Dr. William S. Gray.

HELEN M. ROBINSON

* Copies of titles marked with asterisks are available. All other volumes are out of print.

TABLE OF CONTENTS

✳

INTRODUCTION

✳

HELEN M. ROBINSON

✳

THE theme of this conference, "Developing Permanent Interest in Reading," was chosen because of the genuine concern, both inside and outside the profession, for promoting the habit of turning to reading as an intellectual and emotional resource. For example, Grambs reports that the Committee on Reading Development made this recommendation, along with others: "Professional conferences of educators and librarians also could contribute much to arousing teachers' awareness of their responsibilities for developing the reading habits of students."[1] Many other groups and individuals have supported this recommendation.

Furthermore, often-heard criticisms of the teaching of reading at all educational levels are that children and youth do not read to any extent and that the quality of that which *is* read remains exceedingly inadequate. Many critics point out that schools are falling short in promoting an abiding interest in reading.

SUMMARY OF CRITICISMS

Although criticism of the teaching of reading has been voiced for many decades, lay criticism has increased steadily since World War II. In 1952 Gray and Iverson summarized the lay criticisms of the schools with special reference to reading. At that time they concluded that "neither the public nor the profession is entirely satisfied with the results thus far achieved in teaching reading."[2] Among the many dissatisfactions discussed is one dealing with our theme:

Of the many current criticisms of reading, none is more persistent than the assertion that schools are failing to promote wide interest in personal reading among children and youth. Stated differently, the view prevails among many parents that pupils have either lost, or have never acquired, the art of reading regularly for recreation, stimulation, and enlightenment. Many teachers and librarians concur in these judgments. As a rule, neither lay nor professional critics present convincing evidence in support of their views.[3]

After making a careful appraisal of the available research, Gray and Iverson conclude that there is more independent reading in the earlier grades than formerly and that, in the upper grades, almost all pupils do some free reading but that the amount decreases in the high-school years. Concerning the quality of reading,

[1] Jean D. Grambs, *The Development of Lifetime Reading Habits*, p. 4. New York: National Book Committee, Inc. (24 West Fortieth Street), [1954].

[2] William S. Gray and William J. Iverson, "What Should Be the Profession's Attitude toward Lay Criticism of the Schools?" *Elementary School Journal*, LIII (September, 1952), 15.

[3] *Ibid.*, pp. 27–28.

they conclude that never before has so much material of poor quality, and of good quality, been published and read by children and youth.

The years since this penetrating article was published have brought increased lay criticism and concern. Perhaps it reached a peak with the publication of Flesch's book.[4] This book kindled frenzied arguments among specialists, school personnel, parents, and publishers of magazines and newspapers. As the smoke has cleared, there has emerged a more rational and constructive attack on the problems of teaching reading, now faced by schools. In addition to increased care in appraising methods of teaching children to read, exploration of a wide variety of factors related to the use of reading has become prominent.

A recent example is the article by Dupee entitled "Can Johnny's Parents Read?" In his discussion of the heated arguments about methods of teaching reading, Dupee states:

I would like to suggest that this battle is a sham, and the victory is not to be won on the present terrain at all. . . . Johnny is likely to do what is honored in his own home and what is honored in the society of which he is becoming aware. And ours is a society which does not honor reading. We turn our own depreciation of reading to indignation and blame the school.[5]

To support his conclusion, Dupee cites evidence secured by the American Institute of Public Opinion, showing that, in 1937, 29 per cent of all adults in this country were reading books, in contrast to 17 per cent today. In addition,

he states that only 13 per cent of our citizens borrow books from public libraries, and, according to the judgment of librarians, about 5 per cent of the books borrowed are good reading.

A second example of recent criticism of the schools comes from an exchange teacher, based on her experiences. She came here from India to learn how American schools use materials which coincide with children's interests. Following her observations and experimentation, she concluded that our children are "suffering from intellectual malnutrition."[6] Her solution to the problem of discipline and to creating interest was to supply "some solid intellectual subject matter." She believed that American educational experts had made the error of "equating interest with entertainment."[7] Thus she preferred to rely "upon two powerful allies: children's natural intellectual curiosity and their desire to succeed."[8]

On the basis of the criticism just cited, we may well ask: "What is the nature of children's interests?" "Where do they arise?" "What factors foster reading interests, and which kill interest?" Answers to these and similar questions are sorely needed by school personnel at present.

Few of our teachers and parents today will agree with Dupee when he says:

To presume that public education under public control will conspire with Johnny to reverse the American trend to illiteracy is nonsense. We are asking the next generation to exhibit a virtue of mind which we our-

---

[4] Rudolf Flesch, *Why Johnny Can't Read.* New York: Harper & Bros., 1955.

[5] Gordon Dupee, "Can Johnny's Parents Read?" *Saturday Review,* XXXIX (June 2, 1956), 5.

[6] Frances V. Rummell, "Are U.S. School Children Being Cheated?" *Reader's Digest,* LXVIII (June, 1956), 43.

[7] *Ibid.*, p. 43.

[8] *Ibid.*, p. 44.

selves have debased through indifference and disuse.[9]

Furthermore, many would challenge Dupee's reference to "a trend to illiteracy," since reports show a high level of literacy in this country. But "literacy" has usually been defined as the limited ability to read and write or the ability to read at a given level, perhaps fourth grade. Are we approaching a new era in which, to be literate, one must be able to use reading for important purposes? In other words, is the ability to go through the mechanics of reading a real asset, or is the ultimate value of instruction the ability to read for personal and social purposes?

The trend toward a new emphasis was described at the recent meeting of the International Reading Association. William S. Gray pointed out that society is now demanding that children read better than their parents and that schools learn more about better ways to help children read for personal purposes and for solving urgent problems in society. If schools are to meet this challenge, obviously they must do more than just teach the mechanics of reading, important as these are. During the school years, from the kindergarten to the end of formal education, children and youth must be stimulated by being given contact with all kinds of printed matter; they must experience satisfaction in reading, rather than frustration; they must return again and again to print to form the habit of reading. In other words, children and young people must develop a permanent interest in reading if they are to be really literate in the newer sense.

SIGNIFICANCE OF THE THEME

The aforementioned criticisms, and especially the most recent ones, point up important problems for the schools today. We are challenged to change the reading habits of today's masses. Can we do it? If so, how?

We are challenged to produce a new kind of literacy. We are challenged to be certain that youth who leave school have come to "understand that reading a serious book is an experience between author and reader that is frequently more intense, more demanding, and more rewarding than most of the face-to-face encounters made during a given day."[10]

THEME OF THE CONFERENCE

This conference was planned with the hope and expectation that we might be stimulated and guided toward the solution of some of the vital problems in developing a lasting interest in reading. The theme, "Developing Permanent Interest in Reading," was not so worded by accident. It was reasoned that, if young people develop an interest *in* reading, they will follow varying paths in the pursuit of their goal. In other words, the purposes for reading, and the topics read, will be individual matters—but the interest in reading will be common to all.

The conference papers consider the nature of reading interests in the first chapter. Of special significance is the distinction made between interests, preferences, and needs. Furthermore, the psychological and the sociological bases for children's interests, particularly reading interests, are explored.

The second and third chapters are concerned with the goals that schools should seek to achieve. A description of the reading interests of selected adults provides a background for the over-all

[9] Gordon Dupee, *op. cit.*, p. 34.
[10] Jean D. Grambs, *op. cit.*, p. 5.

goals of the schools and for specific goals at each stage of reading growth.

The fourth chapter includes an appraisal of how well schools are achieving the goals set up. In chapter v research and experience are synthesized to present conclusions about the reading interests of children and young people of different ages.

Chapters vi and vii turn the reader's attention to the purposes for developing reading interests. These purposes are stated as both personal and social in nature.

Chapters viii through xv emphasize various agencies which influence reading interests. Although it is recognized that these agencies often restrict interests, generally the papers adopt the positive position, pointing out clearly how each may foster reading interests. Among the agencies considered are the mass media, such as films, radio, and television; the school, including instruction in both the basic reading program and the content areas; the home, and the school and public library.

Chapter xvi explains the steps taken to promote an interest in reading in a school where students had previously rejected reading. The author shows the necessity for co-ordinating classroom procedures, the selection of materials, and the use of library books with students' reading levels, social backgrounds, and personal interests.

Chapter xvii includes seven papers designed primarily for administrators and supervisors. In each paper, emphasis is placed on ways to help the school staff so that each member may make a maximal contribution to the development of abiding interest in reading.

The last chapter offers information about outstanding books for children and young people which were published during the last half of 1955 and the first half of 1956.

The papers are designed to suggest some principles and procedures for developing a permanent interest in reading. Furthermore, they point up the fact that concentrated efforts are needed on the part of all school personnel, parents, and allied agencies to change the reading habits of today's masses so as to meet the challenge of society.

CHAPTER I

THE NATURE OF READING INTERESTS

✳

PSYCHOLOGICAL ASPECTS

JACOB W. GETZELS

✳

LET me confess at once that my field of specialized competence is not the field of reading. But I do have a vital personal and professional interest in the problems raised by the theme of this conference. For I believe, first, that, if we do not succeed in engaging our children's interest in reading, they will not learn to read; and, second, that the reading interests our children acquire and maintain are a matter of crucial concern to a democratic society.

CURRENT DEFICIENCES IN DEFINITION, THEORY, AND ANALYSIS

Despite the crucial nature of the problem, current work in the area of reading interests does not seem promising. It is clear that both the empirical effort and the speculative writing are at present peculiarly deficient in three factors which are, from my point of view, the *sine qua non* for growth in a given field of inquiry. These factors are precision of *definition*, rigor of *theory*, and depth of *analysis*.

What do we mean by the concept of "interest"? I found a half-dozen significantly different definitions, and my inquiry was by no means exhaustive. Sometimes an "interest" is defined simply as a personal preference, some-times as a trait of character, sometimes as a positive attitude, sometimes as a feeling of pleasantness accompanying a particular behavior, sometimes as an individual need or drive, sometimes as a value characteristic of an object in the environment. My quarrel is not with the rightness or wrongness of any of these definitions. My quarrel rather is that the data obtained in terms of one definition are used interchangeably as if they were appropriate to any definition. And this leads to confusion in research, in speculation, and, I venture to add, in practice.

The second problem is one of theory. This is an unpopular subject, and I would like to say just as little as I can about it here. But it is a subject that is at the very heart of both research and practice, and we cannot avoid it. There is a misconception among educators that what is theoretical is not practical and what is practical has nothing to do with what is theoretical. Nothing can be further from the truth. The theoretical and the practical are necessarily interrelated aspects of professional behavior. The educator whose behavior is based merely on pat techniques for specific situations is operating in an intellectual vacuum. Intelligent action cannot be maximized

5

without some guiding principles or theory, however tentatively these may be maintained.

Finally, I should like to say something about the problem of analysis. While progress is being made in this area, much of the work remains of the following sort. The teacher or the researcher decides that a particular book represents a particular meaning or interest. Every time a child takes out the book, it is attributed to the operation of this interest. Now it can readily be shown that there is no one-to-one relationship between the meaning or interest which *we* may attribute to a book and the meaning or interest which the actual *reader* attributes to it. We are dealing with shabby data indeed if we make an analysis based on a one-to-one relationship between the manifest nature of a book and the nature of a reader's interest in the book.

I should like now to direct my remarks to what seem to me to be three major issues in the psychology of interests, especially as they affect reading: (1) What is the nature of interests? (2) What are the determinants of interests? (3) How do interests find expression in reading? In effect, we shall be dealing with the problems I have raised: those of definition, theory, and analysis.

THE NATURE OF INTERESTS

Every human being has a characteristic *style of life*. He is not only a creature of his biological drives or animal necessities, but he strives to fulfil wants that have no apparent relationship to the maintaining of merely physiological well-being. He seeks to know and to discover, to create and to master. An artist perseveres despite rebuffs; an anchorite forswears all earthly joys; a test pilot daily risks life and limb. Each is expressing a particular system of interests constituting his *style of life* or *basic identity*.

If we study the actions of an infant, we observe that initially his entire behavior seems given over to the gratification of primary drives. But in due course there is a change; he no longer remains at rest when fed, cleaned, and made comfortable. On the contrary, he now reaches out and becomes absorbed in the world around him. The infant has become a child; he is gaining a pattern of characteristic dispositions, a distinctive style of behavior, a personal identity. By the time the child comes to school, he does not come as a *tabula rasa* to be written upon as the curriculum directs. He comes with a system of interests, which determine in a very large measure what he will see and hear, what he will remember and forget, what he will think and say, and what he will do gladly and what he will do only under duress.

The critical difference between what he learns and what he does not learn in the classroom will in most cases be more a function of his interests than of his intelligence. The child who remembers the batting averages, to the third decimal place, of a dozen members of his favorite baseball team may also be the one who cannot remember the single date of the discovery of America. It is silly to think of him as having baseball intelligence and history stupidity. What he has is baseball *interest* and history *indifference*.

It is in terms of these observations that I should like now to examine more formally the nature and meaning of the concept of interest. Let me, then, first differentiate the intent of the concept of interest from its acquired quasi-synonyms. In this way we may both make clear the specific meaning of the term itself and also point to the misapplication of some of the current definitions. Despite present usage, an interest, it seems to me, is not merely a preference. I have a preference for broccoli over asparagus. I have no interest in either. I would not expend a minuscule effort to learn more about the one than about the other. The difference between a preference and an interest is that the preference is relatively passive, while the interest is inevitably dynamic. A preference is a readiness to *receive* one object as against another; it does not induce us to seek out the object. In contrast, the basic nature of an interest is that it does induce us to seek out particular objects and activities.

Again, despite present usage, an interest, it seems to me, is not merely a positive attitude. I have, for example, a positive attitude toward the Eskimos. I confess that I have no particular interest in them. In contrast, I have a decidedly negative attitude toward the Soviets. But I am keenly interested in them. An attitude implies merely the *readiness* to react in a particular direction with respect to the given object. We do not ordinarily speak of being driven by an attitude; we are necessarily driven by our interests.

Finally, I want to make clear the distinction between a drive and an interest. A drive has its source in a specific physiological disequilibrium, and the individual seeks conditions that will reduce the drive or need. An interest has its source in experience and challenges us to exert ourselves even though there is no necessity in any biological sense. Technically speaking, we may say a drive is a function largely of our *instinctual* processes, an interest largely of our *ego* processes.

Against this background, we may now attempt a working definition of interest. *An interest is a characteristic disposition, organized through experience, which impels an individual to seek out particular objects, activities, understandings, skills, or goals for attention or acquisition.*

THE DETERMINANTS OF INTERESTS

What are the sources of these characteristic dispositions of individuals which we call "interests"? What determines why one man will give himself unstintingly to one goal; his neighbor, to another? Although our knowledge of the foundations of human interests is meager, we may identify the following seven major determinants.

1. *Constitutional givens.*—Certain factors in our genetic structure carry with them varying potentialities for directing a person toward one interest as against another. The obese child is not so likely to acquire an interest in ballet, for example, as is the slender child. And of course constitutional differences in the sex of children make a difference in the interests they can develop.

2. *Favored capacities.*—Individuals are born with different capacities. There are differences in reaction time, in energy level, in color vision, in strength, in intelligence, in motor co-ordination, and so on and on. The relationship between capacity and interest may never be disentangled; it may very well be another of the chicken-or-egg problems. But there is little doubt that capacities are related to interests and that, in general, special fitness does make the acquisition of related interests congenial.

3. *Personality structure.*—"Personality," as frequently used, is such a broad term that an individual's interests may be considered an integral part of his personality structure. In this sense it is silly

to talk of personality as a determinant of interests, for an interest is itself a characteristic of personality. But if "personality" is defined in Murray's terms as a system of conscious and unconscious *needs*, then personality, like constitutional and capacity factors, is of course a determinant of interests. The individual is driven to the satisfaction of these needs —the need for affiliation, or for achievement, or seclusion—and the satisfaction of these needs will inevitably influence the interests the individual will acquire. But it must be made clear that, in this formulation, "needs" and "interests" are not synonymous, for the same need may find expression in numerous differential interests, depending on the other determinants. Need for *achievement* may, for example, find expression in the arts, sciences, politics, and so on. The need is the same; the interests, different.

4. *Sociocultural determinants.*—This class of determinants has a particular significance. They not only contribute to the idiosyncrasies of individual interests, but they establish the uniformity of interests among individuals who are members of the same enduring groups. The interest patterns of Americans as a group, for example, seem similar when contrasted with the interest patterns of Japanese as a group. And within the American population itself there are geographic, ethnic, and social-class divisions, each again with intragroup similarities and intergroup differences. The kinds of neighbors we have, the kinds of institutions to which we belong, the kinds of schools which we attend—all play their part in determining the interests we develop.

5. *Role requirements.*—The human organism is not born into the world with a ready-made set of socially appropriate behaviors or values. Rather he is born into a world that already has social norms to which he must conform. The child learns, on the one hand, to renounce, suppress, and redirect drives and behavioral impulses that are at variance with proper social standards. He learns, on the other hand, to acquire interests and values which are in conformity with expectations of the society in which he lives. He comes to realize, for example, that there are certain interests appropriate to his age and sex roles. At age five it is acceptable to play house; at age fifteen it is not. A girl may continue to play with dolls for quite some time; a boy must drop this interest sooner.

6. *Family influences.*—The family is the most important single factor in our development. The process of socialization is essentially a family function, and all the sociocultural and role determinants are brought to bear upon the child through the agency of the family constellation.

7. *Accidental events.*—In addition to the constitutional determinants and the forces which confront individuals who live in the same physical environment and who play the same roles, there are things that "just happen" to people. Even casual contacts of relatively brief duration may be crucial in determining whether a person's life will proceed along one path or another and whether he will acquire one pattern of interests or another.

THE EXPRESSION OF INTEREST THROUGH READING

These determinants provide the context for understanding the reading interests of children; for reading interests are determined by the same factors that we have remarked upon as underlying interests in general and have outlined in the preceding section.

It must be emphasized that teachers, librarians, and reading specialists do not alone determine whether a child will read and what he will read. They are one of the determinants—they are not the whole show, and, in fact, they are ordinarily not even the most decisive part of the show. For how do children develop one interest as against another from the range of interests that society nominally makes available to them? Learning, imitation, conscious emulation—*in* school and *out*—surely play a part. But the fundamental mechanism by which we interiorize interests is *identification*. The child's struggle to integrate the self-image from his piecemeal perceptions of what he is and who he is lead him to view himself as one with another person. The original and most important objects of identification are the mother or mother-surrogate and the father or father-surrogate. If reading is important to these figures, reading will ordinarily also be important to the child. For in making his identifications, the child attempts to incorporate their values and interests.

We may identify five types of interests which the child will attempt to take over:

1. Instrumental interests—that is, dispositions to attend to certain kinds of problems, to acquire particular kinds of educational and vocational skills.

2. Status interests—dispositions to hold certain types of activities, events, or persons as particularly admirable or prestigeful.

3. Transcendent interests—dispositions to attend to certain kinds of ultimate ethical

and religious ends, to seek out certain kinds of spiritual experiences.

4. Aesthetic interests—dispositions to seek out particular kinds of activities, events, and objects as beautiful and harmonious.

5. Recreational interests—dispositions to seek out diversion and relief from tension through certain kinds of activities.[1]

It is plain that reading can be an integral part of these types of interests. Whether it will or not is another matter, and this depends on the nature of the identifications the child has made with his parents and the identifications he has continued to make as he has grown with other important figures in his environment; with playmates, older siblings, movie stars, local heroes, societal prestige persons, and so on.

It is here that the teacher becomes a significant figure. He occupies a high status position for children and is perceived as a powerful person. By means of the identification process the child incorporates the expectations, values, and interests of the teacher. And of course, if the teacher has a genuine interest in reading himself (I do not mean only *teaches* reading), the child will interiorize this interest. One cannot so much *teach* interests as *offer appropriate models for identification*.

This is not to say that identification with the teacher may not present serious problems. For incorporating the teacher's interests may require rejection of other interests, including those of mother and father especially, as is not infrequently the case if the values of the home and of the school are not in accord. And this is of course the psychological dilemma involving interests and education. Everyone may agree on the need for reading; not everyone agrees on what are appropriate reading interests.

[1] I wish to acknowledge the debt of this section of the paper to D. Waples, B. Berelson, and F. R. Bradshaw, *What Reading Does to People*, Chicago: University of Chicago Press, 1940; and to M. L. Hutt and D. R. Miller, "Value Interiorization and Democratic Education," *Journal of Social Issues*, V (1949), 31–43.

SOCIOLOGICAL ASPECTS

WILLIAM S. GRAY

✳

THE preceding discussion has made us keenly aware that reading interests are influenced by all aspects of personality. Obviously, many types of experience help to mold the interests and curiosities that lead to reading. Because of their great importance, I have been asked to focus attention on some of the social forces that influence reading interests of children and adults.

✳ SOCIAL FORCES THAT INFLUENCE READING

Such an approach to the study of reading interests is by no means new. For decades teachers have recognized that a child's social environment and relationships are potent factors in determining his attitude toward reading and what he may want to read about. As commonly reported, these attitudes are acquired through contacts in the home, the neighborhood, the church, and other social institutions.

During recent years sociologists and cultural anthropologists have made intensive studies of the personal characteristics, behavior patterns, understandings, attitudes, and interests of various groups in our country. They have found that the most important social influences on both children and adults stem from three sources: the common experiences of all who participate in our American culture; the distinctive experiences that are acquired through being reared in groups that occupy different levels in the social structure; and the unique experiences shared by those belonging to different ethnic or nationality groups.

It is our fond hope that, as a result of these and other types of experiences, all boys and girls will develop into good American citizens with desirable reading interests and habits. The social experiences acquired, however, vary widely among children or do not play with equal force upon them. As a result, when they enter school, children differ notably in their understandings, beliefs, behavior patterns, and inner drives. Experience teaches that they differ also in their predispositions toward reading and in the things they want to read about.

As revealed by the studies reported, the most vital social experiences in the early development of children are those secured as members of their respective social classes and peer groups. During preschool years the essential aspects of a given class culture "are transferred through the subtle processes of informal learning from the parents to the child."[1] What the child learns at home is reinforced and expanded as he participates in the life of the community. The social experiences thus derived set the stage for his later development by establishing distinctive behavior patterns, attitudes, and interests. They also reveal the roles he

[1] A. B. Hollingshead, *Elmtown's Youth*, p. 442. New York: John Wiley & Sons, 1949.

10

can play, how to play them, and the rewards and punishments he may expect, and they accord to him a specific status position as a member of his group. He is thus being molded into a personality that is a product of his experiences and a determiner of later behavior.

CHARACTERISTICS OF DIFFERENT
SOCIAL CLASSES

The foregoing statements assume large importance because of the wide differences in the basic characteristics of the groups in which children are reared. Although as a nation we tend to reject the idea that people occupy different levels in the social structure, experience and the results of research supply striking evidence that such is the case. Three levels are generally recognized, as evidenced by the wide use of the terms "upper," "middle," and "lower" classes. Investigators usually subdivide these into five or six levels, which vary widely in size among communities. As a background for understanding their influence on reading interests, let us examine briefly the characteristics of five classes which were identified by Hollingshead in his study of Elmtown. The descriptions that are given will doubtless not apply specifically to any of the communities in which my readers teach! Rather, they are presented to illustrate the diversity of conditions that help to mold the attitudes and interests of children.

Group I occupied the highest level in Elmtown and included from 1 to 2 per cent of its population. The families of this group attain their social position through inherited wealth and heredity. In almost all cases they trace their origin to early American stock and believe that essential abilities and traits are largely inherited. Because great importance is attached to leisure-time and social activities, only a limited amount of time is devoted to earning a living. Financial advisers take care of such matters. Families in this group live in spacious homes and travel a great deal, spending summers in the North and winters in the South. The requirements of the social code of their class are followed rigidly. They relate to such matters as clothes, stationery, and manners. The chief training given by parents to children pertains to these matters.

Members of Group I attach only moderate importance to education except as it prepares the individual to play the social role of his group. The average number of children per family is fewer than two. The children receive their training chiefly from tutors, private or public schools, and in finishing schools for girls and colleges for boys. As implied by this description, the children of this group are reared in an exclusive environment that inculcates distinctive attitudes, interests, and behavior patterns.

Group II included about 7 per cent of the population of Elmtown and occupied the first level below Group I. Most of the families belong to early pioneer stock. They attained their position in the social structure either through effort or through inheritance. The men are vigorously engaged in business or the professions and are outstanding civic leaders. They possess a sense of personal assurance, self-mastery, and knowledge of the way in which leadership is exercised. In addition to managing their homes, with full-time help, the wives are very active also in club and civic-improvement activities.

Both parents of families in Group II devote some time to the proper rearing of their children and to inculcating the dominant ideals of their social group. Most of them belong to church, provide leadership in its various activities, and see to it that their children go to Sunday school. They attach great importance to education, take genuine interest in the school progress of their children, and strive to provide a college education for them. They send their children to carefully selected camps and provide social contacts for them with children of other parents of Group II. Whereas the children are somewhat sheltered socially, they are reared in a stimulating environment, which provides broad experiences and aspirations on which the schools can build in promoting reading interests.

Group III was the so-called "middle class" in Elmtown and was the largest single group. Only about a third of the families of this group trace their ancestry to early American stock. They see Group II above them and aspire to membership in it. The family income is earned largely by the husband, but his earnings may be supplemented by those of the wife. About half own small businesses or farms or are members of some profession. The others work for wages or a salary. The income of most families is sufficient for essential conveniences and comforts, but there is little to invest in income-producing enterprises. Most families live in houses of five, six, or seven rooms. They belong to church, study groups, and missionary societies, and the children go to Sunday school.

Although education is highly respected in Group III, only 63 per cent of the women and 26 per cent of the men had completed a high-school education. Most parents urge their children to succeed in school work, and many strive to make it possible for them to go to college. Both parents aid in the home training of their children. They teach them early that their future success depends on their own efforts. Because of the heavy obligations of their parents in earning a living and in keeping house, the children have much freedom. Although many of the latter belong to Scout and other organizations, they acquire most of their social contacts on neighborhood playgrounds and at public recreational centers. As a result their experiences and interests are more or less different from, and their attitudes more democratic than, those of children in either Group I or II. Furthermore, their life-purposes are, as a rule, not so specific or so well defined.

Group IV comprised about one-fourth of the population in Elmtown. Its members are characterized as poor, hard working, and honest. They are aware of their inferior position in the socio-economic scale and resent it. The men work on farms, in mines, and in shops. The wives assist in earning a living in about 30 per cent of the families. Savings are meager, and only about 35 per cent of the families own their homes. One-third of the homes are broken. The wife does all the housework and is discriminated against if she attempts to join women's clubs or other social organizations. The men do not belong to civic organizations but do join fraternal organizations. As a rule, religion is either shunned or embraced enthusiastically.

Among members of Group IV, marriage occurs early, and there are on the average 4.3 children per family. Formal education of the parents is limited to elementary- and secondary-school training. Many left school during the elementary-school period. They want their children to go to high school but are not altogether sure of the value of an education and often let them drop out of school. Practically all leisure time is spent at home, at the movies, or in the park. On Saturday evenings and on holidays everyone is on the street, listening to the latest gossip, scandal, and jokes. The children are given wide freedom at all times to play on the streets and in open lots and parks, usually in groups, cliques, or gangs. Here they make a place for themselves the hard way and often acquire information, attitudes, interests, and aspirations which run counter to those which prove most effective in achieving the broader purposes of schooling and in cultivating reading interests.

Group V occupies the lowest rank in the prestige structure of Elmtown. Its members bitterly resent their lot but see no escape from it. They desire money and prestige but are not qualified to attain them by the usual methods. All ethnic groups are represented in this group. As viewed by the upper classes in Elmtown, the members of Group V have little respect for themselves or the law. They live in boxlike houses of about two rooms, which are occupied by the parents, children, "in-laws," grandparents, and often other families. As a group they are loud in speech, vulgar in manners, and indifferent as to their appearance. The men traditionally do only odd jobs, and the women do scrubbing, washing, and cleaning. Fortunately these conditions are gradually improving.

Marriage among members of Group V occurs in the middle and later teens. The average number of children is 5.6, the range being from 1 to 13. The parents spend much of their free time in low-class taverns and give little attention to the training of their children. Each child acquires his basic attitudes and interests as he seeks to satisfy his hunger and to maintain his status through physical aggression, and he derives immediate satisfaction through participation in the often questionable activities of associates.

READING AMONG DIFFERENT SOCIAL CLASSES

Let us examine next the reading interests and habits of the five groups described and the amount of stimulus to reading thus provided to children. The most important general conclusion justified by all the evidence secured is that the level occupied in the social structure influences reading interests and habits to a notable extent.

The members of Group I are by no means the widest readers. They prefer newspapers with a conservative policy, a good financial page, and a good treatment of national and international news. They are little concerned with local events other than society news and sports. The magazines read include *Time*, *Harper's*, *Atlantic*, and, to a lesser extent, the *New Yorker* and *Fortune*. The books read relate to biography, history, war, detective stories, social techniques, character novels, and standard classics. Obviously, the reading atmosphere is that of an adult leisure class. Because the children are rarely with the parents, the latter exert little direct influence on the reading interests of their children during their early years.

The adult members of Group II are the outstanding readers in American society. Because of their wide participation in business, professional, and civic-improvement activities, they have varied and compelling reading interests. As was true of Group I, they prefer conservative newspapers but read current events widely in an effort to find out what is behind the news and in search for clues to the solution of local and national problems. The magazines are similar in type to those read by Group I but include a wider range. These adults spend about thirty minutes a day in reading books— a time allotment which is twice that of Group I. The kinds of books read not only relate to their business, professional, and civic interests but include many which are recreational in character. A significant distinction between Group I and Group II is that most parents of the latter encourage their children to read. They also provide many attractive books for their children and take an active interest, insofar as time permits, in what they read.

Group III ranks next to Group II in variety of reading interests but devotes far less time to reading. The members of Group III prefer newspapers with a liberal policy and read less to secure a penetrating understanding of current trends and problems and more to learn about local events, accidents, and crime. They evidence widest interest in the more popular types of magazines, such as the *Saturday Evening Post* and *Woman's World*. They respect books but do little book-reading. However, some try to provide books for their children to read, encourage them to use the public library, and often discuss with them the books read both in school and at home.

The members of Group IV are very moderate readers. Most of them take, or have access to, a newspaper which has a liberal policy, gives much attention to local news, and is usually of the tabloid type. While reading, they focus attention on sensational stories, sports, and crime. They read magazines on an average of ten minutes a day, preferring such types as *True Story*, *Woman's World*, and *Needle Craft*. Not more than 5 per cent read books. Those read are usually de-

tective stories, adventure thrillers, and ardent romance. Because of the limited reading interests of parents, crowded home conditions, and distance to the public library, children receive little stimulus or guidance in reading outside of school. The responsibilities of the school are correspondingly great.

The adult members of Group V have very limited reading interests. They do read sensational stories and crime news in newspapers and look at pictures in lurid magazines that emphasize crime and sex. Rarely does a member of this group read a book. Furthermore, parents give their children little or no encouragement to read, and, from their home and neighborhood associations, the children acquire few interests and motives that lead directly to the kinds of personal reading normally expected of children in school.

SUMMARY AND IMPLICATIONS

The foregoing discussion has emphasized the fact that children grow up in radically different social and reading environments. As a result they enter school with varying backgrounds of experience and different attitudes, interests, and behavior patterns. Those acquired by one group are just as real and compelling as those acquired by other groups. The challenging problem which schools face is to start with these varied backgrounds and strive to promote levels of personal competence, good citizenship, and reading interests which are as high as the capabilities of each child permit.

As we reflect on the wide diversity in the attitudes and interests of the children reared in different social environments, we may rightly wonder if desirable reading interests and habits can be developed on the part of all. Much evidence exists to support the view that we have made distinct progress with pupils reared in Groups II and III. Our progress is due in part to the fact that the reading materials provided in school relate more closely to their background and interests than to those of the other groups. Thus far we have been far less successful in promoting keen interest in reading among children from Groups IV and V. This may be due, in some cases, to greater limitations in mental ability on the part of many and to slower progress in learning to read. Of major importance, however, is the fact that their previous experiences have not predisposed them toward reading or awakened interests that can easily be satisfied through reading.

That notable improvement can be made both at the adult level and among children has been demonstrated repeatedly. An analysis of the steps adopted indicates that the following requisites and guiding principles should be observed in further efforts to promote reading interests:

1. Teachers must be given a clear understanding of the nature and importance of the problem faced and be imbued with a genuine desire to do something about it.

2. Teachers should make detailed studies of the social environments of their various pupils and the nature of the understandings, attitudes, and interests of each child.

3. Each child must be accepted as he is, and a classroom atmosphere be developed in which the personality and the views of each are respected.

4. Through individual and group activities, pupil experiences must be expanded, and interests that can be satisfied through reading must be aroused.

5. The school must provide books that are sufficiently varied in theme and difficulty to enable each child to find many that make rich appeal and that can be read with reasonable ease and genuine pleasure.

6. The teacher must give the pupils freedom to choose books for personal reading, while making persistent efforts to cultivate interests that will insure a growing acquaintance with books which enrich experience, provide real pleasure and satisfaction, and help to provide for the developmental needs of children.

7. Underlying the effort to promote desirable reading interests should be a sound basic program which cultivates increasing competence among pupils to read with ease and understanding.

The foregoing suggestions provide merely a springboard for the intensive study that this conference will give to ways in which we may stimulate and guide the development of keen interest in reading among all the children of all the people.

CHAPTER II

AIMS TO BE ACHIEVED IN PROMOTING
READING INTERESTS

✳

THE READING INTERESTS OF MATURE READERS

B E R N I C E   R O G E R S

✳

WHAT do we know about the reading interests of mature readers? This is one of the areas with which research in reading has not usually been concerned. Many studies have been made of interests—children's interests, adolescents' interests, adults' interests—but none of the interests of mature readers.

This fact suggests that we may have been more concerned with minimal technical reading skill than with maximal growth in the use of reading as a tool for full social and intellectual growth. However, at a meeting of the International Reading Association in Chicago in May, 1956, Dr. William S. Gray described a shift during the last few decades from studies of the basic process of reading to the study of reading as an aid to social competence. Another sign of this change in emphasis is the growing body of research in the fields of journalism and communications, which is dealing with reading as part of a larger behavioral syndrome including social participation, opinion leadership, and the like.

In line with this trend is the study, recently completed by Dr. Gray and the writer,[1] which attempted to identify and interpret the interests of mature readers

and to determine the role that reading plays in the total process of the individual's growth toward intellectual and social maturity. By means of a case-study approach, two types of populations were sampled: (1) a cross-section of adults of varying amounts of education and (2) a carefully selected sample of adults whose professional skills and activities indicated that they might be highly competent readers.

Brief excepts from a few of the case studies will illustrate the types of material secured. These excerpts may also show something of the way in which interests grow—the kinds of roots from which they spring and the way in which they may be related to school experiences. Of course the names used are fictitious.

READING INTERESTS OF MATURE
READERS

Mr. Kent is an example of a man whose interests have led him, through reading, to levels of maturity far beyond those which might have been anticipated

[1] William S. Gray and Bernice Rogers, *Maturity in Reading*. Chicago: University of Chicago Press, 1956.

on the basis of the extent of his formal education. Mr. Kent did not go to college and had only two years of high-school education. When he left school, he secured work of a routine, uninspiring nature, which would not of itself have predisposed any man to read.

Today, however, Mr. Kent is a retired corporation executive with a background of reading which would match, if not exceed, that of many college graduates with higher degrees. He exhibits a philosophy of life, carefully developed, which serves as a focus in his choice of reading and as a frame of reference in his interpretation and reorganization of the ideas he gains from reading. He has accepted the civic responsibilities which he sees as part of his role as a citizen and has served with distinction as president of the board of education for a large, city school system. In all these activities, professional and civic, reading has been his guide and his tool. Through independent reading he learned the intricacies of finance in one of today's big businesses. Through independent reading he learned the essentials of his demanding position in relation to schools. Possibly most important, he has become, through reading, an alert citizen, well informed on social and political problems, not only in the United States, but in virtually every corner of the globe.

What was it that ignited the spark which led to this spiral of professional, intellectual, and moral growth? In Mr. Kent's case there was superior instruction in language arts in his high school. Scanty though his high-school education was in duration, it was high in quality. And remote as were his recollections of those distant years, this one thing still stood out in his memory: his contact with great literature in high school. It

was an experience of a positive nature—learning to know, in the sense of understanding and appreciating.

A second example is that of Mr. Ted Lauterbach, whose growth through reading was reinforced continually by his own awareness of his use of reading in the intellectual growing process. Mr. Lauterbach grew up in a small, uncultured, river town. He went to public schools, which he described quite simply as "lousy." His home background offered limited cultural stimulation. His mother had gone no farther than fourth grade in school; his father died when Ted was only a few years old. There were few books in the house, and little money. His interests were football and baseball and the corner "hangouts" of the boys with whom he chummed. He referred to all of them and to himself as "river rats." His clear recollection of this period of his life was that reading anything of the "better class" was sheer pain.

Yet today Mr. Lauterbach is one of the most broadly, most profoundly educated men among the scholars of a great university. He is a shrewd, insightful student of political and social problems all over the world, a philosopher of first rank in the field of higher education, a master of literature from Stendhal to Thomas Mann.

What happened? What miracle opened up to him the endless world of ideas? Quite simply—he read. He arrived in college by way of an unexpected scholarship, and fortunately it was a good college with a solid curriculum in Freshman English. He was confronted with something solid which he could take as his own and to which he could respond. Previously the attitudes of his peer group had been anti-intellectual, and the standards of the public schools had been set for the group, not for him. Now, in college, he was able to build his own intellectual edifice, stone on stone, hewing it out of the great ideas from great writers. He read Ruskin, Carlyle, Steele, Conrad, Thomas Aquinas, Chaucer, Dante, Dostoevski, Tolstoi, Stendhal. His innate intellectual competence, until then unstimulated, grasped this new and exciting world of ideas. An inner urge had been awakened which drove him on in a steady path of intellectual and social growth.

When the war took him to England, he became acquainted with the British newspapers. When he moved on to the Balkans, he took advantage of the situation to become steeped in the history of Balkan political developments. A copy of Hutchins' *Higher Learning in America* (Yale University Press, 1936) fell into his hands, and he remembers clearly coming to the decision of wanting to read more things of that type. He pursued novels, reading all of *Buddenbrooks* in German and all of the rest of Mann in English. The spark had been set to the tinder, and the fire of ideas drove him steadily forward. As he is still a very young man, it will continue to lead him to explore, as well as to broaden and deepen his interests in all directions.

Another case is that of the pastor of a large metropolitan church. Reverend Bettmann's early experiences were not so limited as Mr. Lauterbach's. But like Lauterbach, he found, in college, the reading which eventually set him on his life's course. He went to college planning to major in English. He took courses in English literature but found that Victorian poetry and Elizabethan drama left him unmoved. These works seemed to him to be cold and lifeless, with humanity excluded. Then he discovered the literature of theology, which brought human-

ity back into his world. His interest was awakened, and, like Mr. Lauterbach, once the crucial stimulus was felt, he moved on to ever wider and deeper interests. His current reading interests embrace all of history because he feels that he can secure information from other civilizations which will shed light on the problems of our own. He seeks a broad and deep background of understanding in all sorts of social problems so that he can interpret trends for his congregation. He accepts seriously his role as a community leader and as a world citizen. His competence as a leader derives from his wide reading and his untiring capacity for organizing, reorganizing, and rethinking the ideas he gains from a wealth of sources—from Gilbert Murray to Rollo May. His own comment is most revealing: "I'm living in this world, and I've got to live in it two years from now, three years from now. You try to interpret trends so you can interpret them for other people."

A case whose intellectual growth had an early start was Mr. Ellsworth. He attended good private schools. His parents were actively interested in political and social problems, and he heard enlightened and literate discussions of these problems at home. By the time he was fifteen, he was not only reading but writing at an adult level. His own intellectual ambitions were developed early enough so that he could plan to take part of his university work at Munich and obtain a broad base in political science and language. Mr. Ellsworth has become a top-level radio and television news-analyst, whose interests are as wide as the problems that confront our world. A quick survey of his usual reading gives some notion of their breadth and depth: *New York Times, New York Herald Tribune,*

Christian Science Monitor, Des Moines Register, three Chicago dailies, the *Washington Post Times-Herald*, the *Reporter;* popular magazines like *Life, Look*, and the *Saturday Evening Post* "to see what the public is getting"; the *Neue Züricher Zeitung*, the *Observer, Die Zeit* (Hamburg), the Kiplinger letters, the *American Political Science Review, London Calling*, the *Listener* (London), *Harper's*, the *Atlantic*, the *London Economist, U.S. News and World Report, United Nations World*, and *Foreign Affairs*. In addition, he reads many publications of the Federation of British Industries; the Council on Foreign Relations; and current reports on foundations, community projects, and the like. For relaxation he reads novels in French or German, either of which he uses as easily as English.

READING INTERESTS OF
AVERAGE ADULTS

Some of the average adults had a college education, some had part or all of a high-school education, while others had only eight years of school or even less. Here are a few thumbnail sketches.

Miss Masters is a high-school graduate. She is interested primarily in getting married and having a family. Her leisure-time preferences are movies and embroidery. Her reading consists of a few books which her pastor recommended as preparation for marriage and occasionally, about once a month, a look at the *Reader's Digest*. On Sunday she usually looks at the Sunday paper. She said that sometime she might "read up" on having a family. Other than that, she couldn't see how reading of any kind would be of any interest to her.

Mr. Gerve is an eighth-grade graduate, from the Ozark country. His vocational experiences have included a "hitch in the Navy," a try at farming, and the operation of a freight elevator. He reads the papers, he says, but his real interest is hot-rod cars, because his sons are interested in them. Sometimes he looks at a "book" about hot-rods, which his boys buy.

Mr. Rhodes, a merchandising executive, is a college graduate. He is interested primarily in his business, in providing security for his family, in giving his children a good education, and, in general, in doing the things his social crowd does. He and his wife belong to four book clubs, and he reads all the books the book clubs send.

Mr. Busby left school in ninth grade to go to work. He is now just about twenty years old and likes being a receiving-room clerk because "it's easy" and "you get sick leave" and "if you want to, you can work until you're seventy and then retire." His favorite leisure-time activities are movies and "ridin' around." He knows literally nothing of magazines and books. He looks at the newspaper to see if anybody he knows has been killed in any of the automobile accidents. He likes the funnies, and he says he reads the headlines.

These cases are typical of the unselected adults interviewed in the maturity study. It may be noted that they were all engaged in occupations which did not require wide or comprehensive reading.

CONCLUDING STATEMENT

It seems reasonable to conclude that the interests which are characteristic of mature readers are shared by a relatively small portion of the adult population. These mature interests relate closely to the over-all maturity of the individual. They include an area as wide as the world we live in, are characterized by the quality of social awareness, and are centered in persons other than the readers themselves. The mature and competent readers were uniformly aware of their role as responsible citizens in a changing and challenging world. In their lives, reading served the double purpose of alerting them to current problems and contributing to their participation in the solution of those problems.

Almost without exception, readers who were immature in all respects, including serious deficiency in basic reading skills, limited their interests to their own concerns, their own and their family's survival, the welfare and the status of the immediate family group. They were almost totally, even blissfully, ignorant of the problems confronting the society and the world around them.

When mature interests are thus compared with the interests of average adults, it becomes apparent that the learning process is much more than a superficial acquisition of information about a variety of topics. It is part of the much more profound process of the growth of the individual toward social,

intellectual, and emotional maturity. As has been shown in several of the case studies presented, the ideas in great literature have the power of stimulation and conversion. Thus, to the ready mind, reading can open up new worlds to conquer. It can result in a magnificently endless process of intellectual growth of a completely self-generating nature.

The latent power of great ideas to perform this miraculous change in people must cause some tremor of awe to flash through the soul of even the most experienced teacher. And, by the same token, the loss to society because of the never-consummated intellects who missed contact with the vital spark is equally awesome. The conclusion seems inescapable: we should never stop giving, in the public schools, the best and the most stimulating materials which we can find. Many of the students, perhaps most of them, will not be able to rise to the full heights of the challenge, but all have some capacity for growth. And the few whose latent capacities may enable them to rise to truly mature levels of accomplishment may well be the leaders of tomorrow—of whose fully developed talents we stand desperately in need.

✳ ✳ ✳

GOALS IN PROMOTING PERMANENT READING INTERESTS

LELAND B. JACOBS

✳

TEACHING a child to read is an act of faith and hope—faith that a child can convert black marks on a printed page into meanings, and hope that, in and through this conversion process, the young reader will find sufficient satisfaction and success that he will want to do more reading.

Teaching a child to read is a process of exploring and motivating—exploring the life and mind of the potential consumer of printed pages, and motivating him to master the skills necessary for becoming an able consumer of what writers have to offer.

Teaching a child to read is an act of

creation and criticism—creation of an environment and climate and specific situations in which a child is intimately involved in ideas and feelings that others have put into printed symbols, and criticism (or diagnosis) of what needs to be done next to help the child to be a better reader than he now is.

Teaching a child to read gives the learner direct and vicarious experiences—direct in the sense that, as he reads, the child is behaving immediately and precisely as an individual, and vicarious since the intellectual content and emotional intent of what he is reading take him outside himself.

Teaching a child to read involves the confirmation and the extension of a child's experiences—confirmation of his ability to think, organize, select, evaluate; extension of his potentialities to relate, resolve, reflect, refine.

Teaching a child to read is an immediate end in itself and a means to further ends—an immediate end in that what the young reader currently knows he uses, and a means to further ends in that his present reading accomplishments are only an undergirding for future reading developments.

For what purpose is all this teaching done? Toward what goals is all this teaching directed? For the purpose of developing a civilized, cultured citizenry that is capable of coping with the manifold problems confronting the human race. Toward the goal of individual maturity in achievement and permanence of interest in reading.

From the professional educator's point of view, there are responsibilities for teaching the child to read that must be undertaken. From the lay person's viewpoint, there are achievements in teaching a child to read that must be demon-strated. These adult perceptions of teaching reading are surely important. But what about the child who is being taught? He is a major stockholder in this transaction. He is ultimately the one who is either "in the red or the black." His goals cannot be minimized if the teaching that we do is to be successful.

CHILDREN'S GOALS IN READING

When a child learns to read, what seem to be his goals? Why is he willing to discipline himself to the confining act of pursuing lines of little black marks across pages of paper? Is it to please the adults who demonstrate that they want him to be able to do this mechanical trick? Is it to win some reward, or to avoid the punishments that may come from failing to comply with adult demands? Is it that he wants to be superior to other children because he cannot compete with them successfully in certain other ways? Such goals as these (and they may be the child's goals) are surely not sufficiently worthy ones to encourage. Nor do they lead to maturity in achievement and permanence of interest in reading. In fact, they are not truly goals in reading at all.

As one watches a child learning to read, he is involved in interpreting printed symbols. His primary goal is not the symbols, though they may be great fun in and of themselves. Their shape, their general configurations, their sounds may be pleasantly diverting. To be able to note likenesses and differences visually and orally may be pleasurable. But the child is conditioned early to know that these symbols are more than attractive, abstract designs of seeing and hearing. They are maps to meanings. They are vehicles to carry the reader into the mind of the writer. The child's real goals are to exploit the symbols for what they can help him to know, to be.

And children want to learn a great deal from their reading. They want information, many kinds of information. They want to know about the physical world and its phenomena, the social world and its relationships, the people who live on this earth and the great among them. While each child differs in the specific questions to which he seeks answers, he also joins with all other children in the general kinds of informational reading that he is willing to do. He is willing to read well-written information concerning life and its manifestations on this earth.

Children also want to be entertained. They expect that their reading time will be devoted to books that delight them. They want high adventure and romance and laughter. They want literary fare that carries them out of their mundane, workaday world. They want the stimulation of identifying with worthy heroes. Through their reading, they want the enjoyment of possessing pets, and friends, and even, perhaps, relatives whom they may not have in real life. They want to be cloistered with a writer who so magnificently creates his extramural world that one virtually exists in the time, place, and character which his fertile imagination has made manifest. For this is the essence of entertainment—a worthy goal that children seek in reading.

A third goal is that of self-understanding and enhancement. The search for self is as basic to living as breathing. Whatever a person does must somehow affect his perceptions of himself as a human being. Granted that some experiences more strongly affect a person's self-portraiture than do others. Nonethe-less, all human activities contribute in some way to this strong urge to know and feel one's own self emerging. And so children read to find themselves. They read to see themselves like others, to see themselves different from others. They read to test their accomplishments against those of personages found in books. They read to put themselves inside the skins of others, the better to know their own skins. They read to test or reinforce their own beliefs, perceptions, ways of behaving. Unless reading has done something to the reader, it probably has not been a very vital experience.

Why does a child learn to read? Probably to be knowledgeable, to be entertained, to become more sure of himself, to grow in stature and wisdom.

TEACHERS' GOALS AND CHILDREN'S GOALS

The teacher's goals and the child's goals are not, at best, incompatible. The child's goals of reading for meaningful contributions to everyday living do not belie the need on the part of a teacher to help the child improve his reading abilities and skills. The child wants to behave effectually in a world of time, place, people, and culture. If reading aids him to find his way more maturely into what he is going to do anyway, he will welcome the aid which a teacher can give him to learn to read better. If the child sees a purpose for reading better, he is willing to try to improve. Children are not averse to learning skills; they are only opposed to practicing skills for which they see no particular need—practice that is play-acting rather than reality.

Thus the teacher earns the right to teach for reading improvement. He hinges instruction to the child's observable reading wants. Instead of creating pressures for making a child go through mechanical procedures that may positively or negatively change his reading habits, the teacher lets the child's own needs create the pressures, and the teacher is available to alleviate the pressures by teaching the child functionally, at the point of demonstrated lack in reading power.

No, children's goals and teachers' goals are not necessarily incompatible. Readers are developed in classrooms by teachers who have the imagination to perceive the potentialities of children's purposes for learning and who help children, through reading, achieve their purposes. Readers are taught to be better readers by teachers who square the skills of mastering written symbols with the blueprint of the observable human potential of the individual.

PROMOTING PERMANENT READING INTERESTS

The teacher who would promote permanent reading interests on the part of children, then, is clearly one who knows that communication not only is essential to human behavior but is also a truly individual achievement. Such a teacher has felt the import of reading in his own living: the pursuit of stimulating ideas; the impact of lasting impressions of beauty garnered from authors' creative uses of written language; the challenge to stretch to new meanings and insights; the testing of old ways of behaving; the delight in coming again to familiar writings; the sharp pang of awe in the presence of greatness; the tingling anticipation of new worlds, in words, to come.

Such a teacher would want to share this splendid bequest with children, not by weighting them down with cumbersome paraphernalia that impede their progress toward their goals, but rather by helping them map out the territory and setting up appropriate guideposts so that, as they carry their reading equipment, they move ahead with confidence and comfort toward their destinations.

As has just been indicated, to promote permanent reading interests is first and foremost the art of making reading a tremendously satisfying experience—one to which a person comes again and again with pleasurable anticipation. But there are some specific practices which are worth suggesting.

1. Keep immediately available an attractive and well-balanced collection of reading matter that is just right in content, form, and readability for this particular group of children.

2. Help the individual child find the reading content that he cannot resist. Starting with his present achievements and tastes is the surest way to lead him to higher achievements, more discriminating taste.

3. Encourage children to share their reflections on the reading which they have done. Encourage them to think independently and share genuinely their reactions to the ideas and feelings that they find in others' writings.

4. Relate school reading experiences to other communication arts, particularly television, radio, motion pictures, recordings, the comics, and picture magazines. Make constructive use of the various mass media to complement and reinforce one another.

5. Read to children. Let them know the delight of words brought to life through oral interpretation. Let them thus locate new sources of reading matter that they previously had not known. Let

them sample new genres, new types of content.

6. Develop with the children suggested reading lists on topics that relate either to content areas or to special interests or to human relations or to personality development. Make such reading lists available to parents as well as children.

7. Encourage children to interpret what they have read in other forms of symbolism—dramatics, painting, dioramas, sculpturing, puppetry, for example.

8. Utilize the facilities of book exhibits and book fairs for extending children's awareness of the great variety of stimulating reading matter available to them.

9. Have children keep informal records of their independent reading, which will serve the teacher as a means of seeing, at long range, their reading interests; of helping them evaluate their reading; of making suggestions for further reading; of getting to know the individual child better as a reader.

10. Use only those evaluating procedures that concretely aid the child to assess realistically his present reading accomplishments and his blocks to even greater reading prowess.

IN CONCLUSION

Goals, neatly packaged as verbalizations, may be static and inert, an impediment rather than an aid to progress. Goals, as mere words, can lead to complacency, superficiality, self-deceit.

On the other hand, goals are behaviorally a necessity. Statements of goals that help one achieve their meanings in action are dynamic. They are useful to the extent that they guide one in his doings. They become central in the assessment of accomplishments. They help to inventory the present, and, from this inventorying, one can gather leads for next moves, new developments. In those situations where teachers' and children's goals in reading are compatible, permanence of interest in reading is encouraged.

And what about promoting reading interests? Here the teacher can, by sales techniques, contests, games, external rewards, seem to be promoting permanence of reading interest when, in reality, this show of the spectacular is really only transitory, a mirage. On the other hand, a teacher can, in more subtly creative ways, so make reading an integral part of school activities that, day by day, almost imperceptibly, the child himself makes reading a seemingly natural component of his total life. He reads because teachers have helped him to see himself as a person who not only knows how to read but also as an individual who finds in reading the succor, satisfaction, and stimulation that he currently needs. Such promotion is rarely spectacular while it is being carried on. Such promotion can never be called spectacular unless we believe that the achievement of enduring habits of reading for rich living is a show, an exhibition, a dramatic display. But it can be demonstrated as a great and satisfying accomplishment, an important means of making life good.

And what about reading interests? The interests themselves may be evanescent or abiding. This does not matter so much. That a boy reads avidly about cowboys for a year, or that a girl reads about ballet for eight months and then moves on to new reading interests, is somewhat common. It is not the school's task to make of a child a lifetime reader about dinosaurs or cowboys or ballet.

The permanence desired is not in such interests. The permanence to be developed is purpose for reading, whatever the content may be; for the person who senses the integrating effects of reading for being and knowing has a touchstone to more interests than he can ever fully pursue. His is the permanence about which Emily Dickinson wrote so eloquently:

> He ate and drank the precious words,
> His spirit grew robust;
> He knew no more that he was poor,
> Nor that his frame was dust.
> He danced along the dingy days,
> And this bequest of wings
> Was but a book. What liberty
> A loosened spirit brings![1]

Or, in the words of the *New England Primer:*

> My Book and Heart
> Must never part.

[1] Emily Dickinson, *Poems for Youth*, p. 70. Boston: Little, Brown & Co., 1942.

CHAPTER III

OBJECTIVES FOR IMPROVING READING INTERESTS

✳

IN KINDERGARTEN THROUGH GRADE THREE

CHARLOTTE HUCK

✳

DESPITE criticism to the contrary, primary-grade teachers have been successful in teaching the majority of our children the mechanics of reading. However, Russell[1] reported in the *Saturday Review* that 48 per cent of American adults read no books last year. Evidently yesterday's schools did a better job of teaching children *how* to read than in teaching children *to* read.

TEACHING CHILDREN TO WANT TO READ

In light of these facts, it seems evident that the major objective for improving reading interests in the primary grades should be the development of children who want to read; for our work will be to no avail if, having taught children the mechanics of reading, they never read.

In what ways, then, can we strengthen the child's interest and desire for reading? First, we can see that he has successful experiences with reading; for we truly like only those things at which we can succeed or at least see the possibility for success. This principle implies a developmental reading program and a willingness

[1] David H. Russell, "We All Need To Read," *Saturday Review*, XXXIX (February 18, 1956), 36.

on the part of teachers to let each child read on the level at which he can be successful.

Lately, in our eagerness to satisfy demands of parents, board members, and other laymen interested in education, we are in grave danger of discarding that which the research of years has proved to be necessary for success in learning to read. For example, we cannot afford to ignore the fact that many children require a rich readiness program prior to their initiation into the complexities of reading print. Without such a program, certain boys and girls will be placed in the impossible position of being expected to do that which they simply cannot do. These children will be building attitudes toward reading, but they will be attitudes of permanent dislike.

The second factor in helping children to like to read is the attitude of the teacher. The teacher must create in the classroom a climate which not only is conducive to promoting reading interests but also contributes to the well-rounded development of boys and girls. This kind of climate requires teachers to broaden their concepts of what they consider acceptable. Few children ever come to a first grade discouraged with their own abilities, but many, before they leave the grade, have been made to feel unhappy with themselves. If we really recognize individual differences, each child should be proud of his own forward-moving progress and not feel defeated because he is reading at a primer level while others in his group may be reading second-grade books. His attitude is likely to be a direct reflection of his teacher's attitude. If the teacher becomes discouraged with him, he will become discouraged with himself.

DEVELOPING A VARIETY OF READING INTERESTS

The second major objective for improving reading interests in the primary grades is to be certain that we expose children to many books and to many different kinds of books.

Textbook-reading alone is not enough to make a child want to read. Basic readers are important, but they cannot serve as the whole reading program. Their function is to serve as the foundation stone upon which the child may build his own superstructure of education. The controlled vocabularies of these readers necessarily limit their content. Publishers claim that their stories are based upon the here-and-now world of the primary-grade child. But what constitutes the here-and-now world of today's six-year-old? With a twist of a television dial he vicariously projects himself through outer space, or he may return to the days of the dinosaurs. The hunger for excitement which is so characteristic of today's child is hardly satisfied with the pallid plots of the primer family.

Children need a diet of balanced reading—one which will include modern stories with the old favorites; one which mixes the fanciful with the realistic, sprinkles the serious with the humorous,

adds the informative to the fictional, and is topped with well-chosen poetry! We need not be too concerned if such a diet includes the comics. It is only when comics become the major portion of the child's reading fare that we can expect literary malnutrition.

Not only should children have access to a wide variety of books, and preferably in their own classroom libraries, but they should have time to read them. Teachers and children should be sufficiently flexible to adjust their reading programs to their needs. Rather than always reading from readers, the children might better profit from reading some number stories or one of the fine weekly newspapers for children. How often do we take the time to have children read the booklets which they themselves have made? Nothing can destroy home-school relations faster than to have children consistently bring home worksheets or booklets which they have made but cannot read. Finally, recreational reading should be a part of the daily program of every grade, including kindergarten. One book in a child's hands is worth ten on the shelf.

Teachers, too, can do much to promote a wide variety of reading interests among boys and girls by the use of the daily story hour. Only by reading to children can we fill in the gap between their highly developed level of appreciation and their slowly developing reading ability. Books can provide competition for television. Watch a group of primary-grade children as they listen to the story of *The Biggest Bear* by Lynd Ward (Houghton, 1952). No TV western ever received more rapt attention! The audible sigh of relief and contentment which invariably accompanies the solution of Johnny's problem indicates the degree to which children have identified themselves with Johnny and his almost-human bear. Certain choice literature has to be read to children to be appreciated. *Charlotte's Web* by E. B. White (Harper, 1952) is such a book. Sheer fantasy, this story depicts the gamut of human emotions, including humor, pathos, loyalty, and courage, all through the experiences of a spider and a pig! The animals in *Winnie the Pooh* (Dutton, 1926) are also people in disguise. We have all known a gloomy Eeyore and a Bear of little brain! Unknown to us but hilarious in their extravagant nonsense are the imaginative animals of Dr. Seuss. These books provide the genuine laughter which our children need. The beauty of both the story and the pictures of Virginia Lee Burton's *The Little House* (Houghton, 1942) or Flack and Heyward's *The Country Bunny and the Little Gold Shoes* (Houghton, 1939) should be part of every child's experience with books. More than twelve hundred juvenile titles are published each year. Teachers have the responsibility to share with children certain choice books which the children themselves might not read.

ENCOURAGING CHILDREN TO REACT TO READING

A third objective for promoting permanent reading interests in the primary grades is to help children do something with the stories and poems which have been read in order to make them meaningful and vivid. It enhances the child's enjoyment of literature if he can be encouraged to react to stories in a variety of ways. Pictures may be drawn of the most exciting events; cereal box movies may be made; dioramas may depict scenes of a story. Certain favorite tales, such as *The Rabbit Who Wanted Red Wings* or Wanda Gág's *Nothing At All* (Coward-McCann), are particularly adapted to use with a felt board. "Who Am I?" bulletin boards, showing favorite story-book characters, could be arranged by the children. Pictorial maps of certain stories could be made. Frequently children like to "continue" favorite stories and write their own "further adventures." This can be done through illustrations, too. One third-grade group drew their own pictures similar to *On beyond Zebra* (Random, 1955) but called them "On beyond Seuss." Fantasy also lends itself to a puppet show, a favorite with children. If at all possible, we should try to acquaint children with the authors of some of their books. The children might arrange an author's party or write to their favorite author. There are so many ways, other than the deadly dull book report, that children can share their favorite stories and poems. Their enthusiasm can be contagious and so encourage others into wider reading.

HELPING CHILDREN SEE THE USE OF READING

Closely related to the third objective of encouraging children to do something with their reading is the fourth objective of helping children see that reading is really useful. Today reading is faced with many competing agencies: television, radio, movies, picture magazines. As a six-year-old, one might well wonder if there is any real reason to have to learn this tedious process. As teachers, we may need to point out the many ways in which the children have used reading or have seen reading used by others.

Long before boys and girls come to school, they have had many opportunities to observe the functional use of reading. They have watched their fathers reading the newspapers in the evening. They have seen their mothers make shopping lists or follow a recipe. Some have even experienced the dire results of a recipe which has been incorrectly read! Many have experienced the disappointment which comes when new clothes are the wrong size; perhaps an aunt has failed to be a critical reader and has sent the same size as marked in her birthday-book last year! Children themselves learn to look up the time and channel of their favorite TV programs long before they attend school.

Once children are in school, the use of reading becomes even more outstanding. In kindergarten we write the child's name on his picture, and he sees that this prevents it from being lost among many others. Letters of appreciation are frequently dictated by the children to their kindergarten teacher and then delivered with care to some deserving person. As the teacher writes the words in front of the children, they begin to gain an appreciation for the fact that those "squiggly" lines carry a message which can be read by almost anyone except five-year-olds.

We want to keep reading meaningful in the primary grades also. Some children see no reason to read about the gay jaunts of the primer family to grandfather's farm. However, children's own experiences are meaningful to them, and we can capitalize on these through the use of experience charts or individual booklets. The frequent interruptions in our classrooms for announcements of assemblies, movies, and luncheon menus could be turned to good use if they were written to be read by children. A bulletin board for messages might well stimulate certain children to read. Teachers could write occasional notes to children. The children could be encouraged to write birthday cards and letters to their friends. In this way, both writing and reading would serve the functional purposes of the children.

Boys who are having difficulty with reading frequently can be reached if they have a real purpose for reading. Help them to read the directions for making their model airplanes or submarines. Then lead them into wider reading through factual books rather than fictional: books by Bertha Parker, Herbert Zim, and the "First Books," to mention just a few. We need to be increasingly sensitive to the opportunities which present themselves for primary-grade children in order that they may use their reading.

HELPING CHILDREN FIND JOY IN READING

Finally, the fifth objective in promoting reading interests is one which is inherently the result of all the others, namely, helping children recognize the joy and zest which can be theirs through reading. Once the six-year-old has learned to read, he has the key to the gates of all knowledge; for all that man has thought, dreamed of, despaired of, and determined as fact is written down in books somewhere. As primary-grade teachers, we do not want to be so concerned with the forging of this reading key that we neglect to show our children its many uses. It is a key which can open the gates to the exciting realms of fantasy, poetry, biography, fiction, and fact. The true test of our success or failure in teaching children to read is not to be found in the results of a battery of tests but in the reading habits of these children twenty years from now. Will we have taught them to be readers or only to read?

IN GRADES FOUR THROUGH SIX

MAUD C. CLEWORTH

✳

THE central theme for this conference embraces the development of permanent interests in reading. Hence the first step for us to consider concerns the *objectives* for improving these reading interests. In thinking through this problem, we find that the objectives are twofold: the first, to provide for the immediate needs of the child and to supply materials within his level of knowledge and experience; the other, to develop skills and interests for his future needs. Both types of objectives are mutually significant, require direct and simultaneous attention, and demand long-term planning if permanency is to be assured. In other words, the immediate interests must be nurtured day by day to feed into the pattern of the more complex interests of the well-rounded person.

Consider the field of science, for example. Pupils must learn to observe, to think, and to draw conclusions. But how? Topics such as weather, rock formations, electricity, or plant life may be introduced again and again at differing levels of complexity so that extension of knowledge parallels the child's capacity and ability to understand. Each presentation must aim toward a spiral development that takes into account the ascending levels of maturity. This is the stage where the teacher must play his most tactful role in meeting the immediate interests of children and in cultivating the unknown or latent interests.

It has been said that man's survival is dependent upon his ability to adjust to his surroundings. No longer are people of any country living in a little sphere of their own. Therefore young people must be awakened to the realization that they are a vital part of a larger sphere where pressures demand a citizenry made up of persons who *can* and *will think*, who *can* and *will adjust* to an ever changing world. Because of these circumstances, general interests and the objectives for promoting them, either from the teacher's or from the pupil's point of view, must keep pace with present-day living. Today we cope with today's needs, neither yesterday's known ones nor tomorrow's anticipated ones. True, we may reach back to yesterday or stretch out to clasp tomorrow, but *today's* reading interests and the objectives concerning them must be in *today's* thinking and planning. Today's problems are real, and they must be met directly, squarely, and honestly. This is no time to clack our tongues at what has not been done, but it is an opportune time to plunge on to new heights.

What, then, are the objectives? In the following discussion I have listed the seven objectives I deem most essential in sequential order so that one blends into the next. No one objective outweighs the others; all are necessary to bring about the desired results, and all must be developed simultaneously.

TO ENCOURAGE WIDE READING AND A BROAD INTEREST SPAN

Individual interests of preadolescent children have changed greatly in the last several years even though the general categories remain about the same. Boys prefer adventure, history, science, and hobbies. Girls' interests center in home life, careers, some fantasy (though that is on the wane at this age level), and boy-and-girl relationships that tend toward romance. Both sexes enjoy "thrillers" and stories of space travel and of seeing the world. The teacher's objective here should be to keep the range of interest broadly based and to provide materials varied in type and purpose. Of course one starts at the level at which the pupil is (and knowing that level is a must), but one does not let him stagnate. In too many instances such stagnation has been a fault that has been ignored in our schools.

What makes Abraham Lincoln step from a book and walk the Illinois prairies? What makes Dick Tracy or Skeezix so real to all America? Why is Mark Twain quoted so often? Why is Joan of Arc the heroine of all time? Is it not because someone was able to "live" the experiences of these characters and to make the reader "live" them, too?

Through wide reading, a pupil may learn how to satisfy a curiosity, verify a fact, solve a problem, or follow specific directions. Equally important is the realization that this type of reading should be an enjoyable, rewarding, and enriching experience.

TO GAIN INDEPENDENCE IN ALL SKILLS

Gaining independence in reading skills is the crux of all reading and should be dealt with at all levels. Improved interests lend themselves to experiencing quicker recognition of, and attaching deeper meanings to, a greater number of words, groups of words, and idiomatic expressions. The expansion of interest provides both motivation and source material for developing readers who think in thought-patterns rather than single words. Remember, one who cannot read well substitutes other means of gaining information. Therefore one's interest, in addition to broadening one's background, may serve as an incentive to improved reading habits.

Furthermore, varied interests promote opportunities for using the dictionary, encyclopedias, and source materials of all kinds. Learning how to use the library advantageously is a vital part of this objective since it is an essential factor in locating information. Many students have gone far beyond the intermediate-grade level before they have any knowledge of how to use a card catalogue, the *Readers Guide to Periodical Literature*, or even the most simple indexes. Early training in how to locate information promotes greater interest, for the know-how is an important phase in achieving a goal.

TO INCREASE READING VOCABULARY

Studies reveal that the reading vocabulary of many pupils is inadequate to cope with today's needs. This situation has arisen in part because too often only a *general* comprehension of the material read is expected. But if one reads for precise meanings, shades of meanings, or exacting recognition, words in themselves must take shape in both a visual and an auditory sense as well as a meaningful sense. Vocabulary-building is being stressed increasingly by educators who see the need for reading beneath the surface to improve comprehension, interpretation, and appreciation. If interest is used as a leverage, teaching to build a good reading vocabulary can and will be effective. Let us not lose sight of this objective, for it is the foundation of future study and present understanding.

TO ENCOURAGE SELF-DIRECTION AND MENTAL ACTIVITY

If pupils throughout the formative, preadolescent years begin to learn how to read with a purpose in mind, they will soon be able to read *into* rather than *through* selections. Interests, varied and new, lend themselves to individual growth. Mental laziness—or, perhaps more appropriately termed, mental inertia—is too often the status quo in many classrooms. This is particularly true among groups of average and above-average ability. Because pupils in these categories have the capacity for learning, they perform the rudimentary requirements with comparative ease but do not have the self-direction to broaden or intensify their knowledge. With proper incentives, these students could go far.

It has been said that first one sees, then he visualizes. That is, "seeing" is perceiving, and "perceiving" means understanding. Seeing must have more depth than the creation of a single image, more breadth than citing from a single instance. To get desirable mental activity, all senses must be brought into play. For example, one may see, hear, touch, or read about an airplane. But does he actually get the full significance of it until he zooms off the ground into space? Again, how does one form attitudes about peoples throughout the world? How does he learn to appreciate their differences, to understand their beliefs, their traditions, or their sense of values? What does it take to be a good winner or a good loser? These and other understandings can only come by broadening and deepening our knowledge about them. It takes varied

reading interests to exchange ideas intelligently and to broaden horizons. But it is in this way that a pupil will begin to understand himself, his strengths and his weaknesses, and may even direct his efforts toward an occupational future.

TO STIMULATE CONCEPT-BUILDING AND SYNTHESIZING OF MATERIALS

This is the day of seeking workable solutions to problems, not memorizing facts alone, but putting facts together in a logical, sequential manner so as to synthesize the whole. This type of reading invites inquisitiveness, logical thinking, and a knowledge of facts. Again, to make this kind of learning a vital part of individual thinking, strong motivation is required, because it is too easy to take the line of least resistance. This objective demands the ability to distinguish fact from fiction, truth from fantasy, and reality from imagination. It leads to that type of good organization in which one must read with a purpose in mind, see facts in sequential order, draw inferences, and arrive at a logical conclusion.

For instance, how does one form a point of view? Orville Prescott in his book, *The Five-Dollar Gold Piece* (Random, 1956), explains the importance of becoming a discriminating observer, listener, and reader. He relates how the Civil War jumped out of books and into a world of direct experience for him. There was Uncle Frank, who had been a prisoner at Andersonville; there was Cousin Ida, who told of Sherman's march to the sea; and there was Gibson, the silent Negro who had been a slave in Alabama. To form a point of view, one must see *all sides* of a question. To insure this type of thinking, we must capitalize on broad and varied interests.

TO EXPAND READING POWER

When we talk about expanding reading power, we are delving into that more remote type of objective that develops the pupil's sensitivity to things about him, a reasonable imagination, an understanding of figurative language, and the realization that integration of ideas can only come when one has acquired a broad background on any given subject. It is through this expanding power, too, that individuals may receive therapeutic treatment for their own problems. Take a disturbed child, an only child, or a selfish child; individualized reading keyed to his problem may give him the solution to it.

This objective includes the expansion of reading interests both vertically and horizontally. A person who wants reading power needs to dig deeper, climb higher, and encompass a larger area if he expects to integrate his thinking intelligently. Let me explain. The study of Thomas A. Edison may reveal certain scientific facts or historical facts or sociological facts, but it takes the integration of all these facts to give a real understanding of the man. Thus the power to read with breadth and depth of interpretation kindles and feeds the flames of reading interests.

TO PERPETUATE SELF-STIMULATION FOR MEETING FUTURE NEEDS

Youth merge into adulthood at an early age these days. There are too few years to promote those reading interests that will meet a person's needs in everyday living through his entire life-span. There are the leisure hours, when good reading can be a real joy if one has learned to read with ease. There is a career to be carefully selected if one is to be happy during his working years. There are the privileges and the responsibilities of an intelligent citizenry—voting privileges, community responsibilities, and the need for understanding peoples around the world. There will be family problems, community problems, national problems, and world-affairs. Thomas Carlyle said, "All that mankind has done, thought, gained, or been: it is lying as in magic preservation in the pages of books." It is only fair then that, by promoting reading interests at an early age, we teach our youth the necessity and the rewards of developing reading power.

✳ ✳ ✳

IN GRADES SEVEN THROUGH NINE

CATHERINE HAM

✳

SINCE I am a teacher of English and since the major responsibility for guidance in reading inevitably falls to the English teacher, it seems reasonable to discuss the objectives for improving reading interests in the junior high school from the point of view of teachers of English. Why do we want to improve the reading interests of our students? What kind of readers do we want to produce? Our ideal, or course, is that our students will grow into discriminating adults who read widely, with perception, with pleasure, and with appreciation. To attain this ideal, we must develop not only interests but also skills and standards. At this point the job of English teachers becomes complex and contradictory because, in our efforts to develop the latter, we sometimes destroy the former and even turn students away from reading—or so we are frequently told. Is it fair to lay the blame for lack of interest in reading on the already heavily burdened shoulders of the teachers of English?

A NEGATIVE OPINION

In 1937 Betzner and Lyman reported that school guidance in reading had not been successful; preferences in voluntary reading, perhaps as a relief from required reading, were mainly for inferior materials.[1] In 1948 Paul Witty found that "in general, recent studies . . . reveal the failure of high schools to develop permanent interests among students in reading increasingly worth-while materials."[2] In 1955 Elizabeth Rose reported that 75 per cent of our adults read no books, 25 per cent read one book a year, and only 1 per cent read as many as five books a year.[3] In the same year a report by the Committee on Reading Development stated: "Although the spread of education tends

[1] Jean Betzner and R. L. Lyman, "The Development of Reading Interests and Tastes," *The Teaching of Reading: A Second Report*, pp. 189–90. Thirty-sixth Yearbook of the National Society for the Study of Education, Part I. Chicago: Distributed by the University of Chicago Press, 1937.

[2] Paul A. Witty, "Current Role and Effectiveness of Reading among Youth," *Reading in the High School and College*, p. 20. Forty-seventh Yearbook of the National Society for the Study of Education, Part II. Chicago: Distributed by the University of Chicago Press, 1948.

[3] Elizabeth Rose, "Literature in the Junior High," *English Journal*, XLIV (March, 1955), 141.

to increase the proportion of the population that reads regularly, it appears that reading is still unattractive to a majority, and that most students are not motivated to continue reading after the years of formal education."[4] For almost twenty years, then, we have been concerned about improving reading interests, but still the surveys show that we do not produce readers.

Recently the fact that Johnny can't read has become a national issue, but no one outside of school people and a few booklovers seems to be concerned about the fact that, even when Johnny can read, he doesn't. Do parents read? Do teachers read? Isn't "bookworm" often misapplied, and isn't it always a pejorative term? Aren't people more impressed by the doer, the "go-getter," the man of action? Must we not conclude that we shall not be successful in our efforts to improve reading interests until society looks upon reading as a pleasurable, admirable, and useful activity?

CRUCIAL YEARS

If this radical change is to be accomplished in the future, the junior high school teacher will have a part to play in the pre-revolutionary activities. According to most surveys, these middle years are crucial ones in the life of the child; reading interest begins to flag, and frequently it drops sharply in the years that follow. It is not surprising that this should be so; these are crucial years in general—years when the student is part child and part adult, and each part wars with the other. Juvenile stories are often pushed aside as being too childish, but

[4] Jean D. Grambs, *The Development of Lifetime Reading Habits*, pp. iv–v. New York: National Book Committee, Inc. (24 West Fortieth Street), [1954].

adult books are often too slow moving, even when the subject matter is interesting. Novels dealing with universal human experience seem remote and meaningless to children of this age. Books dealing with the problems and activities of adolescents are significant, because these books fulfil their need for role-playing, assure them of their own normality, and allow them to test themselves without having their privacy invaded.[5] They like excitement and adventure, especially when boys and girls of their own age achieve great things. Through such books they are able, albeit vicariously, to live lives of surpassing accomplishment and to gain emotional release and satisfaction. They like books about young people who face and solve problems similar to their own. Through these books they may learn that their problems are not unique and may come to have a more objective understanding of themselves and their relationships with others. If the teacher is able to find and to suggest suitable books, he may lead students successfully over this rocky portage to the next navigable river and send them paddling happily on their way. If he requires them to read books that are dull or meaningless to them, their burden may become too heavy, and they may decide that getting to the next river is not worth the struggle.

READING FOR FUN

One of our objectives, then, is to try to convince our students that reading is pleasurable. Reading for fun is, and always has been, a worthy leisure-time pursuit. Our library shelves and our reading lists should be filled with humorous books, attractive narratives of youthful escapades, and adventure thrillers, whose

[5] G. R. Carlsen, "Behind Reading Interests," *English Journal*, XLIII (January, 1954), 9.

only aim is to delight and to entertain; and a generous proportion of our time should be given to guidance in this area. Whether they read series books or literary classics, our students must enjoy what they are reading or they will most probably not continue to read.

But in emphasizing reading for pleasure, there are pitfalls and problems. It is here that the question of standards arises. If we could be concerned only with fostering interest and stressing pleasure, we could ignore quality and could count ourselves successful if our students read a mystery a month for the rest of their lives. But as teachers we cannot content ourselves with this kind of achievement; we cannot condone the continual reading of cheap thrillers (not that all mystery books fall into this category) or sentimental love stories or watered-down problem novels where everything is black or white, where virtue is always rewarded, and where solutions are superficial and contrived. Although we recognize that reading furnishes a temporary escape from a humdrum existence or from the demands besetting most of us, we are constrained by our role as guide to see that our students escape into a fictional world that is honest and truthful, and we must combat the possible substitution of reading for doing. Reading purely for escape may lead to living in a dream world where wishful thinking takes the place of action. This, I grant you, is one of our minor problems, but it is something we should weigh in our programs.

READING FOR PROFIT

If we want to suggest books that are enjoyable, we want also to suggest books that are worth while; but students' definition of "worth while" is not always ours. Not that we insist that they read only literary classics, nor do we emphasize style or aesthetic appreciation in Grades VII, VIII, or IX. Such matters must be taught obliquely, if at all. Certainly we cannot answer the ever recurring questions, "What does it get me?" by saying, "Good books will improve your taste and your appreciation." We cannot even answer, "Pleasure," because the student who asks this question does not enjoy reading.

How can we answer this question? Such rewards as learning about one's self and others and discovering answers to personal problems have already been mentioned and might be acceptable answers. Certainly an important answer is that, through reading, we can get information—information about atomic energy, contour plowing, baseball strategy, or table settings. We can learn how to do almost anything, from how to prospect for uranium to how to break the ice at a party. In our hurried, practical world these reasons for reading may prove acceptable. If our students won't read for pleasure, they may read for possible profit.

If we did not have to fit the answer to the questioner, we could say that reading, and the study of literature, acquaints us with our cultural heritage and gives us a sense of belonging to a tradition; that it induces intellectual curiosity and reflective thinking; that it gives us an opportunity to re-examine our sense of values; that it helps us to develop critical appreciation; that it is a way of identifying, extending, and intensifying our interests; and that it enables us to develop social insight through the reinforcement of challenging attitudes.[6] That these are excellent objectives for improving reading interests no teacher would deny, but we cannot hand a book to a pupil or as-

sign a selection for reading with the words, "Here, re-examine your sense of values," or "Develop your social insight." The realization that reading can do these things for us comes slowly through years of experience. Our job is to lay the foundation for this realization by keeping these objectives firmly in mind when we suggest books for outside reading, when we plan lessons, and when we conduct class discussions.

These last two activities are, it seems to me, particularly important. These objectives cannot be realized through guided reading alone, not if guided reading means merely suggesting books and hearing reports. We must force our students to think. Force has unfortunate connotations, but thinking is hard work and hard work requires discipline. We must stimulate our pupils and make them aware, not by inspirational homilies, but by challenging and thought-provoking questions. We are often told that, by probing and analyzing, we make reading a chore rather than a delight. Close reading need not be dull, and I question whether our enthusiasm lessens as our understanding increases.

Although our task is a formidable one, we may, through wise counsel, stimulating guidance, and infectious enthusiasm, inspire our students not only to read but to read with discernment and sensitivity. If we do not reach all of them we must be comforted by the hope that "the girl who becomes truly excited over *Seventeenth Summer* may quite possibly become a fine reader eventually and understand Lord

[6] Dora V. Smith, "Guiding Individual Reading," *Reading in the High School and College*, pp. 180–205. Forty-seventh Yearbook of the National Society for the Study of Education, Part II. Chicago: Distributed by the University of Chicago Press, 1948.

Jim, Anna Karenina, and the archbishop,"[7] or even that the boy who is bored by *David Copperfield* may, ten years later, read *Our Mutual Friend* with genuine interest and appreciation.

CONCLUDING STATEMENT

The objectives at the junior high school age are to move students as rapidly as possible toward wide reading with perception, with pleasure, and with appreciation. During these crucial years the teacher must find books about young people who face and solve significant problems. Reading must be fun, but it must also yield a profit if it is to play a significant role in the years ahead.

[7] Elizabeth Rose, *op. cit.*, p. 143.

$$\star \quad \star \quad \star$$

IN GRADES TEN THROUGH FOURTEEN

HAROLD A. ANDERSON

$$\star$$

IT IS commonly assumed that the well-educated man can be distinguished from the poorly educated one by what he reads. There is even some objective evidence to support the belief that maturity in reading is an index of general maturity. In brief, we say that reading makes the man.

Our specific assignment is to analyze the problem of improving the reading interests of students at the senior high school and junior-college levels. The heart of our topic is centered in the term *improving*. I take this to mean that our task is to improve both the quality of the interests and the choice of reading matter used to satisfy those interests.

People read for a wide variety of reasons. They read to free the mind; to develop allegiances to core values; to extend horizons beyond the limits of immediate problems and needs; to open new intellectual vistas; to achieve interpersonal, intergroup, and international understanding; to understand self and to achieve self-realization; to find rational solutions to personal and social problems; to heighten personal feelings of prestige and power; to reinforce attitudes presently held or to seek new ones on a wide variety of controversial issues; to seek relief from tensions, anxieties, and frustrations. These are lofty goals. And there are more.

SOME OBJECTIVES FOR IMPROVING READING INTERESTS

The foregoing goals for reading make a strong case for improving the reading interests of young people. Indeed, there are many valid and forceful reasons for developing in young people abiding interests in good reading. I shall have time to develop only five.

1. *Extension of human experience vicariously.*—One important function which reading can serve is the extension of human experience vicariously far beyond that which real life affords. I need not elaborate the proposition that life can be immeasurably enriched by vicarious experience. This has always been true, even before the invention of print. Centuries before man learned to communicate with written symbols, he communicated by word of mouth. Indeed, for ages

listening was the primary means possessed by man for enlarging his own experiences vicariously. In those days, one who did not know how to listen well lived a life of limited horizons. Bonaro W. Overstreet put it this way: "The individual who, in the long preliterate stages of history, had no keen ability as a listener must have remained a prisoner within his own small cell of experience."[1]

Today one who does not read widely and well likewise remains a prisoner within his small cell of personal experience. But the consequences for both the individual and the nation are more tragic, for the complexities and demands of modern life virtually compel us to seek the fullest possible contact with the "wide, wide world." The economic, social, political, and ideological interdependence of all peoples makes all men neighbors today, even though they do not live together as neighbors should.

Let me explore this concept further. Reading can expand experiences geographically. Most of us are forced by circumstances to live in a relatively restricted geographical area, and our firsthand experiences are confined to it. But reading affords to all who would read a vagabond journey around the world.

Experiences can also be expanded historically. At best, the span of life is a brief seventy years, and our direct experiences are limited to these seventy years. Through books, students can live imaginatively with peoples remote in time and place and sometimes foreign to his understanding and sympathy. Thus, through the medium of print the spirit of the past communicates with us today, welding each new generation to the past and giving to successive generations an intellectual, social, and moral cohesion so necessary to the survival of civilization today.

There is yet another way in which reading may extend experiences vicariously—socially. We need to know better not only the peoples of the far corners of the earth but those near at hand. Some people are born in favored places; others are born in slums. Some are reared in rural areas; some in urban centers. All should know, indeed must know, something of how the other half lives no matter to which half they belong. Wisely selected and properly read books can produce in us a sensitivity to, and a sympathetic understanding of, the trials and tribulations, failures and triumphs, hopes and aspirations, problems and perplexities of people in high places and low.

2. *Provide a balance to the content of vicarious experience.*—The foregoing discussion of the value of a wide range of vicarious experience through reading should not be interpreted as suggesting that there are no other media by means of which vicarious experience may be had. But the various media differ in their usefulness.

This is not tantamount to saying that in all media there is good and bad and that it matters little on which we rely. An examination of studies of the content of motion pictures, radio, and television reveals that far too often the central theme relates to unrealistic romance, violence, crime, and lurid treatment of sex. In many ways these media present an unwholesome and distorted picture of life. Their center of interest lies too often in the senstational and pathological aspects of life. May I reiterate that there are many good motion pictures and television programs. Some are superb.

Our objective is not to wean students

[1] Bonaro W. Overstreet, "After This Manner, Therefore, Listen . . . ," *Wilson Library Bulletin,* XX (April, 1946), 598.

away from the mass media. Rather, it is to stimulate and encourage students to read good books as a means of gaining a realistic, comprehensive, and mature view of life. Such a view of life is not likely to be gained by those who rely largely on the mass media.

3. *Extension of intellectual horizons.*— There is grave danger, in a society as complex as ours, that we shall develop such high degrees of specialization of interests, of talents, and of capacities that barriers to communication result—in a society which because of its complexity demands a high degree of mutual understanding.

According to Gray and Rogers,[2] one mark of general maturity is a catholicity of reading interests. These authors also point out that the mature reader usually begins with some focus or central interest in some aspect of his environment. His reading at first revolves around it, but in time his reading interests expand into ever widening circles.

If a mark of growing maturity is an ever widening circle of reading interests, our task is clear. Somehow we must identify the present interests of our students and introduce them to reading matter related to these interests, no matter how limited these at first may be, and then through skilful guidance open up newer and wider horizons. If promoting maturity is a goal of education, one means to that end is improving the reading interests of young people.

4. *Enrichment of emotional and moral life.*—Actual everyday living affords to very few a well-balanced and full emotional life. For many young people, life has not yet presented any real problems.

[2] William S. Gray and Bernice Rogers, *Maturity in Reading.* Chicago: University of Chicago Press, 1956.

No one in the family circle has been seriously ill, in material need, disappointed in love, or frustrated in ambition. Life moves along on an even keel. But in due time crises will come—disappointments in love, family disunion, shattering of hopes, illness, death. Faced with these problems, or even in anticipation of them, the reader may identify himself with fictitious characters who have faced and met similar crises. If the problems faced and the characters who have met them are true to life, the reader can gain confidence, strength, and resourcefulness to meet his own.

Literature may also open to us a whole gamut of healthy emotions which might otherwise be foreign to us. The poet's peculiar sensitivity to the beautiful, to the aesthetic, to the artistic in the everyday world, and his ability to communicate his emotional experiences to others make it possible for all to share the emotions aroused by beautiful sunsets, cloud formations, line and symmetry, noble deeds and thoughts, and the things of the spirit.

Somewhat different, but I think not unrelated, is the role which literature can play in the development of the moral virtues. I should make clear at once that I am not proposing that literature be taught didactically or that a moral lesson be tagged on every piece of writing. But I am contending that the moral virtues are best exemplified in the great literature. No, as teachers we need not point the moral; but, properly motivated, read under appropriate circumstances, sheared of the usual incumbrances of classroom assignments, *Idylls of the King, Macbeth, Self-reliance, Up from Slavery, The Spirit of St. Louis,* and a long and impressive list of other titles will afford the reader vicarious living on a high moral plane.

I should like to make one further comment relating to the role of reading in the development of healthy emotions. We are living in an age of speed, noise, and tension. Life is lived at a high tempo. Man needs, perhaps more than anything else today, moments of quiet contemplation. Anne Morrow Lindbergh makes this clear in her lovely book *Gift from the Sea* (Pantheon, 1955).

Mass media of communication appear to increase the tempo. The blaring radio, the overloud television, and the relentless forward movement of the motion picture sound track hardly contribute to the contemplative mood. Too, these mass media tend to call for mass participation. They stampede the listener and viewer into mass response. Everybody is expected to laugh in unison or weep together. Humor is timed, calculated. A premium is placed on group response.

Reading provides a different fare. It can be a quiet, thoughtful, and contemplative experience permitting a private response. One of our objectives is to help young people discover the satisfactions which such moments can bring.

5. *Reading as a meaningful and rewarding experience.*—I submit that one of the most vital factors in developing the habit of good reading is to make certain that the act of reading is a meaningful and rewarding experience. Much reading in school and college is done under compulsion—to satisfy demands largely extrinsic to the interests of students. Altogether too often the literature we recommend for young people consists of "profound and difficult classics written by men of uncommon powers," men who have passed through the experiences of mature life. If students are prematurely introduced to these books or required to read beyond their level of maturity or largely outside their range of interests, their reading is likely to end with graduation. In fact, there is disturbing evidence that such is the case. The reading we succeed in persuading, if not compelling, our students to do while in high school and college is of little avail unless it impels them to read on their own the remaining fifty years of their lives.

Unless the reading experience, whether it be in a course in literature, economics, history, or science, is a meaningful and rewarding one, the student is not likely to turn to the printed page on his own volition. What is worse, he is likely to develop lasting aversions to reading and become easy prey for the purveyors of life rendered superficial, sensational, and distorted.

SUGGESTIONS FOR INSTRUCTION

I shall close this paper with some brief suggestions concerning instructional practices. First of all, may I suggest that all teachers subject their reading assignments and suggested reading lists to these criteria: Is the reading matter within the range of the student's reading ability; his social, emotional, and intellectual maturity; and his current and potential reading interests? If these criteria are met, the reading experience is likely to be a meaningful and rewarding one.

May I further suggest that, whenever possible, reading be related to broad, flexible units of instruction. For example, an appropriate unit in a literature course might be organized around such a broad theme as "Protests against Social Injustices." From the beginning of preserved writing we have a record in our finest literature of protests against man's inhumanity to man. Most young people are sensitive to some form of social injustice. Each student will bring his special sensitivity to the unit of study and find in its broad scope a point of contact. Class discussion is likely to extend the areas of concern and evoke wider and wider reading. All of us have had the experience of dropping a pebble into a body of water and have marveled at the growth of ever widening concentric circles. Growth in reading interests is something like that.

CHAPTER IV

THE STATUS OF PERSONAL READING

✳

IN SCHOOL

MARGARET HAYES

✳

To DEVELOP permanent interest in reading has long been a primary objective of the reading and library program of the school. Concern about how well the schools are achieving this objective has become widespread in recent years. Many parents charge that the schools no longer teach children how to read or transmit to them an enduring enthusiasm for reading. Parents and teachers fret that magazines, television, and movies are making books obsolete. Are these fears well grounded on facts of the present, or are they ill-founded on myths about the good old days? Do children and youth read less today than they did formerly? Has the quality of their reading deteriorated?

These are difficult questions to answer even though hundreds of studies have been made during the past half-century about the reading habits of children and young people. Differences in the test conditions and in the methods used to gather and analyze the evidence make valid comparisons about the reading of youth in different periods of time exceptionally difficult. Yet some statements of approximate fact can be made, which may provide some understanding of the status of personal reading among children of our own and earlier generations.

AMOUNT OF READING

One method that investigators have used to answer the question, "Do children read as much as they used to?" is to compare statistics about the number of children's books published and the number of books children borrow from the library. Such indirect evidence about the current status of children's reading appears encouraging. There has been a tremendous increase both in the number of new titles of children's books published and in the total volume of juvenile publishing. In 1925, 710 new books and 318 new editions were published;[1] in 1950, the number had increased to 1,059;[2] and in 1955, to 1,485.[3] The total number of copies of juvenile books produced in 1925 was 25,214,000,[4] and in 1945 the total number of juvenile books sold was 53,752,000.[5] Gains in the circulation of

[1] *Publishers' Weekly*, CIX (January 23, 1926), 233.

[2] *Publishers' Weekly*, CLIX (January 20, 1951), 240.

[3] *Publishers' Weekly*, CLXIX (January 21, 1956), 223.

[4] United States Department of Commerce, Bureau of the Census, *Biennial Census of Manufactures: 1925*, p. 662. Washington: Government Printing Office, 1928.

[5] United States Department of Commerce, Bureau of the Census, *Biennial Census of Manu-*

children's books from public libraries are also impressive. Circulation statistics show an increase from about 138,000,000[6] in 1938–39 to over 162,000,000[7] in 1950. Similar data are not available for school libraries, but there is every reason to believe they would reveal an equally striking gain.

Although these figures show that more books are available and are being used today than during any period in our history, they do not answer two important questions about amount of reading. Are a larger proportion of children reading voluntarily today than yesterday? Are children reading more?

Analytical summaries reported by Gray and Munroe in 1929[8] and by Gray and Iverson in 1952[9] provide a chronological comparison of the reading of children and young people. Studies made between 1890 and 1928 showed that the per cent of children who read books voluntarily increased rapidly in the primary and intermediate grades and approximated 100 in the junior high school. In some high schools, voluntary reading continued among almost all students. In other high schools, there was a marked decrease in the proportion of

students who read and in the average amount of reading of those students who did read. Almost all children above the third grade read the newspaper and, to a lesser extent, magazines. The proportion of children reading them increased steadily during elementary grades and reached a high level in the junior high school. Almost all high-school students continued to read newspapers but in some schools read less in magazines.

Few major changes in this general pattern were reported in the summary of those studies made since 1940. The chief differences are the greater popularity of magazines and newspapers at practically all grade levels and the more rapid increase in the proportion of children reading books voluntarily during the elementary-school grades. The decline in book-reading among high-school students was as great as before, if not greater. Not only do high-school students read less, but fewer of them read. This fact has sometimes been misinterpreted to mean that high-school students read less than elementary-school students. However, a few recent studies of both required and voluntary reading show that there is actually an increase in the total amount of reading during the high-school period because students read more for assignments.

Facts about the numbers of books read voluntarily by children and youth also provide an interesting basis for comparison of the reading patterns of today and yesterday. Gray concluded from data summarized in the twenties that the number of books read by sixth-, seventh-, and eighth-grade pupils averaged from one to two a month.[10] A survey of similar

---

factures: 1947, II, 358. Washington: Government Printing Office, 1949.

[6] *Public Library Statistics: 1938–39*, p. 5. United States Office of Education Bulletin 1942, No. 4.

[7] *Public Library Statistics: 1950*, p. 38. United States Office of Education Bulletin 1953, No. 9.

[8] William S. Gray and Ruth Munroe, *The Reading Interests and Habits of Adults*, pp. 104–5. New York: Macmillan Co., 1929.

[9] William S. Gray and William J. Iverson, "What Should Be the Profession's Attitude toward Lay Criticism of the Schools?" *Elementary School Journal*, LIII (September, 1952), 28–29.

[10] William S. Gray, *Summary of Investigations Relating to Reading*, p. 159. Supplementary Educational Monographs, No. 28. Chicago: University of Chicago Press, 1925.

studies made during the past decade convinced him that the average number of books read by children today is not radically different from that of three decades ago.[11] Henne, analyzing studies of high-school students' reading made during the period from 1900 to the early forties, also found no marked difference in the amount of voluntary reading during the four decades.[12]

RANGE AND QUALITY OF READING

Obviously, sound appraisal of children's personal reading cannot be based solely on data about how many children read and how much they read. Information about the range and quality of their reading is even more significant.

Studies made during the past half-century reveal few major changes in the range and the general subject matter of children's reading. The broad subject pattern of their reading in both fiction and nonfiction is almost identical, although the specific books and magazines read vary from decade to decade as a consequence of what is published and made available.

At all ages, children read more fiction than nonfiction and like it better. They read increasingly more difficult children's stories until the junior high school period. Between the ages of twelve and fifteen, they shift from the juvenile and teen-age story to adult fiction. For a while children read from both fields, but usually the transition has been completed by the age of sixteen. The reading of nonfiction tends to increase progressively during junior and senior high

school grades; this trend is particularly evident at the high-school level. In recent studies a somewhat larger proportion of nonfiction is reported in the personal reading of primary- and intermediate-grade children than in former investigations. This shift probably reflects the tremendous increase in the number of informational books published during the past decade for younger children.

If we cannot find any significant difference in range of material read by children and youth from decade to decade, can we find any difference in the quality of material read? Many parents and some teachers complain that children and youth are not reading the classics today as often as they formerly did and that they are failing to develop a taste for good literature.

One approach to the question of quality of reading is through reports of favorite books. The major conclusion to be drawn from studies made during the past fifty years is that the quality of children's choices is much the same from one decade to another. Children's preferences encompass several classics and "good" modern stories, a large number of acceptable but undistinguished titles, and a few pieces of trash. The high-school students' formula is a mixture of classics and standard titles of adult and juvenile literature, adult best sellers, and very light adult fiction. Such classics as *Tom Sawyer*, *Little Women*, *Huckleberry Finn*, and *Treasure Island* appear as frequently on current lists as on earlier ones. A 1955 study[13] of the favorite books of some 5,500 boys and girls in Grades V through

[11] William S. Gray and William J. Iverson, *op. cit.*

[12] Frances Henne, "Preconditional Factors Affecting the Reading of Young People," p. 76. Unpublished Doctor's dissertation, Graduate Library School, University of Chicago, 1949.

[13] Mary A. Schneider and Marion W. Taylor, "Children's Reading Interests in the Chicago Public Schools," p. 34. Unpublished Master's thesis, Graduate School, Chicago Teachers College, 1955.

VIII of the Chicago public schools indicates the range in literary merit and the division between the old and the new that are typical of children's choices. The books preferred by the boys, ranked in order of their popularity, were: *20,000 Leagues under the Sea*, Walt Disney's *Davy Crockett*, *Tom Sawyer*, *Homer Price*, *Black Beauty*, *Black Stallion*, and *World Series*. The girls' favorite books were: *Double Date*, *Little Women*, *Class Ring*, *Black Beauty*, *Boxcar Children*, *Going on Sixteen*, *Practically Seventeen*, *Black Stallion*, *Lassie Come-Home*, and *Andersen's Fairy Tales*.

Another recent study[14] offers more insight into the place of the classics in children's reading. One year's voluntary reading of some 750 Chicago school children in Grades IV through VIII was analyzed to determine how many of the 300 titles found in publishers' reprint series had been read. Although adults might not agree that these 300 titles were classics, the titles of many of the series indicated that the publishers considered them as such. Half of the 300 titles were not read at all, and the other half were read by only 43 per cent of the pupils. At first glance this evidence seems to support the charge of neglect made by apprehensive parents. Before such a conclusion can be reached, however, it would be necessary to know whether any other titles were read more widely by students. A similar study of 300 contemporary books might reveal no greater incidence of reading than was shown in this report.

Probably the most valid appraisal of the quality of reading is that based upon an analysis of individuals' total reading. In the limited evidence of this type available about children's reading in earlier and later periods, there is little agreement about the relative amount of good or poor material. There is agreement that the quality ranges from the classics to rubbish, but the relative portion of each in children's reading diet is still open to question. Some investigators have found children in intermediate and junior high school grades reading a number of juvenile series of the "Tom Swift" and "Nancy Drew" variety in recent times, the "Rover Boys" and "Tarzan" in earlier periods. Other researchers, however, report only a small number of undesirable titles on the list of books read voluntarily by children. To what extent these inconsistencies are caused by real differences in the reading of children and to what extent they are caused by children's reluctance to report books they think adults will not approve allow interesting speculation.

At the high-school level the majority of surveys from 1900 on show that light fiction predominates in the reading of students. There exist minority reports, as exemplified by the high-level reading of the secondary-school students of the Ohio State University school,[15] that suggest the potential influence of the free yet guided reading program upon the reading habits of young people.

Any appraisal of the quality of youth's voluntary reading must consider magazines as well as books. Most of the studies are based upon reports by secondary-school students of the magazines they read regularly or the maga-

[14] Mary Katherine Eakin, "The Reading of Books from Publishers' Reprint Series by Children in the Elementary Grades." Unpublished Master's thesis, Graduate Library School, University of Chicago, 1954.

[15] Lou L. La Brant and Frieda M. Heller, *An Evaluation of Free Reading in Grades Seven to Twelve, Inclusive*. Ohio State University Studies, Contributions in Education, No. 4. Columbus, Ohio: Ohio State University Press, 1939.

zines they most enjoy reading. The lists of high-ranking titles among high-school youth have changed but little over a period of years. The *Saturday Evening Post, American, Collier's,* and *Ladies' Home Journal* typify the perennial favorites, joined recently by such newcomers as *Life* and *Look.* Neither the quality periodical, such as *Harper's* and the *Atlantic,* nor the pulp magazine, like *Detective Story* and *True Romance,* appears on these lists. These preferences can be misleading. They tell nothing of the proportion of good and inferior magazines in the students' reading. That a large part of their magazine-reading may be of questionable quality is suggested by a study of the magazine-reading of some 3,000 Chicago high-school students in 1941.[16] Approximately 10 per cent of the reading was in pulps or movie magazines and another third in magazines characterized as "generally mediocre."

And then there are the comics magazines. Studies are not needed to testify to their universal appeal to children. Research does tell us, however, that the height of their popularity is reached in the middle grades. After this time the proportion of children reading them and the number of magazines read decrease steadily, although some high-school students continue to read them. Obviously, this trend cannot be interpreted as improving the quality of modern children's reading. The best that can be said about the best of the comics is that they are harmless and sometimes comic.

IN CONCLUSION

What do all these scattered findings about personal reading add up to? Children today, as their parents and grandparents before them, read a mixture of the good, the bad, the indifferent. Their interest in book-reading starts earlier in the grades and develops more rapidly, but it declines as much during senior high school, if not more. The number of books read is neither greater nor less than it formerly was. Interest in reading newspapers and magazines has increased. This evidence may mollify our critics, but does it reassure us? What are the implications in these findings?

Does the fact that children are devoted to comics magazines, to "Tom Swift," to "Nancy Drew," give evidence only of their desire for effortless reading and vicarious thrills? Or is it evidence of the scarcity of books in our libraries that appeal to their craving for adventure and excitement without distorting human abilities and values?

The spate of books on the market today which are thinly disguised sermons on social consciousness and character development is scarcely the kind of fare to answer children's demand for a "really good" book. Such titles, in their attempt to make good citizens, may only make poor readers. Books are not medicine to be prescribed for Bill who is too timid, for Sue who is too bossy, for Joe who is too fat. Let us leave bibliotherapy to the therapist and concentrate on helping children find good books in whose pages they can lose themselves—to find themselves.

Why do senior high school students lose interest in book-reading? Are we destroying youths' interest in reading by keeping them overlong in the "junior novels" with their patterned plots and happy endings? Critics denounce the stock characters and the contrived and

[16] Wilma S. Mater, "Sources from Which Chicago High-School Students Obtain Reading Material," pp. 32–34. Unpublished Master's paper, Graduate Library School, University of Chicago, 1943.

wholesome—"disgustingly wholesome" —boy-girl situations which fill the pages of many teen-age novels which in turn fill many school library shelves. Are we frightening youth away from continued reading by insisting upon *Silas Marner* and *The Scarlet Letter?* The best of the current adult literature gives an honest, albeit an often frank, portrayal of the world that youth must live in and strive to understand. Are we depriving youth of the very books that will make reading seem worth the effort because we fret unduly about an occasional "damn" and a frank presentation of the facts of life?

Should we worry because the high-school youth spends less time in casual and personal reading as long as the total amount of his reading is increasing? Perhaps yes, perhaps no. If assigned reading is introducing him to the enjoyment and stimulation to be found in contemporary adult literature, and if class discussions are helping him to sense the provocation and artistry of writers who have something important to say, the reading requirement may well be a potent motivation for permanent interest in reading. It is highly doubtful that the student will like *The Caine Mutiny* less because he is reading it for English class.

What are the implications of the increase in magazine-reading, particularly among high-school students? We know magazines are far more popular with adults than books. Should the schools buy more magazines and make greater attempts to interest students in the better ones? Or are these facts a challenge to renew effort in motivating students to read books? A case might be made for the fact that much of the most rewarding adult reading is to be found between the covers of a book rather than on the pages of a magazine and that the schools are failing if they do not keep alive in students the desire to read good books.

How many people will never be readers, in the sense that they turn to reading voluntarily as a source of pleasure, enrichment, and stimulation, we know not. Certainly, we cannot be satisfied that the group of adult readers is as large as possible until such time as every child is given an opportunity throughout his school life for personal reading. The formation of sound and enduring reading patterns among children and young people is important for them, not only in 1956, but also in 1976. The reading habits formed by children and youth influence society today and tomorrow; the good society will be the society of good readers.

* * *

IN ADULT LIFE

LESTER E. ASHEIM

*

To establish with any certainty the status which reading holds in our society is a very subtle and difficult task. It is one with which social scientists have been much concerned and which they have tackled in many different ways. But a survey of the reading studies reported to date reveals that most of the devices now available for measuring reading are still too gross and unrefined to provide us with the kinds of insight we seek.

The kinds of measurements we make

are primarily indirect ones. They tell us something about how much reading is *possible* in our society much more frequently than they tell us how much reading is actually done. Certainly it is true that the United States is particularly fortunate in almost all the correlates of reading. A greater proportion of our population is educated; we have more leisure; our ability to pay for such amenities is greater; and the number of public libraries far exceeds that of other countries. Yet "at any time, only 17 per cent of the adults in the United States may be found reading a book . . . [whereas] in England, where schooling is far from universal, 55 per cent of the population at any given time may be found reading a book."[1] Thus the kinds of figures we like best to quote reveal only that most of our people *can* read and that some of them do. It does not tell us what they read, for what purposes they read, or, most especially, what role reading plays in their lives in relation to their other life-activities.

To find answers to questions such as these, the research device has usually been to ask the people themselves. But to ask the people themselves about something as intangible and complex as the status of reading is to ask them for answers which they cannot properly give. People do not know how important reading is for them; they cannot remember accurately how many books they have read in the past month; they do not analyze with any insight the factors which led to their choices. It is not always that people deliberately misrepresent but that they plain do not know. Of course misrepresentation is a problem, too, since a kind of prestige attaches to

reading, and respondents are often loath to put the worst—that is, the true—light upon the kind and amount of reading they do.

Some insights, however indirect, are provided for us by these researches. From the over-all figures of publication, circulation, and sale of printed materials, we know that reading is rapidly becoming an essential part of the daily activities of more and more people. We know that between 85 and 90 per cent of the adult population reads a newspaper with at least some regularity and that 60–70 per cent read at least one magazine regularly. In terms of the mere spelling-out of the meaning of black marks on white paper, a lot of reading is being done throughout the United States. As a matter of fact, literacy is assumed in our society, and a great deal of information which it is essential that our citizens know is made available to them through the medium of print. As a tool of survival, a basic kind of literacy is virtually mandatory.

When we direct our attention to reading at a level above basic literacy, we find a somewhat less encouraging picture. The number of persons likely to be reading a book at any given time seldom exceeds 17–25 per cent of our adult population. If we try to limit our analysis to books of some stature, some seriousness, some profundity, the likelihood is that the proportion is not going to be much more than 5–10 per cent. This 10 per cent is represented in all the other figures of communication activities: they are the readers of magazines and newspapers as well as of books, the viewers of television, and the audience for the theater and film, forming what has been termed by Berelson a kind of "communications elite."[2] But they are a very small segment of the

[1] Gordon Dupee, "Can Johnny's Parents Read?" *Saturday Review*, XXXIX (June 2, 1956), 6.

[2] Bernard Berelson, *The Library's Public*, p. 15. New York: Columbia University Press, 1949.

population indeed, and there is a group just as large in which no reading, not even of newspapers, is ever done.

When we come to the questions which try to provide more direct evidence about the status of reading in our society ("For what purpose did you read this?" "How did you hear of it?" and the like), we begin to get answers which make more gratifying claims than observed reality would tend to support. Asked why they read a newspaper, a large number of respondents will claim something like "to be better informed about current problems," which is exactly what we would like to hear them say. But any pollster, or any quiz program, or any general examination reveals how badly informed about current events the average newspaper reader is. His newspaper-reading could be a source of important information about the world he lives in and the decisions he will be called upon to make affecting it, but, when we probe beyond the high-sounding responses our reader gives us, we find that he knows very little about the events and the issues on which he allegedly sought enlightenment. This does not mean that he does not read; he may not be able to name the premier of France, but he will know who plays first base for the Giants. It means only that his answers may not have quite the meaning they appear to have and that we should use extreme caution in generalizing about his motivations for reading and the effects of it.

Similarly respondents will frequently supply (or check) answers concerning their reading of books and magazines which make us feel a little better about the role that reading plays in our lives. "To broaden my view and my knowledge," "To keep abreast of the times," "To stimulate my imagination"—these are the reasons we often find in our studies. So far we have not often correlated these reasons with the actual readings themselves, but it is at least possible that in popular reading the situation is very like that in popular communication experiences of other kinds. The average person tends to over-evaluate that which is easily understood, instantly assimilated, and readily adapted to some practical purpose. And since terms like "educational," "informational," "intellectual" are dependent upon the subjective standards of the respondent, I mistrust a literal acceptance of the reader's own evaluation of the level at which he reads and the effects he imagines he derives from his reading. Though it be treason, on this campus, to say so, I am inclined to believe that the investigator's informed impressions of the role which reading plays in society may describe it more accurately than do the data he gathers from the readers themselves.

These data can be used, with caution, to tell us a great deal. What they reveal most clearly to me—in the contradiction they present between what the respondents say and what they actually do—is the strange ambivalence toward reading which is characteristic of the present-day attitude toward all things intellectual. Our respondents really want to think highly of education, of reading, and of knowledge. But the effects of reading, particularly of serious and important reading, are difficult to recognize, to appraise, and to pin down. When we ask for answers from respondents, they can reply accurately only about things which can be weighed, measured, and held in the hand. The greatest values of reading are not of this nature, and so what our respondents tend to appreciate in reading are not its greatest values.

It is a revealing reflection of our thinking that, on the "$64,000 Question" program, the master of ceremonies said to the lady who had just won the prize money for her knowledge of the Bible, "Well, all that Bible-reading finally paid off, didn't it?" Neither the contestant, nor any member of the audience, nor any commentator that I have seen since then has been moved to suggest that there might have been other pay-offs in all those years of Bible-reading.

On the other hand, there is a tradition of respect for learning in what has been called the "book and reading culture of the West." Unfortunately the benefits of education and of reading have come to us almost through hearsay; we cannot, in any of the tangible ways which carry weight in our society, prove to ourselves that they really have the value they are supposed to have. Time and again in the interviews for our reading studies, we find a somewhat apologetic tone in the responses ("I do mean to read a lot more, but somehow . . . ," "I know I should read more than I do, but . . ."), and always the gist of the apology is that more important and more interesting things have intervened.

Here we begin to get to the heart of the matter. Society acknowledges a certain importance to reading in its scheme of things, but it finds many things much more important. Despite its alleged respect for reading, it is just a bit suspicious of someone who does what it calls "too much" reading. In our society it would be unutterably shocking to find among our friends and acquaintances someone who did not know *how* to read. We also consider education to be basic, at least a high-school education and, generally, some college. But when we reach the college level, we begin to think in terms of the tangible pay-off. We state quite baldly that there are many who will

go into fields of endeavor where they don't "need" a college education; that is, where the financial rewards will not be increased by education. It is clear, therefore, that financial rewards and business success are considered more important than the nonvocational benefits of higher education. Erudition, or learning (which in some societies in some periods was seen as a great good in itself), is somewhat suspect today. We can accept a man who is college educated, but we don't want it to show unduly. The well-read person is acceptable, but the bookish person certainly is not.

This odd ambivalence derives in part, I think, from our heavy emphasis on social values in the narrowest sense. Today we are concerned with group activities, with participation, with (as the Madison Avenue copy writers have it) "togetherness." But reading, unfortunately, is a kind of antisocial activity. The reader reads by himself; he seeks privacy; he closes the door. Today's parents are much more likely to be concerned about the children who read too much than they are about those who read too little. It isn't that Johnny can't read; it is just that the social environment is constantly operating to discourage his reading. His fellows don't read; his parents don't read. Except in the case of a few best sellers, he cannot even have the pleasure of talking about his reading with others, as he can about last night's television program, or the current movie, or the outcome of yesterday's ball game. And today's Johnny is, of course, tomorrow's John, Sr.

It is important to remember the child as father to the man. We cannot talk about adult attitudes toward reading without facing the fact that those attitudes have their effect on the development of the young person on his way to adulthood. In high school, and in the early years of college, our young people are beginning to make career decisions; they are beginning to look in the direction they will want to go as adults. Naturally they look to the adult world for the models they will follow. Consequently most of our high schools and colleges, reflecting that adult world, place their emphasis on the non-book aspects of education. Would most parents prefer to have their daughter selected for Phi Beta Kappa or chosen as the queen of the Senior prom? Would they prefer to have their son made president of the honor society or captain of the football team? With whom would they most want their children to be popular: with their teachers or with their fellow-students? In most cases, I believe, the preference would be for peer-group popularity. How often have we heard, not only from parents, but even from educators, that—in a university, mind you—you can carry the emphasis on education too far!

The failure of the teachers, then, is not that they have turned out people who cannot read. In teaching the technique of reading, our present educational system must be accounted a considerable success. What little personal reading is done, is done by the few with the most education—and by children. But the child who reads has to live in the world, and that world is essentially hostile to reading. What the teacher has failed to do is demonstrate to the student the personal value which reading can have for him, quite probably because the teacher himself is not really that kind of a reader. To answer the characteristic question of our time, "What's in it for

me?" teachers, and librarians and parents, have sought to build up the instrumental values of reading: "It helps you get a job." "It teaches you how to do something." "It brings some tangible nonreading reward." If this is all that reading does—make certain facts available—then it is logical that the book should be displaced by films, radio, and television.

The teachers are not the solely responsible villains, of course. They are merely reflecting the society of which they are a part, and, for most people in our society, reading is not a good in itself. It is seen as a tool skill which may lead to other goods, but it is not its own reward. One does not gain prestige for being a reader; reading's value is that it may help one to reach other goals which do carry prestige. Thus those who do read, read what they must or what will have an instrumental value for them. The drop in book use which inevitably follows at the point of leaving school is overwhelming evidence of this fact.

Even pleasure reading is generally undertaken less for its own sake than as a refuge from complete inactivity. People do not stay home to read; they read because they are forced to stay home. They read on buses and on the subway, in dentists' offices, and in isolated vacation spots—on rainy days. They did a lot of reading while in the army, but this did not fix a continuing habit. This is not to say that pleasure reading does not give pleasure, but it is to say that, if some other diversion requiring less effort presents itself, the book is usually cast aside.

And there we have another key to our puzzle: the effort. In any human endeavor the effort one is willing to expend is dependent upon the resulting rewards. A young man will work very hard over a difficult technical manual if it will lead him to the job he wants. A young woman will follow with care the charm book which is guaranteed to make her more popular. But personal reading, in its best sense, seeks for rewards which are intangible and long-term, and thus on a second level of urgency. If reading is to assume a more important role, the goals of our society will have to be on a higher plane than those dictated by immediacy, expediency, material values, and the easy way out.

One thing that our studies strongly suggest is that the social role played by the individual is a basic determiner of his reading pattern. To raise the status of reading, we shall have to alter our present concepts of what constitutes an admirable social role. The task of education, therefore, is much broader than that of teaching reading or even that of developing a deeper appreciation of reading. It is one of making society better than it now is. But, in a sense, this is always the task of education.

CHAPTER V

A SURVEY OF CURRENT READING INTERESTS

✳

IN KINDERGARTEN THROUGH GRADE THREE

MARTHA LOU AUSTIN

✳

W HAT do we mean by "reading interests" of children? Reading interests
are, of course, the things boys and girls
want to read about, but basically the
interests include the things they like to
do, the people they like to know about,
the things they want to learn how to do.
Really to learn about children's reading
interests, we must first investigate all
the interests of children: what they like
to do, say, hear, see, and feel. What,
then, are children looking for in books?
Lewis says:

Stories that present, either realistically or
symbolically, the problems and emotional
situations faced by real children in and out of
their families, at different stages of their
growth; stories of warmth; of the courage
and tenacity that lead even the small and
weak, or the old and worn-out, to successful
achievement; stories of the overcoming of
fear and danger; stories that bring new
perspectives and discoveries flashing onto the
page, with surprise or suspense, or adventur-
ous turns and twists; stories made for
laughter and peopled with ourselves, as we
are, and as we would like to be—these are
essentially what all children are looking for.[1]

Through the years, noted authorities,
writers of children's books, librarians,
and teachers have attempted to discover
the reading interests of children at different age and grade levels. They have
learned that certain general patterns become evident at different stages of
maturity. They have also learned that,
although we can predict general trends
in the reading interests of primary-grade
children, we cannot even begin to say
what children as individuals will be
interested in reading. In our quest for
information about the interests of primary-grade children, let us examine
briefly a few of the earlier studies.

EARLY FINDINGS OF PRIMARY-GRADE
READING INTERESTS

Dunn[2] in 1921 made a scientific study
in Grades I, II, and III to determine the
elements in primary-grade reading material which arouse the interest of children. Pairs of stories were read to children, their written preferences were
secured, and the results were statistically
analyzed. Dunn's findings indicated that
children's tastes are legion; that, if we
give children a few important elemental
qualities of fact or fiction, prose or verse,

[1] Claudia Lewis, *Writing for Young Children*,
p. 81. New York: Simon & Schuster, 1954.

[2] Fannie W. Dunn, *Interest Factors in Primary
Reading Material*. Teachers College Contributions to Education, No. 113. New York: Teachers College, Columbia University, 1921.

real or fanciful situations, they are attracted and pleased. The children in Dunn's study liked the story, or plot element, but they liked it whether it appeared in fiction, in verse, or in historical prose.

Dunn found the elements contributing most to reading interest were surprise, plot, narrativeness, liveliness, repetition, conversation, childness, familiar experience, animalness, and moralness, with the latter two being attributed only to boys. She also said that age, sex, advancement, comprehension, the experience upon which reading matter is based, and the method of its presentation—all appeared to share in the modification and development of the original stock of interests.

Wilson[3] reported a study made in kindergarten and in Grades I and II of the Model School of Hunter College. This study was of the questionnaire type and was made with the co-operation and help of the parents. Replies suggested early and persistent interest in hearing nursery rhymes, simple fairy and folk tales, animal stories, nature stories, how-to-do-it books, and adventure stories. The range of interest in the types of stories enjoyed seemed limited only by the supply of story material available to children. No grade differences were conspicuous, with the exception of the Mother Goose rhymes, whose interest value tended to decrease from grade to grade. Variety rather than favoritism seemed to be the rule in connection with "acting out" stories.

Witty, Coomer, and McBean[4] conducted a study in the Chicago public schools. Children in kindergarten and the first three grades were asked to name stories they liked best, and their home-room teachers wrote down the pupils' choices. Choices of stories were found to be animal, fairy, and humor in narration, with predominance of animal stories as favorites. Whether wild or tame, real or fanciful, these creatures seemed to stir the feelings and imaginations of boys and girls. Only one book of poetry received enough votes to appear in the composite list of favorites. Humor in narration and in illustration was characteristic of many of the books chosen by kindergarten and primary-grade children.

In the studies mentioned above, poetry has seemed to suffer in comparison with other story forms. But McCauley[5] says it isn't so! She says that young children love poetry and that they enjoy listening to poems of singsong rhythm. Even at play, poems beat out the rhythm of jumping ropes and of pounding rubber balls. On dark or drab days a humorous poem or nonsense jingle is welcomed and relieves the sober or tense atmosphere.

Limitations of some of these studies are evident. Adult classification of the elements in stories is an arbitrary process; children may choose a story for a reason other than the one the experimenter had in mind. For example, a story may have been classified as an animal story, but the children may have chosen it for its conversation. It is difficult to measure the interests of young children, since they change from day to day and are greatly influenced by motivations of teachers

[3] Frank T. Wilson, "Reading Interests of Young Children," *Journal of Genetic Psychology*, LVIII (June, 1941), 363–89.

[4] Paul Witty, Ann Coomer, and Dilla McBean, "Children's Choices of Favorite Books: A Study Conducted in Ten Elementary Schools," *Journal of Educational Psychology*, XXXVII (May, 1946), 266–78.

[5] Lucille McCauley, "Little Children Love Poetry," *Elementary English*, XXV (October, 1948), 352–58.

and classmates. The main contribution of this kind of study is that it indicates to us what children in general like in stories.

What methods can be used to ascertain the reading interests of primary-grade children? The questionnaire is not ideally suited to the primary level because supplying the answers is too difficult for very young pupils. Examination of books in libraries for wear and tear may give an indication of the titles that children in general are reading, but not the specific age at which the books are read.

Most of the recent studies of primary-grade reading interests have been made by those who actually work with children, see the activities they engage in, hear them talk about the things they like to do, and see what books are freely sought. And who are these people? Those in contact with children's likes and dislikes: the classroom teacher and the school librarian.

RECENT STUDIES OF READING INTERESTS

Gunderson[6] made a study in Grade II to determine the particular qualities in books that appeal to these children. In the attempt to discover which qualities in books were especially liked, the teacher asked, "Why do you like it?" The most frequent responses were: "It's funny," "It's interesting," "It's exciting," "It's scary," "It's magic." "Funny," according to the writer, is used by children to indicate the ridiculous, the unbelievable, surprising, imaginative, and the absurd. In summarizing, children liked the books

for qualities of humor, excitement, suspense, adventure, kindness to animals, magic or fancy; ability of the leading character to accomplish the unusual or unexpected; and an ending in which justice triumphs.

Claudia Lewis, whom I have quoted earlier, also says:

It is likely that the animal story, in which animals act as people, will not outgrow its popularity among young children. Animal characters are scarcely ambiguous symbols, yet they are one step removed from human beings, and for this reason invite the child to project himself freely into them. When a bunny is pictured running away, or a puppy is shown rebelling against the things he should do, the child can . . . experience vicariously what he might not otherwise feel free to experience.[7]

Frank[8] has given the results of years of experience in learning what children of different ages enjoy in reading. She indicates that everything points to the love of preschool children for color, especially the primary colors, in illustrations of picture-books. Young children delight in word sounds and word sensations. Humor must be direct and obvious, hinging on situations within their range of understanding. Children cannot understand incongruities and mishaps based on experiences that they have not yet had. They like real and fanciful animal stories. They attribute human qualities to their toys and pets and do not find it at all strange that the three bears should sit in chairs and sleep in beds or that Peter Rabbit should disobey his mother and be properly punished for it. Along with

[6] Agnes G. Gunderson, "What Seven-Year-Olds Like in Books," *Elementary English*, XXX (March, 1953), 163–66.

[7] Claudia Lewis, *op. cit.*, p. 92.

[8] Josette Frank, *Your Child's Reading Today*. Garden City, New York: Doubleday & Co., Inc., 1954.

picture-books, young children delight in verses and jingles, and nothing so far has succeeded in displacing Mother Goose.

The seven- or eight-year-old usually prefers the realistic to the personified; not only the things, but the people, that do the world's work are important to children in these years. In their reading about animals, children turn first to stories about the more familiar creatures, with dogs and cats leading all others in popularity. As the children grow older, they enjoy reading about all kinds of wild creatures in their natural surroundings.

The place of fantasy is firmly established. We may ride on a space ship instead of a magic carpet, but the purpose is still the same. The fairy tale offers escape and wish fulfilment and provides experience beyond the realm of the possible. Satisfying, too, is the punishment that comes to the wicked. It is their very elemental appeal to the emotions which has kept these stories alive. The height of interest in fairy tales seems to be reached around eight, or perhaps nine, years of age.

CONCLUDING STATEMENT

Observations, checking of reading lists, and interviews with librarians bear out Frank's conclusions as to reading interests in general. At the primary-grade level, both boys and girls tend to be interested in a variety of reading material because they are interested in a variety of things.

Can we say then that, if we have a variety of animal stories, fairy tales, stories about children, and so on, we have provided for the reading interests of our pupils? No. For these qualities in stories are those that children *in general* like. These findings cannot take the place of the information obtained by the teacher for himself, through any means necessary, concerning the individual interests and tastes of the children within his own classroom.

✳ ✳ ✳

IN GRADES FOUR THROUGH SIX

GRACE S. WALBY

✳

CHILDREN read for many reasons. Curiosity may send them to books. They may read for self-discovery. Reading also provides emotional safety valves —outlets for aggressive feelings, satisfying the need to feel big or the desire to outwit others by cunning or to digress from righteousness and be punished. Much of children's reading is a quest for information, a desire to know more about the world of which they are a part. Often reading may be, just as with adults, an escape from the anxieties of a too pressing world. However, it would be a mistake to assume that each child has a single specific motive which leads him to books. Children's motives may be mixed or even merged.

Whatever their motives, children are reading. But what are they reading? This is a question which has long been of concern to parents and educators. Investigators have sought the answer in many ways. They have devised questionnaires;

analyzed library withdrawals; observed children; and talked with teachers, librarians, and parents. Let us look briefly at some of their findings.

REVIEW OF FINDINGS

One of the early "classics" in the field is the study by Terman and Lima[1] of the qualitative and quantitative aspects of children's reading, with special reference to individual differences caused by age, sex, intelligence, and special interests. Their findings were based on questionnaires to children, teachers, and parents; on children's reading records; and on the memories of a group of university students as to their own favorite childhood books. At about the same time Washburne and Vogel[2] also developed a list of titles, using the additional factor of the amount of reading ability necessary for maximum interest. In both these lists, the selection was made on a dual basis: what children like and what, according to adult judgment, was felt to be worth while.

A summary of these studies and of others done before 1930 indicates that there is a certain constancy in reading preferences at different periods of a child's growth and development. Such factors as differing rates of physical and mental growth, school environment, social or economic status, home training, and past experience affect individual preferences. Therefore Sister Celestine cautions: "The varying influence of these numerous factors indicates clearly that no sharp line of demarcation can be made in determining exactly the books that appeal to children at any specific age."[3]

However, there seem to be certain typical trends. In the middle grades there is evidence of the diverging interests of boys and girls. Although both enjoy animal stories and tales of other lands, boys are demanding realistic adventure, while girls continue to enjoy the imaginative and stories of home and school. Girls read more than boys but have a narrower range of interests. Biography, history, travel, and science have greater appeal for boys, but these interests are minor. Both boys and girls prefer prose to poetry. Poetry, however, has some appeal for girls, but none for boys. The dominant interest of both boys and girls is fiction.

Although boys and girls fail to read informational materials widely, it has been shown that they will read, with keen interest, informational material prepared expressly for children if it is well written. Thus it may not be the theme, but the manner of treating it, which contains the vital appeal.

There are qualitative and quantitative differences in the reading interests of gifted children. They read more, and over a wider range, than do those of less intelligence. They read more informational material and nonfiction and show a greater preference for humor. The most striking contrast is in the ages at which books are read. Superior children will read at an earlier age what appeals to the average or dull child at a later age.

---

[1] Lewis M. Terman and Margaret Lima, *Children's Reading: A Guide for Parents and Teachers.* New York: D. Appleton & Co., 1926.

[2] Carleton Washburne and Mabel Vogel, *Winnetka Graded Book List.* Chicago: American Library Association, 1926.

[3] Sister M. Celestine, *A Survey of the Literature on the Reading Interests of Children of the Elementary Grades,* p. 35. Catholic University of America Educational Research Bulletins, Vol. V, Nos. 2 and 3. Washington: Catholic University of America, 1930.

Thorndike[4] developed an instrument which he felt would enable him to obtain an estimate of reading interests quickly and conveniently, apart from the influence of availability, readability, and past experience with particular books. He did this by preparing a questionnaire of fictitious, annotated titles. Responses of children in Grades IV–XII were analyzed with particular attention to the influence of age, sex, and intelligence in determining interest patterns.

His findings agree with earlier studies in revealing consistent patterns of boy interests and girl interests cutting across all age and intelligence differences, and in showing reading interests of younger bright children to be like those of older children of less intelligence. However, he noted that the acceleration of interest of bright children appeared as clearly in an early interest in violent adventure and mystery as it did in an early interest in science or invention. His finding of relatively small changes in interest in many topics over a wide age span is of particular concern to those who must meet the needs of retarded readers.

Children for whom reading is not yet an easy task, Frank suggests,[5] can be intrigued into a book only if the story gets under way at once and if it moves rapidly. Books will seem more inviting if they are not too thick, have readable type and wide spaces between the lines, and are generously larded with pictures and quotation marks. If the contents are rewarding and the material is not too difficult, such books may help children acquire the facility which can make reading a pleasure. With such children as well as with all whom we seek to guide, the trick is to know which book to offer to a particular child and to know when to offer it.

Many other studies relating to reading interests and the factors which influence them have been made. Perhaps, however, it would be profitable at this time to consider briefly two types of reading which flourish in spite of adult concern. A good book has been defined as one which gives to the reader a good reading experience.[6] A good book, by adult standards, is not a good book for a particular child if it does not give him a good reading experience. If, then, we can find out the values that children get from the comics and series books, we may learn something of value in guiding children toward better reading experiences.

Virtually all children read comic books. These books are read to some extent by children of all ages, but the peak of popularity is reached during the middle grades. Why do children read comic books so avidly? Research[7] indicates that comics satisfy the desire for action, excitement, and adventure and that they provide an escape from the routine of everyday life. They are accessible, inexpensive, easy to read, episodic. They establish a child as a member of a group and even satisfy the collector's urge. They allow children to overcome, in imagination, the limitations which age and ability impose. They may serve the very real purpose of stimulating an

---

[4] Robert L. Thorndike, *Children's Reading Interests*. New York: Bureau of Publications, Teachers College, Columbia University, 1941.

[5] Josette Frank, *Your Child's Reading Today*, pp. 98–99. Garden City, New York: Doubleday & Co., Inc., 1954.

[6] *Ibid.*, p. 40.

[7] Paul Witty and Robert A. Sizemore, "Reading the Comics: A Summary of Studies and an Evaluation," *Elementary English*, XXXI (December, 1954), 501–6; XXXII (January and February, 1955), 43–49, 109–14.

initial interest in reading, serve as a bridge to books.

Children's persistent interest in the series books has been noted in almost all studies of children's reading interests. Many have dismissed this interest as worthless. Frank suggests that these books cannot be dismissed as unworthy of interest, because children so thoroughly notice them. She feels that they have values for the child which adults are likely to underestimate: chances to meet, again and again, familiar characters and situations. They are not a waste of time if they provide for a child his first enjoyable reading experience. They are a transitory pleasure, on which we can capitalize by offering well-written books that come in series form and thus give the series addict a more enriched reading experience. Growth is our goal, and, if we are alert to children's needs, we can help them progress from the lesser to the greater values and to a wider use of reading to meet a variety of needs.

RECENT TRENDS

In recent years there has been a tremendous increase in the number, scope, and accessibility of children's books. Schools, radio and television, and world events have done much to widen children's horizons. What effects, if any, have these factors had on the reading interests of today's children? To find an answer to this question, I interviewed librarians who have been in close contact with children for a number of years. Many interesting trends in this age group have been noted. Career books, especial-ly those concerned with ballet and nursing, are in great demand. Biographies are very popular, as are science fiction and aviation. Increased interest has been noted in mythology, tales of other lands, stories about such inventions as the atom bomb, and in religious books. Family stories still form the bulk of reading. Animal and sports stories are perennial favorites. Many of these interests can be traced to the stimulation of television and to world events. Many are undoubtedly also due to the increased availability and appeal of books on many subjects.

SUMMARY

Children read for many reasons and to meet many needs. At this age level, new interests are opening up to them, and their reading is therefore likely to be varied—a reaching-out in many directions. They will be reading comic books and the series books, but they will also be reading adventure, history, and fiction; about the lives of real people and heroes of mythology; science fiction; sports; information; and animal stories. The differences in interests between boys and girls become increasingly marked throughout this age period. Many factors influence individual reading preferences.

Therefore our success in guiding children to better reading experiences will depend on how close we can get to the individual child's own tastes, needs, and capacity for understanding. Children can come to good literature only by their own routes, stimulated by thoughtful adult guidance.

ALICE R. WICKENS

✳

Teachers of reading hope to develop in children the variety of skills needed for reading many different kinds of material, as well as an abiding interest and continuing pleasure in extensive reading as a useful and as a leisure-time activity. It is not encouraging that research has disclosed that the majority of adults do little reading of any significance. Teachers therefore should look carefully at the reading interests of adolescents, to find clues to the development and maintenance of a desirable quality of reading as an adult activity.

RELATION OF AGE TO READING INTERESTS

Research reports over a period of years show amazing agreement on the nature and effect of certain factors on reading interests. The first of these factors is chronological age. The junior high school years bring the peak in amount of reading done. Only a very few children do no reading at all during this three-year period.

Although this is the period of maximum reading, it is also the period in which reading definitely declines. The amount of individual reading increases rapidly toward the middle and upper grades and then begins to drop off in Grade IX. Pupils in junior high school read an average of 19 per cent more than do pupils in senior high school. This pattern has been repeatedly verified.

A current survey of individual reading over the past year for these three grades at the Laboratory School of the University of Chicago shows a seventh-grade range of 5 to 79 books read, an eighth-grade range from 1 to 108, and a ninth-grade range from 1 to 55.

In an interview with this writer, Mrs. Yolanda Federici, young people's supervisor for the South Side Division of the Chicago Public Library system, notes that a similar decline occurs at the ninth-grade level in the general population, except in isolated instances. With this conclusion, Miss Catherine Adamson, general supervisor at the central library, concurs.

Both the literature and the opinion of experts advance reasons for this decrease in reading. Academic expectations increase considerably at this age, requiring additional homework and reducing time available for free reading. There are more extra-curriculum activities in school and a marked increase in the demands of social life outside of school.

In our culture, reading once tended to be looked upon as a waste of time as youth began to assume adult responsibilities. But since current living puts a rather high premium upon the ability to read, it is quite likely that these young people literally do not have time to read. This conclusion would imply that, since the decrease in quantity cannot be prevented, steps should be taken to insure a high quality of the reading done.

What is the quality of reading during

60

early adolescence? In 1928 Jennings[1] noted the wide range of interests and the general preference for wholesome reading on the part of junior high school boys and girls. Holy[2] found a much wider range of interests in the junior high school than in the senior high school. For example, more magazines are read at age thirteen. Newspaper-reading shows the beginning of a genuine interest in world events. Rather specialized interests begin to appear at fourteen. Esther Anderson[3] called this the age of exploring. All the research studies agree that the major interest is in fiction, mostly juvenile, with a dawning interest in adult fiction. Among the top favorites in all reported lists, however, are the classics, both juvenile and adult.

Data indicate that young people select books because of interesting titles or pictures or because they know and like the author. Literary elements with appeal for them include action, human interest, imagination, humor, direct discourse, colorful descriptions and names. Particularly they dislike preaching or moralizing. Other interest factors are suspense, happy endings, and situations in which students can imagine themselves. Elements of style which appeal are a free and easy manner of writing, brevity, sincerity, and straightforwardness of language, joined with rapidity of movement.

Norvell determined the order of preference for types of literature as follows: novels, plays, short stories, biographies, essays, poetry, letters, and speeches. He summarized the changes in interests when he stated: "The results of five studies . . . indicate that the year-to-year changes in children's reading interests between Grades VIII and XI are usually gradual and small."[4]

At the junior high school level, Lyness[5] found that certain interest patterns tended to cluster in certain subject-matter areas and to carry over from one area of mass communication to another. Included were violence and adventure, educational content, love, private life, and glamour.

Josette Frank[6] summarizes the general areas of interest in a descriptive and comprehensive manner. Young teenagers enjoy the series books, stories of families, of life in other lands, and of adventure on land and sea. They like stories with historical backgrounds, stories about animals, and the teen-age and career books. They are interested in informative and how-to-do-it books, in biographies, science, and discovery. Stories about school and about sports have appeal. Students read the classics, both juvenile and adult. They read mysteries, science fiction, poetry, and comic books.

[1] Joe Jennings, "Leisure Reading of Junior High School Boys and Girls," *Peabody Journal of Education*, VI (May, 1929), 343–47.

[2] T. C. Holy, *Survey of the Schools of Euclid, Ohio*, pp. 139–42. Ohio State University Studies, Bureau of Educational Research Monographs, No. 22. Columbus, Ohio: Ohio State University, 1936.

[3] Esther M. Anderson, "A Study of Leisure-Time Reading of Pupils in Junior High School," *Elementary School Journal*, XLVIII (January, 1948), 258–67.

[4] George W. Norvell, *The Reading Interests of Young People*, p. 38. Boston: D. C. Heath & Co., 1950.

[5] Paul I. Lyness, "Patterns in the Mass Communication Tastes of the Young Audience," *Journal of Educational Psychology*, XLII (December, 1951), 449–67.

[6] Josette Frank, *Your Child's Reading Today*, pp. 138–68. Garden City, New York: Doubleday & Co., Inc., 1954.

Since they do read comics, it is well to note Arbuthnot's opinion: "There is probably little cause to worry about children and their comic strips as long as they are also enjoying good books."[7]

Recently public librarians have observed some trends suggestive of interest changes. Career books have dropped from eighth-grade to sixth-grade level in popularity, while teen-age girls are increasingly demanding books about the ballet and about ways in which to develop personality and popularity. Science fiction has also moved from junior high school level to the elementary school, where both boys and girls read it. The demand for biography has increased, with emphasis upon the lives of living persons. There is considerable increase in requests for informative books. It has been suggested that television is largely responsible for these changes. Librarians have noted that television stimulates areas of interest among young people on the one hand, while on the other hand the vast publishing industry turns out more and more books to meet this interest demand. These new books, in turn, provide television with additional subject matter. A dynamic interrelationship exists between the various media of mass communication, each stimulating the other.

SEX DIFFERENCES AND READING INTERESTS

At adolescence, differences in reading interests of boys and of girls sharpen. Norvell[8] has pointed out that the influence of sex differences upon selection of

[7] May Hill Arbuthnot, "Children and the Comics," *Elementary English*, XXIV (March, 1947), 183.

[8] George W. Norvell, *op. cit.*, p. 46.

reading material is a dominant and highly significant factor. Girls read more than boys, but their interests are more homogeneous; boys cover a wider range of subjects and read more nonfiction than do girls.

Girls read boys' books, but boys do not like girls' books. Boys like biography and history, inventions and mechanics, adventure stories, and tales of athletic prowess. Girls read stories of home and school life, with *Little Women* reaching its height of popularity. Girls read adventure stories, too, but prefer them to be of the mild variety rather than the grim and desperate type which engross boys. Both sexes read biography, girls preferring the life-stories of women, although they read about men. Boys will not read biographies about women if they can avoid it.

About 90 per cent of the reading of both sexes is fiction. Of this, boys prefer outdoor adventures, mystery and detective stories, stories about sports and about animals, especially wild animals. They enjoy comic books, the boys' series, tales of war and patriotism, and those of humorous incident. They turn to adult fiction about a year later than girls, usually to the adult adventure story. In nonfiction, boys read over a wide range: biography, history, science, travel, and sports.

Girls also read mystery and detective stories, comic books, adventure and animal stories. The adventures, however, are mild, and the animals are pets or domestic animals. They read the girls' series, stories of home and family life, and romance. They read adult fiction earlier than boys, generally turning to adult romance. Much of it is likely to be sentimental trash. So heavily do girls read in this area that, unless they have some guidance, they are in danger of developing a persistent habit of inconsequential reading. Girls read and like drama and poetry much more frequently than do boys. Their narrower range of nonfiction tends to be confined to biography, some history, and subjects related to feminine interests.

INFLUENCE OF INTELLIGENCE ON READING INTERESTS

A third factor having some influence upon reading interests is intelligence. Exceptionally bright children read an average of three or four times as many books as do children of average intelligence, and the bright children generally read books of better quality. The socioeconomic status of bright children is usually high and may influence the amount of reading done. Lazar[9] found that bright children from homes of lower socioeconomic status read a great deal but that the quality tends to be less satisfactory.

Girls read more than boys, bright children more than average children, average children more than dull children, while dull girls read more than dull boys. Dull children tend to choose simpler and less realistic materials, while bright children seem to be more interested in the realities of life. Bright and average boys usually read adventure, history, and science. Slow boys tend to read history, mysteries, fairly tales, and stories of home and school life. There is little difference between the reading done by bright, aver-

age, and slow girls, except that the slower girls read more fairy tales and seem especially interested in useful feminine activities.

In surveying the reading of the bright population in Grades VII–IX in the Laboratory School, the most interesting observation about their reading was the catholicity of interest of both boys and girls. It was as though they were dipping into, and savoring, all kinds of literature, almost all of it of good quality and much of it classic.

READING AND ENVIRONMENTAL FACTORS

There are also certain environmental factors which determine reading interests, such as the influence of parents and the recommendations of friends, librarians, or teachers. More reading and a better quality of reading are associated with higher socioeconomic level. They are also correlated with the education of parents and their occupational and leisure-time pursuits, as well as with the amount of value which families accord educational attainments. Availability of books is a factor which librarians stress. Possession of library cards varies with the proximity of libraries. The kind of books available is of utmost importance. It has been found that amount and quality of reading are related to the number and kinds of books, magazines, and newspapers found in the home. A less measurable environmental factor is the early experiences of children with reading. Woellner[10] reported that 91 per cent of the children in her study had

[9] May Lazar, *Reading Interests, Activities and Opportunities of Bright, Average, and Dull Children*, p. 101. Teachers College Contributions to Education, No. 707. New York: Bureau of Publications, Teachers College, Columbia University, 1937.

[10] Mary H. B. Woellner, *Children's Voluntary Reading as an Expression of Individuality*, p. 117. Teachers College Contributions to Education, No. 944. New York: Bureau of Publications, Teachers College, Columbia University, 1949.

enjoyed having books and stories read to them.

We must not fail to take into account, as an environmental factor, the influence of television, mentioned earlier. Josette Frank has this to say about it:

More young people are growing up with an appreciation of the arts because, through the mass media, more children are exposed to them. . . . Books, newspapers, magazines, television, and radio bring the world into their homes.[11]

INDIVIDUAL PERSONALITY DIFFERENCES

Personality is the last factor considered here, and one of extreme importance. Certain aspects of personality are characteristic of children of junior high school age. Other aspects are highly individual, but all of them operate to determine activities and interests. Children at this age read to satisfy personal curiosity and to satisfy deep needs and wishes. Reading can be a refuge from unpleasant circumstances, a source of companionship, a "ladder to the stars."

Woellner[12] found that the reading attitudes of young people can be classified into three major groups. One is a tendency toward excessive reading, which results from emotional difficulties, with indiscriminate choice or an inadequate balance between purely recreational and purposeful reading. The opposite attitude is avoidance of reading, also rooted in personality problems, with poor reading habits, careless selections, and little progress in critical or creative thinking. Normal interest, the third, is associated with emotional poise, lack of rigidity in intellectual and emotional satisfactions, and versatility in general interests.

It cannot be stressed too heavily that these personality differences must be understood and accepted by the teacher. Each adolescent is still himself, no matter what the generalizations about reading patterns and interests for his age group may be. What, then, are the implications for teachers?

CONCLUDING STATEMENT

It is quite clear that the definite taste for reading characteristic of early adolescence is a guidepost. But if each child is to select the reading materials that will make the most of his personal capacities and interests, the teacher must provide careful guidance. Lack of time will inevitably diminish the quantity of the adolescent's reading. Careful guidance may help him to maintain worthy quality.

Paul Hazard's *Books, Children and Men* is a must for teachers in whose hands lies this intricate problem of motivating children to read and to like reading. The spirit of such leadership and the theme of Hazard's book are both expressed in these sentences from it:

"Give us books," say the children; "give us wings. You who are powerful and strong, help us to escape into the faraway. . . . We are willing to learn everything that we are taught at school, but, please, let us keep our dreams."[13]

[11] From *Your Child's Reading Today*, p. 19, by Josette Frank. Copyright 1953, 1954, by Josette Frank. Reprinted by permission of Doubleday & Company, Inc.

[12] Mary H. B. Woellner, *op. cit.*, pp. 73–75.

[13] Paul Hazard, *Books, Children and Men*, p. 4. Boston: Horn Book, Inc., 1947.

IN GRADES TEN THROUGH FOURTEEN

HELEN K. SMITH

✴

TODAY when many media compete with reading for the time of young people, it is imperative that educators know and understand the interests of youth if reading tastes are to be improved. The results of the many research studies since 1897 vary in some of their details but are in general agreement concerning many of the major premises, regardless of the date of the research.

Methods of studying reading interests have varied so much that it is somewhat difficult to make fair and adequate comparisons. Frequently the following research methods have been used: the questionnaire, the cumulative reading record, analyses of book and magazine withdrawals, interviews, check lists, and observations. In each case the investigators attempted to determine the true reading interests.

GENERAL TRENDS

Certain general tendencies are noted in all research concerning high-school and college students. They do read; some read a great deal. Fiction, especially that having a strong plot, is much preferred to nonfiction. There is a decided preference for the modern books, including those on best-seller lists. Within recent years, frequently mentioned favorites are *The Robe* by Lloyd Douglas (Houghton, 1942), *The Black Rose* by Thomas Costain (Doubleday, 1945), books by Pearl Buck and A. J. Cronin, and Margaret Mitchell's *Gone with the Wind* (Macmillan, 1936). Within every group, however, the titles of favorite books show much variety, ranging from mature and recent books to the old favorites of children. Many students, especially the immature readers, prefer books of a series.

Biography appears to be the most popular form of nonfiction. Perennial favorite subjects of biography are Abraham Lincoln, Will Rogers, Helen Keller, Charles Lindbergh, Theodore Roosevelt, and Daniel Boone. Sports personalities appear to be the current favorites.

Prose of any form is preferred to poetry by most students. Research shows that, outside of required reading, very little poetry is read. A growing interest in books on vocational guidance, psychology, and technical and scientific subjects (especially aeronautics, television, and automobiles) has been noted.

THE READING OF PERIODICALS

More newspapers and magazines than books are read, especially by the older students. Studies reveal that from two to three magazines are read regularly by students, most reading with little guidance.

Having the most appeal to all readers are *Life, Look, Reader's Digest, American Magazine, Saturday Evening Post,* and *Collier's.* In addition to these, boys prefer magazines such as *Popular Science* and *Popular Mechanics.* The girls like *Good Housekeeping* and *Ladies' Home Journal.*

News magazines rank high on only a few lists, with *Time* being the favorite. Such magazines as *True Story* and *De-*

65

tective Story are read by a number of students. Unfortunately, critical and literary journals were seldom listed as being read.

Most high-school and college students read one or more newspapers regularly, spending from ten minutes to over an hour's time each day in this activity. The average time spent by students in reading the newspaper is from fifteen to thirty minutes a day. The three favorite sections, in order, are the comics, the sports page, and the front page. Picture sections are always popular. Many high-school and some college students prefer the tabloids.

When students were asked if they believed what they read in the newspaper, in some schools as many as 90 per cent answered in the affirmative. Almost one-half of the students stated that they had no special method of reading the newspaper. Reading everything concerning their special interests and glancing at headlines only were the two principal plans used. A few read almost everything thoroughly.

FACTORS DETERMINING READING INTERESTS

All investigations agree that sex is a strong determining factor in kinds of reading done by young people. Usually spending more time in reading, girls prefer books to magazines and newspapers, while the opposite is true with boys.

Books of adventure are the decided favorites of boys, while stories of love and romance lead for the girls. According to research, boys also like scientific and technical books, war stories, mysteries, detective novels, some humor, animal and aviation stories, and history. Girls, on the other hand, favor books concerned with home and school life, teen-age

problems, mild types of adventure, and biography, especially of women. They like poetry better than boys do.

Boys do not like girls' stories, while some girls will read and enjoy boys' books. In nearly all cases the girls exceeded the boys in the use of libraries.

Sex differences are shown in newspaper-reading. Boys show a definite preference for sports news; accomplishments in science, aviation, and industry; and crime news. Showing little interest in these, girls prefer the society and women's pages, news of entertainment, gossip, and beauty advice.

In a lesser degree than sex, age is the second factor which influences reading interests. Two general trends can be noted in the results of research studies. Older students in some schools have developed maturity of reading habits and interests. In others, there does not appear to be the broadening of interests one would expect among older students, especially college students.

In the research which shows growth in reading interests, the maturity is seen in various ways. In many cases the juvenile literature read by younger students is replaced by books currently popular with adults. The older students read for information more often than the younger ones do. The older students show increased interest in current news, science, travel, editorials, and technical articles. A decrease in interest in the comics is noticed, with the comic strip being more popular than the comic books. Nonfiction, especially biography, appeals to the older students more than to the younger ones. Often the tabloid newspaper is replaced by one of more liberal nature.

It would be encouraging if all students broadened their reading interests with maturity. In several studies related to free reading in college, immature habits and interests were reported. It was agreed in this body of research that habits were rather permanently formed in secondary school.

Research is not in complete agreement concerning mental ability as a determining factor of reading interests. The research does report that intelligent young people read more and usually over a wider range of subjects than do those having a lower mental ability. One study showed that bright students tend to read the more realistic types of books and articles, while the dull ones seemed to prefer fanciful and romantic types. The latter avoided scientific books, perhaps because of the vocabulary. Other studies, however, found that interests of bright and dull students were not so different as might be expected.

Reasons for liking or disliking selections vary, and what one student likes may be the very selection that another dislikes intensely. Students are not generally inclined to like subtle humor, poetry, long passages of description, letters, editorials and useful information in the newspapers, philosophy, religion, music, art, drama, political and historical subjects. They do not like reading which has difficult vocabulary and sentence structure, wordiness, slow movement, too much sentimentalism, monotony, and characters who are old. Students favored books having the opposite characteristics.

Many young people lack real guidance in the selection of books and magazines. A large percentage stated that no one had helped them select their reading material. Friends were more influential than any other group, including the teacher. The other motivating factors were parents, librarians, book displays, book clubs, relatives, knowledge of the authors, the scoutmaster, hobbies, and advertisements.

THE QUALITY OF THE READING

Most of the investigators show extreme concern about the literary merit of the independent reading of young people. Although the reading is described in various degrees, from commendable to worthless, it is the general agreement that the quality of the reading is disappointing, even though the content itself is harmless. The overabundance of the reading of light fiction, the intense interest in comics and pictures, the dearth of poetry-reading, the undiscriminating choices of newspapers and magazines, the neglect shown toward the better magazines, the continuation even into college years of interest in juvenile literature—all these indicate that little of the students' reading demands minute insight and critical judgment.

Librarians who were interviewed this spring agreed with the findings of this paper. Fiction is still preferred to non-fiction; boys like stories of automobiles, adventure, and sports; girls demand romantic fiction. Poetry and plays are read only when they are assigned, except for a few students in dramatic groups who read drama for enjoyment. Modern books are preferred. Young teen-agers favor authors like Tunis, Meader, Cavanna, and Lambert; older readers seem to have no preferred authors. Many are beginning to show more mature and broader interests than they did formerly.

Additional trends not indicated in the research are noted. Science fiction is in great demand. Boys are enthusiastic about books and magazines concerned with automobiles. In addition to the extremely popular books, *Street Rod* (Random, 1953) and *Hot Rod* (Dutton, 1950), they like biographies of people like Wilbur Shaw. They like all automobile magazines, *Hot Rod* being the favorite. They also show much enthusiasm for sports and aviation magazines. Girls like to look through the magazine *Seventeen* but state that they like to read the small magazine *Compact*.

IMPLICATIONS FROM RESEARCH

The first of four implications derived from the research on reading interests is that students need to have available a variety of good, readable books and magazines. Teachers and librarians need firsthand knowledge of many books suitable for the young people whom they teach. For many students the school library is the chief source of books.

The second implication is the importance of accepting the student on his own reading level with his present reading interests. Beginning with these and leading to a higher and broader plane of interests should be the goal of all teachers.

The third important implication is the necessity for guidance in reading. A number of investigations show that effective guidance in reading results in improved tastes and interests. All research agrees that students need to read more widely. Most of those who do read desirable books limit themselves to the reading of fiction almost entirely.

Guidance should extend to the area of magazines and newspapers, the two media used most by students. Effort should be made to introduce students to magazines of high quality instead of those that merely satisfy the purpose of diversion and light entertainment.

These interests and tastes, as the fourth implication, should be considered by teachers and curriculum makers, especially those who are prone to choose selections according to their own preferences. Norvell found that certain required selections were much better enjoyed than others and asked this question of the reader: "Why should we insist on *As You Like It* or Shakespeare's sonnets when *Macbeth, Hamlet,* and other well-liked plays are available?"[1]

The manner in which reading interests of young people are used in modern education may determine not only the future use of leisure time but also the future thinking of the nation. It is desirable, therefore, that educators continue to study reading interests; environmental changes and new means of communication may create new trends which should be identified and utilized effectively in education.

[1] George W. Norvell, "Some Results of a Twelve-Year Study of Children's Reading Interests," *English Journal,* XXXV (December, 1946), 536.

CHAPTER VI

THE EFFECTS OF READING ON PERSONAL AND SOCIAL DEVELOPMENT

✳

ANNE McKILLOP

✳

To teachers of reading who spend much time analyzing the reading task, urging the young to read more, and seeking out even more printed material, it seems a preposterous suggestion that reading may not have as great effects on people as we like to think. It is difficult to imagine a world without books, but there may be one in the future. It is possible that, with new discoveries, books will go out of date and that, except for scholars who delve into the past, people of the future will rely upon other forms of communication.

Even today many people read little. They glance at the bulletin board in the factory, the headlines in a daily paper, and peruse the television schedule. Occasionally they read a note left by some member of the family. For information, entertainment, and inspiration they turn to other media. However, four hundred million books were bought in 1954 in America; over four million newspapers are sold daily in New York alone; eleven and a half million books were borrowed from the New York Public Library from July, 1954, through June, 1955. What effect does all this have on people?

One way of answering this question is to ask another: What happens to the people who cannot read? Here the answer is

fairly clear. Usually the person who cannot obtain meaning from at least a minimum number of printed symbols is unemployable. The armed services considered that every serviceman needed reading ability equal to that reached by the average nine-year-old child. Most business concerns ask the prospective employee to fill out an application form, and most jobs in industry require some reading skill. In some states literacy must be established before one can vote. The individual who cannot read is thus cut off from military service, from most types of employment in urban areas, and sometimes from the privilege of voting.

In addition to these limitations upon his activities, the illiterate is often humilated by being unable to read. People may be tolerant of, or even rather proud of, their inability to spell or add, but being unable to read is different. One child stopped attending Sunday School because the children were reading "verse about" in the class, and she was unable to face the humiliation of not being able to take part. It is an indictment of our verbal schools that many children consider inability to read a mark of moral failure.

At least limited reading skill, then, is

69

necessary in this society. It is necessary for the basic activities of social life and as a mark of social respectability and adequacy. Beyond opening these doors, what does reading do to people?

READING IS AN INTERPERSONAL EXPERIENCE

In order to explore the effects of reading, it is necessary to examine the nature of the reading process. Essentially it is an interpersonal experience, a meeting of minds, an interaction between the reader and the author. In a rich reading experience the author and the reader communicate with each other; the reader does not passively receive impressions from the author's thought. Some readers argue aloud with an author. Others cannot resist writing in books; this is their way of reacting to the author's ideas. It is true that, in reading, the interaction is somewhat limited since the author cannot react in turn to the reader, but the one-sided, private nature of the relationship between reader and author provides some unique features. The reader may feel safer than in a face-to-face relationship. He may leave a boring book when he would not feel free to leave a boring guest; he may read about subjects which he would find too embarrassing to talk about; he may ask questions of books which he could not ask of people.

Reading, then, can exert the same influences as any interpersonal experience. It may instruct, entertain, inspire, persuade, but with certain limitations and certain strengths. We shall consider three possible effects of reading and some of the limitations that surround them.

READING BUILDS COMMUNITY

One of the effects of reading is to build community, not only with the author and his thoughts, but with others who have read and reacted to the same book or article. Being read to as a young child and later reading with or to others build common bonds between the reader and the listener. It is a sharing of emotional experiences, a knowing of mutual friends. A common step in the building of a friendship is the exploration of one another's likes and dislikes in reading. Urging a friend to read an enjoyed book is often a way of sharing the experience.

These common readings can provide group symbols that consolidate the group and provide a kind of communication shorthand. For example, everyone in a group of gifted adolescents knew T. S. Eliot's "The Love Song of J. Alfred Prufrock," which symbolized for them the dry and empty world against which they were rebelling. In many ways this one poem constituted a strong bond between them.

The common bond afforded by reading may be based upon a genuine sharing of ideas and feelings or upon a desire to be "in the know," to be able to talk about the same books as others. Best-seller lists are often outgrowths of this need to belong, to have something in common with others. A tenth-grade class whose reading skills were deplorably inadequate insisted on reading Shakespeare's *Julius Caesar* because, in that school, all full-fledged tenth-graders read *Julius Caesar*. Undoubtedly the reading influenced them, but it was probably in this area of common understandings and shared experiences rather than in the area of information or aesthetic appreciation. In schools we have often been so concerned with the dissection of a selection or with the correct recognition of all the words that we have failed to see reading as providing this kind of shared experience.

READING INCREASES FREEDOM

Another important effect of reading is to expand the individual's world, to grant him a greater degree of freedom than he would otherwise possess. With the precious key of reading, one can unlock the gates of time and space and can range at will over past, present, and future, under the earth, on the earth and above it. One can learn about the real or revel in fantasy. A person who can read is free to try new experiences. The woman is not limited to making the same meat loaf that her mother taught her to make; she can try the new recipe she finds in a magazine. The man is not tied to the job he learned as an apprentice; he can get a correspondence course in anything from beekeeping to xylophone-playing. The child is not tied to a small midwestern town; he can be a pirate with Long John Silver, find out about animals in central Africa, or plan a trip to the moon.

Books may provide an antidote to the stereotyped conformity which seems to be an increasing danger in our society. In reading there is an opportunity to explore one's own interests whenever and wherever one pleases. Books can be picked up and read at any time; one is not tied to a schedule. In subject matter, too, books provide wider range and greater flexibility than other media of communication.

READING HELPS TO REORGANIZE EXPERIENCE

Reading can do more, however, than expand horizons and build community. It can give the reader an opportunity to reorganize his own emotional experience, to stand back and look at himself and others. It provides a way of participating vicariously in a variety of emotional experiences and of trying on a number of roles "for size." One who has read widely has looked into many people's hearts, known their struggles, their loves, and their hates. He has learned to know them better than he knows many of the people he sees every day, and he has learned to know better the part of him that is Everyman.

One of the ways in which this influence operates is through the psychological mechanism of identification. We say that the reader identifies with the book character; he becomes that character in his imagination; he feels with the character, fails and triumphs with him. In this way he may objectify his own feelings and, when he sees them in another, find them more manageable and less frightening. This process of identification is subtle; it is not always easy for the outsider to see it in operation. One bright adolescent explained the appeal of Terhune's "Wolf"[1] for her in terms of her identification with the dog. He was different, a nonconformist—proud, brave, sensitive, and misunderstood. She identified with him, and the story's appeal for her lay in this identification rather than in the adventure. Reading offers the adult a way of doing what a child so often does in play, when he sorts out his life-experiences, tries to make sense out of them, and tries to find out what it feels like to be different people.

It is possible for a particular book to symbolize a specific conflict for a reader, as T. S. Eliot's poem did for the group mentioned earlier. Perhaps the appeal of the Western adventure tale lies in its

[1] Albert Payson Terhune, "One Minute Longer," from *Buff, a Collie, and Other Dog Stories.* New York: G. H. Doran Co., 1921.

structuring of the conflict between "the good guys" and "the bad guys" in a situation which is quite safe because "the good guys" always win. One can afford to flirt with evil when he is sure it will be vanquished. Such books may help children strengthen their controls over their own behavior.

Books, too, may help children and adults realize that their situation or problem is not unique. Here is someone else who feels lonely and misunderstood or who secretly wants to rebel against the demands made on him. The situation cannot be impossible if others have experienced it; it does not seem so terrifying.

THE EFFECTS OF READING ARE LIMITED

Undoubtedly, reading has influenced many people in many ways and will continue to do so, but, as an agent of personal and social change, it is subject to many limitations. One difficulty lies in trying to match the book to the reader. A book about someone with a similar problem may be helpful, or it may arouse so much anxiety that it is rejected. One undersized child, for example, carried Beim's *The Smallest Boy in the Class* (Morrow, 1949) everywhere with him and read and reread it; another child, equally undersized, said it was a silly book and wouldn't even touch it. An individual may not recognize, or may recognize and then deny, that he and the book's character are facing similar problems. It is always possible, too, that his reactions to an overtly similar situation may be quite different from those of the book's hero.

Sometimes a book which presents a problem not faced by the child in real life but which fits into his fantasy life may be helpful. It is likely that the appeal of *The Boxcar Children* by Gertrude Warner (Scott, Foresman, 1942) lies in this realm. It seems as if many children, in fantasy, have managed without parents, taken care of each other, and proved adequate to the demands of life. This may be a way of trying out in imagination their own independence.

Helping readers find the right book is not easy. The situation is further complicated by the fact that it must not only be the right book but it must be read at the right time if it is to help the individual. This raises questions regarding the use of lists of books dealing with specific problems. Certainly the right book at the right time cannot be handed out like a prescription.

Another limitation in the use of reading to influence behavior and feelings springs from the tendency of people to choose materials which reinforce their feelings and attitudes and to avoid materials which take opposite points of view. It is commonly accepted that one can tell the political leanings of an individual by the papers and magazines on the coffee table. Even when the individual does read material which is out of line with his attitudes, he is likely to interpret it in terms of his biases, especially in the area of judgments and general impressions. This tendency of all of us "to read with our prejudices" limits the effects that reading may have on attitudes and beliefs.

The negative effects of reading on behavior and feelings should not be overlooked. Reading, in itself, is not necessarily good. The literacy rate was high in Nazi Germany and higher in Japan than in other Oriental countries. Apparently, reading can influence people but, in itself, does not insure desirable behavior.

Those who read most are not necessarily the best people, the ones we want for friends, the ones to whom we turn in trouble. It is well to remember this when reading is recommended as a panacea for all the ills of the world, from juvenile delinquency to corruption in government. It does seem that, if one is convinced of the ability of books to change people, one must accept this on the negative as well as on the positive side.

Fortunately or unfortunately, depending upon the effect of which you are thinking, books rarely stand alone in an individual's life. Since they are only one of the influences at work in his life, their effectiveness is limited. If a book reinforces other experiences which the reader has had or is having, it is more likely to be influential than if it stands completely alone. Waples explains changes in attitude as generally resulting "from the reinforcement of an associated but subordinate attitude, which causes it to dominate the matrix of conflicting attitudes and interests."[2] This means that the influence of reading comes into play only when the potential change in attitude or behavior is within the individual in embryonic form. Gibran, speaking of teaching, said: "No man can reveal to you aught but that which already lies half asleep in the dawning of your knowl-

edge."[3] The same may be said of reading. It cannot revolutionize feelings and attitudes; it can only bring into clearer focus something which has already been established within the individual through previous experiences.

CONCLUDING STATEMENT

Of all the many effects of reading, only three have been chosen for consideration: the building of community, the increase in freedom, the help in reorganizing life-experience. Reading is not the only activity which can bring about these effects; indeed it may not even be the most effective instrument for bringing about any of them. It is difficult to steer a middle course between selling reading short and overemphasizing its influences.

We need to know more about the effects of reading mediated through listening. We need to know about the reading of pictures as well as the reading of print. Above all, perhaps, we need to remind ourselves that one can live richly with only limited reading skill. Reading has important effects on personal and social development, but relationships with people and experiences with materials and ideas have even stronger effects.

[2] Douglas Waples, Bernard Berelson, and Franklyn R. Bradshaw, *What Reading Does to People*, p. 119. Chicago: University of Chicago Press, 1940.

[3] Reprinted from *The Prophet* by Kahlil Gibran with permission of the publisher, Alfred A. Knopf, Inc. Copyright 1923 by Kahlil Gibran; renewal copyright 1951 by Administrators C.T.A. of Kahlil Gibran Estate, and Mary G. Gibran.

CHAPTER VII

PROMOTING PERSONAL AND SOCIAL GROWTH THROUGH READING

*

IN KINDERGARTEN THROUGH GRADE THREE

MARGARET M. CLARK

*

INTO the library not long ago came a small girl asking for books on how to be a saint. Unfortunately the do-it-yourself books did not include explicit directions for reaching this particular goal. Instead we substituted stories about people who had achieved it. There are few books for children that supply directives for acquiring the intangible qualities of mind and spirit needed for personal and social growth, but there is a rich supply that can indirectly help children to appreciate, and even to acquire, some of these qualities.

In the fairly limited environment in which most younger children live, books skilfully introduced can contribute more to their growth than can almost any other experience. The teacher who, using books as one resource, can help children to glimpse a world of security, affection, and contentment and can inspire a desire for knowledge and achievement, is making a very genuine contribution to educational and emotional growth. This is particularly true if the reading is a group experience, following which the children freely express their own feelings and reactions.

The past decade has seen an impressive growth in the number of books published which, through fictional situations,

interpret problems common to children living in today's world. The majority of these books are directed to children beyond the primary-grade level. Nevertheless, there is a surprising scope of material, new and not so new, to enlarge the horizons of the younger child. It would be naïve to consider that meeting problems through books is the only way of developing children into richer human beings, but reading can help substantially.

The approach to aiding personal and social growth through reading is a two-fold one: introducing children to books about other children who meet problems similar to their own and introducing them to the broad field of aesthetic experience and knowledge to be gained through books about nature, poetry, humor, and stories from the Bible, to indicate just a few.

INTRODUCING STORIES OF HUMAN VALUES

To find books concerned with human interrelationships, one source that is now almost basic is *Reading Ladders for Human Relations*,[1] recently issued in the

[1] Margaret M. Heaton and Helen B. Lewis, *Reading Ladders for Human Relations*. Washington: American Council on Education, 1955 (revised).

74

third edition. Under eight broad headings, this book groups titles of books pertinent to a wide variety of human experiences and situations. Four of the headings offer substantial bibliographies for primary-grade children: "Patterns of Family Life," "Community Contrasts," "Belonging to Groups," and "Experiences of Acceptance and Rejection." These headings embrace many experiences understandable to younger children. Descriptions of helpful techniques for introducing the material and for stimulating discussion constitute almost one-third of this book.

The themes of the *Reading Ladders* have had wide use in our community. Some teachers follow the techniques therein suggested and select other topics to meet particular situations. For instance, one teacher, coping with a class of rugged individualists, launched the theme of co-operation. She borrowed every picture-book she could find which touched even slightly on the value of working together, in the hope that reading and discussion would stimulate better attitudes. Teachers are of two opinions about ways of introducing these themes of the spirit. Some feel that one or two books carefully introduced are sufficient. Others believe that use of a wide variety of books strengthens the emphasis and leaves more lasting impressions.

INTRODUCING APPRECIATION OF CREATIVE WORK

While the content of books is a source of enrichment, an appreciation of the creators of books can also make a substantial contribution. Many teachers in the upper grades have found that introducing a background on the authors and how their books came to be written adds

to the memorableness of the reading. One of our primary-grade teachers has discovered, too, that introducing such information has won an enthusiastic response from younger children and has been a real stimulus to their appreciation of creative work. It is exciting to discover that Virginia Burton's *Little House* (Houghton, 1942) was inspired after the author's house was moved back from the busy road to the apple orchard, that Hardie Gramatky's *Little Toot* (Putnam, 1939) was prompted by the author-artist's observation of a personable little tugboat on the East River. There are many sources for this kind of material. Montgomery, in *The Story behind Modern Books*,[2] tells absorbing and childlike anecdotes about authors who have written favorite books, and there are at least a dozen with special appeal for primary-grade children. Other sources include the *Horn Book Magazine*, which for years has devoted generous space to authors and artists as well as books, and *Elementary English*, which in recent years has published articles on authors. The *Junior Book of Authors*[3] is another comprehensive source for this background material. And not to be overlooked are the book jackets! Now that cellophane covers are coming more and more into popular use, the jackets are kept on the books because of their attractiveness, and they usually include introductory material about the author. All these sources are potential helps in building a card file of authors and artists, which is studded with interesting details to heighten the enthusiasm for

[2] Elizabeth Rider Montgomery, *The Story behind Modern Books*. New York: Dodd, Mead & Co., 1949.

[3] *Junior Book of Authors*. Edited by S. Kunitz and H. Haycraft. New York: H. W. Wilson Co., 1951 (revised).

reading and an appreciation of the creative imagination that can produce so many kinds of books.

In her Foreword to *Children's Books Too Good To Miss*, May Hill Arbuthnot states that "age is no guaranty of excellence nor are beautiful illustrations and recency any indication of triviality."[4] The title selections given here are current, having been published since 1950. They do not replace, but they do supplement, the beloved books which have become basic through the years because of their substance and genuine appeal to children: *Make Way for Ducklings* by R. McCloskey (Viking, 1941), *Little Toot* by H. Gramatky (Putnam, 1939), *Tale of Peter Rabbit* by B. Potter (Warne, 1902), *Ask Mr. Bear* by M. Flack (Macmillan, 1932), *Story about Ping* by M. Flack (Viking, 1933), *Millions of Cats* by W. Gág (Coward-McCann, 1928), and other such titles that leap to mind the moment the subject of children's books is mentioned. In their essence, all these books offer a satisfying sense of security, no matter how novel is the telling of the tale.

Many of the recent titles also help to fill basic needs and to enlarge horizons in the young child's personal world. An unusual theme and a good one for these hectic times, the beauty and peace of silence, has been the subject of two recent books. Charlotte Zolotow, in *The Quiet Mother and the Noisy Little Boy* (Lothrop, 1953), has written an amusing tale about a small boy, Sandy, whose every word and action was loud pitched. It was not until his even noisier cousin, Roger, came to visit

[4] May Hill Arbuthnot and Others, *Children's Books Too Good To Miss*, p. 8. Cleveland: Press of Western Reserve University, 1953 (revised).

and turned the house into a bedlam that Sandy perceived, as did his mother, that "it can be too quiet or too noisy if there is too much of either." A hilariously funny tale, *The Loudest Noise in the World* by Benjamin Elkin (Viking, 1954), tells of young Prince Hulla-Baloo, the loudest little boy in the city of Hub-Bub, who for his sixth birthday gift wanted all the people in the world to yell at the same moment. The beautiful plan failed when everyone kept still in order to hear the noise that the others made. This unexpected gift of silence delighted the little prince because "for the first time in his life he was hearing the sounds of nature instead of the noise of Hub-Bub. For the first time in his life the prince had been given the gift of peace and quiet, and he loved it." And so did everyone else in the city of Hub-Bub! Since a sense of tranquillity creates an atmosphere in which other qualities may develop, these two titles offer a special contribution.

Several recent stories with family background point up personal and social development in children. The lively little Scotch tale of *The Patchwork Kilt* by Mabel Watts (Aladdin, 1954) is a highly original tale of family solidarity and reciprocity. Small Biddie Biddlewee's family and relatives, sure that she would win the silver cup for dancing the Highland fling at the fair, shared their bits of plaid to make her a handsome kilt. When stage fright overtook poor Biddie, it was the memory of family kindness that helped her through. Alice Dalgliesh, in *The Courage of Sarah Noble* (Scribner, 1954), chose a historically true incident on which to base the theme of personal courage. Timid, eight-year-old Sarah went with her pioneer father to cook for him while he built a new home. Frightened to death at every forest sound, she endured quietly through the period of building and a brief stay with the Indians when her father went back for the family. Distinctive backgrounds add a quiet force to the telling of these two stories. An outstanding here-and-now family tale is Robert McCloskey's *One Morning in Maine* (Viking, 1952). Based on the commonplace and familiar incident of a little girl's losing her tooth, this heart-warming story tells of simple pleasures shared together to mark the extra-special event. Outstanding illustrations of the sea and shore background convey, in addition, a genuine feeling for the beauties of nature in this story of close family relationships.

The novel theme of two other favorite books concerns books and libraries. Sue Felt, in *Rosa-Too-Little* (Doubleday, 1950), tells of a small girl who desperately wanted a library card like the other children, so that she could borrow books. A summer of persistent name-writing practice brought her to triumphant achievement. In *Mike's House* (Viking, 1954), Julia Sauer builds an exciting adventure about Robert's love for his favorite book, *Mike Mulligan*, which he borrows over and over again until, to him, the library has become "Mike's house." When Robert is lost in a heavy snowstorm en route to the library, there is a period of adult confusion because he can identify the building only as Mike's house. In both of these stories the desire for, and the enjoyment of, books are cleverly heightened.

TEACHING AIDS FOR POETRY AND DRAMATICS

In addition to stories which can give to children fresh insight and perspective, the important field of creative experience in drama and poetry is becoming increasingly significant in education.

One of the most distinguished contributions to the literature of aesthetics is Arnstein's *Adventure into Poetry*,[5] a personal account of how the author worked with children to give them an appreciation of poetry and stimulated them to write creatively. She tells of her experiences, both the successes and the errors, describing them with a fulness of detail which will be of tremendous help to other teachers. There are fine criteria for poetry and suggestions as to the kinds that children enjoy most. What children gain in appreciation of beauty and sensitiveness to words and ideas is the underlying theme of *Adventure into Poetry*. Whether it is used as an aid in introducing poetry, encouraging the writing of poetry, or heightening special experiences, the teacher will discover in it a wealth of inspiration and guidance.

Winifred Ward's most recent contribution on creative dramatics is *Stories To Dramatize*,[6] a most valuable book for the primary-grade teacher. It is a collection of stories and poetry from many sources, which have been used successfully for dramatizations with children from five to fourteen years of age. There are about fifty selections for the primary grades and a bibliography of about thirty more to be found in other sources. A few suggestions for direction and production are included, but the author's earlier *Playmaking with Children*[7] offers the comprehensive treatment on this subject.

[5] Flora J. Arnstein, *Adventure into Poetry.* Stanford, California: Stanford University Press, 1951.

[6] Winifred Ward, *Stories To Dramatize.* Cloverlot, Anchorage, Kentucky: Children's Theatre Press, 1952.

[7] Winifred Ward, *Playmaking with Children.* New York: D. Appleton–Century Co., Inc., 1947.

Another title which has many practical helps is Durland's *Creative Dramatics for Children: A Practical Manual for Teachers and Leaders*,[8] directed particularly to the inexperienced worker. Mrs. Durland contributes many constructive ideas for dealing with the varied backgrounds, aptitudes, and personality traits of children in classroom and other groups, as well as for the working-out of programs. Both of these authors emphasize the value of improvised dramatizations in helping to enrich children through shared activity.

CONCLUDING STATEMENT

Whether social and personal development of the child is advanced through the vicarious experience of a story-book situation or through an art form stimulating to the creative imagination, each can contribute immeasurably, especially when used by teachers aware "that guided self-expression opens up important paths not only to cultural living but also to learning, to morality, and to health; that each revelation of the inner spirit thus successfully handled by adult guides has canceled at once a hundred personal and social problems of the faraway future."[9]

[8] Frances Caldwell Durland, *Creative Dramatics for Children: A Practical Manual for Teachers and Leaders.* Yellow Springs, Ohio: Antioch Press, 1952.

[9] Reprinted from *Adventure into Poetry* by Flora J. Arnstein with the permission of the author and of the publishers, Stanford University Press. Copyright 1951 by the Board of Trustees of Leland Stanford Junior University.

✳ ✳ ✳

IN GRADES FOUR THROUGH SIX

RAYMOND A. LUBWAY

✳

OF ALL the responsibilities of a teacher, one of the most important is that of guiding the personal and social development of children. Despite its importance, it is one of the least understood. By virtue of his role of leader in a classroom, a teacher is a powerful force in the development of children who are happy with themselves and others. A teacher may create a classroom atmosphere in which a child may encounter the problems of growing up and living with others with a minimum of anxiety and a maximum of adult support and guidance. A teacher may help a child grow into his place in the adult world by emphasizing the rewards as well as the restrictions of societal living. A teacher may help a child view the problems of growing up as challenges rather than obstacles.

On the other hand, a teacher may create an atmosphere in which the adult world is seen as a forbidding place of restrictions and expectations. The child may see only the disappointments and frustrations of his initiation and then behave so as to arouse the disciplinary function of that world. This situation creates additional problems which are more difficult to solve.

The teacher's job of guiding the development of children is difficult. Children are in school a comparatively short time, and society has specified the academic achievement expected. In the classroom the teacher, responding to the pressure of time, often gives priority to the academic objectives. The personal and social growth of children is sufficiently unique to each that it requires more individual attention than the teacher can give. While many of the factors that influence the personal and social growth of children are beyond the control of the teacher, there are ways in which a teacher can make a positive contribution to their development.

Reading activities are useful because stories describe concrete examples of human relationships. Many of them deal with people whose characteristics and problems are familiar to children. Some stories offer solutions to these problems. While these solutions may or may not be useful to particular children at a particular time, the children may come to appreciate the value of books as a source of information and help as they encounter their own problems.

Many stories may serve to stimulate discussions of the problems of growing up, living with other people, and meeting the expectations of society. I would like to illustrate these remarks with some reading experiences I have had with a fourth-grade class and a sixth-grade class.

THE CHILDREN READ

Some years ago, when I was teaching Grade IV, the children were reading "The Princess Who Could Not Cry" from *Times and Places* (Scott, Foresman, 1947). As you may recall, this is the story of a princess who laughed constantly. Her parents were so distressed that they asked every wise man in the land to try to make her cry. Eventually a clever peasant brought tears to her eyes with an onion.

The children enjoyed the story and were ready to go on to another, but I asked them to explain why the parents were so upset: "After all, doesn't everyone want to be happy? Shouldn't the parents have been glad that their daughter was so happy that she couldn't cry?" The children knew the answer to this, but it took a little discussion before the group could verbalize it: "Of course everyone wants to be happy, but you can't be happy all the time." When I asked them why everyone couldn't be happy all the time, they explained that life consists of happy times and sad times and that a person alternates between them. They explained this with illustrations rather than generalizations, but the point is that, in the process of explaining this to me, they were putting into words their observations about life. I have no way of knowing whether their verbalization will ever give them pause in happy times or hope in sad times, but the discussion provided an opportunity for them to interpret their own experiences in the light of a generalization. If this observation gives comfort, in a reflective moment, to even one child, the time will have been well spent.

My sixth-grade pupils read "The Junior Team's Bargain" in *People and Progress* (Scott, Foresman, 1944). This story concerns a young athlete whose responsibilities on his father's farm interfere with football practice with the Junior Team. His father will not let him play in an important game until the crops are harvested. The Junior Team volunteers to help with the harvest in order to make it possible for the boy to play in the game. I asked the children if they thought the father was fair in not allowing his son to play football. In the discussion that followed, many of the feelings the children had about parental authority and the responsibilities of children became apparent. Some children said immediately that the father was not fair, that he could have permitted the boy to play in this one game. Other children objected, pointing out that the father had to have help in the harvesting and it was the boy's job to help. If the crops were not harvested, the boy would suffer too. I asked them if they had had experience with adults who seemed to act unfairly toward children. We went on then to discuss these experiences and to draw a generalization about the responsibilities of parents and children toward each other.

I do not feel that a teacher should labor the point. A teacher can provide the opportunity and the stimulation, but the length and depth of the discussion must be determined by the children's willingness to talk freely. The vigor of the discussion is a good indication of the significance that the topic has for them.

THE TEACHER READS

Another way of stimulating children to discuss their common problems is to select a book illustrative of such problems and read it aloud to them. Besides being an enjoyable and profitable language experience, reading aloud generates between the teacher and class a relationship which allows for free and easy discussion.

I read *Call It Courage* by Armstrong Sperry (Macmillan, 1940) to my fourth-grade class. Mafatu, the son of a Pacific Island chieftain, is afraid of the sea—a disgrace for the son of a chief and a disaster for an islander. While he has not lost his father's love, Mafatu has lost his father's respect. This situation becomes so painful for the boy that, accompanied only by his dog, he sails to another island. While he is there, his courage is put to the test in many adventures. The most significant one for Mafatu occurs when he must jump into the sea to save his dog's life.

The children enjoyed the story very much, but they did not appreciate the full meaning of the boy's journey by sea until we discussed it in terms of their experiences in conquering fear. I asked them if they had ever been afraid of something. At this point the discussion became spirited. Some were afraid of sliding down a steep hill on their sleds, and others had once been afraid of sleeping without a light. Many, I am sure, had fears which they did not mention. However, the discussion was led by children who described, very dramatically, how they felt when they were afraid and how good they felt when at last they conquered their fears. Children learn so much more effectively from one another that I had good reason to hope that even the most fearful child could not help but feel heartened by the success not only of Mafatu but of his peers. Only when children can be made to feel that even the most deviant point of view will be respected, will they discuss their problems explicitly.

I read *Mistress Masham's Repose* by T. H. White (Putnam, 1946) to my sixth-grade class. This story concerns a little girl, orphaned by an accident, who, under the tutelage of a callous governess and an unscrupulous vicar, lives unhappily in a dilapidated palace. Maria's only friends are a cook and an absent-minded professor, who live on the premises. One day, while exploring a little island in the center of a pond, she discovers a colony of Lilliputians, who become the delight of her life. Her size, a handicap in her relations with the governess, becomes a source of power in her relations with the Lilliputians. As she misuses this power, relations between the Lilliputians and herself become strained. It becomes increasingly apparent that their relations are handicapped not only by her size but by her unwillingness to accept and appreciate the Lilliputians' desire to work for themselves and to maintain their integrity.

As each incident was read, we discussed the cause for the growing coolness of the Lilliputians, but the discussion did not come to life until it touched on the common problem of dominance. I asked them if they ever had the feeling of being "bossed." They certainly had. Only after their accusations against older brothers and sisters had been exhausted, were they able to discuss the distinction between legitimate authority and usurpation of authority. Older brothers and sisters with delegated parental authority were not being bossy in insisting that they go to bed at the prescribed time, but Maria had no authority to require the Lilliputians to play with her whenever she wished.

Maria is most unhappy when the coolness turns to obvious rejection. The author illustrates, in detail, Maria's struggle with herself. On the one hand, Maria righteously asserts that she meant to do only good and the Lilliputians were most ungrateful. On the other hand, in the back of her mind is the disconcerting realization that she brought the situation on herself. After we discussed the significance of this episode, I asked the children what they would do if they were in her place. The decision in such a situation, in which people often find themselves, may hinge on the value that is placed on harmonious group living as opposed to the rights of individuals. The children agreed that, if Maria wanted to continue to see the little people, she should help them only when they asked for help. Implicit in this solution is a recognition of the privileges and responsibilities of group living. Again, there is no assurance that, as a result of these discussions, there will be immediate carry-over into the children's own lives. But if children become more aware of the need for social sensitivity as a result of such discussions, the teacher will have made an important contribution to their personal and social development.

CONCLUDING STATEMENT

I have illustrated ways in which a teacher may use reading activities to promote the personal and social growth of children. This growth is a highly individual matter, but, by providing a classroom climate which is conducive to the free expression of variant points of view and by the reading and discussion of selected materials, a teacher can focus the attention of the children on problems which all must face. Through such discussions, a teacher may stimulate analytical and interpretive thinking, induce a sensitivity to social situations, and encourage the interpretation of personal experience.

IN GRADES SEVEN THROUGH NINE

LLOYD J. MENDELSON

✳

THE period of early adolescence is one of great upheaval and personal groping. To project an effective reading program that will assist young people in adjusting to new responsibilities, the teacher must recognize those areas of need particularly applicable to the early adolescent. Although individuals pass through stages of development at different rates, common areas of growth have been identified at each succeeding level of human development. These have been alternatively expressed in terms of "needs," "values," "goals," and "tasks."

This writer has found it worth while to utilize the concept of developmental tasks as a basis for an understanding of the problems of personal and social growth of the emerging adolescent. As propounded by Havighurst,[1] "developmental tasks" are those learnings and adjustments that all persons must achieve at particular stages of development, successful accomplishment of which leads to personal happiness and preparation for later tasks, while failure leads to unhappiness and disapproval by society.

SELECTING APPROPRIATE READING EXPERIENCES

Organizing the reading program to assist young people with their developmental tasks can be viewed from two aspects, neither exclusive of the other. In the first method, indirect but planned means are

[1] Robert J. Havighurst, *Developmental Tasks and Education*, p. 2. New York: Longmans, Green & Co., 1952.

used to integrate worth-while reading experiences into various phases of the curriculum. The second method uses the direct reading unit focusing on a particular developmental value.

Through the indirect approach the unit of learning might center in one of the content areas. The teacher recommends, and pupils discover, certain books or reading sources which pertain to phases of the unit problem and which bring to light some of the developmental problems facing young people. For example, a seventh-grade unit on the struggles of the American colonies for independence lent itself to biographical study of Colonial leaders, such as Samuel Adams, Paul Revere, and Tom Paine. Reading about how these leaders matured, the difficult decisions they had to make within their emerging code of values and beliefs, their willingness in many cases to risk secure ties for the venture into freedom, not only provided significant understandings of the founding of a free nation but also aided the students in working out some evaluation of social change on the world scene. Biography is an especially fruitful source material for the study of personal values because of the number of available books at all reading levels which have interest appeal to the early adolescent.

Another illustration of the indirect approach is to utilize reading sources to provide information on current problems of student interest. During Brotherhood Week an eighth-grade class in Farren Public School initiated a project on "Getting To Know Other People Better." This was particularly important in a school of homogeneous racial and ethnic background. The primary motivating activity was a series of interviews conducted by the students, functioning in small groups. The committees, after working out a series of pertinent questions, interviewed teachers, community leaders, and other young people of divergent backgrounds. This technique stimulated much enthusiasm and interest on the part of the class to learn more about the culture, desires, and problems of various nationality groups. The teacher was ready to suggest both reference-type material for factual information and appropriate literature sources for additional insight into the topic. Eventually the class prepared a sizable scrapbook, actually a form of a source textbook, bringing together the variety of materials the students had written and accumulated.

In the direct method the class centers its attention on the reading unit. Focusing on some point of interest, such as "Getting Along with the Family" or "Building Teen-Age Friendships," students agree to read and discuss a number of books which treat of the particular topic selected. Under teacher guidance and with assistance from the school librarian, the class prepares a bibliography of interesting materials at different reading levels. These books become the basis of the reading unit, and the sharing of experiences among students furthers awareness of, and insight into, such developmental tasks as adjusting to new peer relationships and understanding one's own role in the family.

Classifications of books according to the developmental values stressed, as well as interest appeal and reading levels, give tremendous aid to teachers in the selection of materials that relate to personal and social growth. The Center for Children's Books, of the University of Chicago, maintains such a continuous cataloguing of young people's books. At Carter Elementary School in Chicago, the librarian classified all books in the school library according to specific moral and aesthetic values served. The Chicago Board of Education Library has issued a publication[2] classifying books according to developmental values, while the recent edition of *Reading Ladders for Human Relations*[3] is an invaluable compilation of annotated titles of books and short stories, with practical suggestions for their use.

SPECIFIC TEACHER GUIDANCE

The teacher, of course, is the key person in stimulating the effective use of reading materials to aid personal and social growth. With the increased range of reading competencies characteristic of the junior high school level, reading problems in this respect are more intensified. The teacher is rightfully concerned with raising the comprehension levels of all students, especially the retarded readers. To the extent that he is able to develop these competencies, he is promoting child growth, since effective reading not only is a basis for academic attainment but contributes as well to the multiple endeavors necessary for success in all aspects of living. For the individual to be

[2] Effie LaPlante and Thelma O'Donnell, *Developmental Values through Library Books.* Chicago Schools Journal, Vol. XXXI, Nos. 7–8, Supplement. Chicago: Chicago Teachers College, 1950.

[3] Margaret M. Heaton and Helen B. Lewis, *Reading Ladders for Human Relations.* Washington: American Council on Education, 1955 (revised).

able to select and adjust his reading to the particular purposes sought—whether it is interpreting a newspaper article, following the directions of a do-it-yourself kit, or reading a novel for personal enjoyment—specific instruction is necessary, for relatively few can accomplish these purposes at the early adolescent level without adequate instructional background.

The teacher, then, directs his reading program in a twofold manner: first, through building the specific competencies dictated by student needs and, second, through encouraging the reading and interpreting of materials that throw light on the developmental tasks facing the early adolescent.

Obtaining the full value of a reading program necessitates the sharing of the students' reading experiences through a variety of means but, in all cases, providing for discussion and interchange of ideas. The teacher's role will vary according to the genuine interest of the material and to the background level of the class. If the group members are skilled in expression, the teacher may serve primarily as a co-ordinator of the discussion, guiding the class to select the more pertinent points, to discard the irrelevant, to modify points of view, and to draw generalizations that seem applicable. In a class of more limited intellectual skills, the teacher may have to assume more direction in initiating and guiding discussion by raising perceptive questions that will stimulate thoughtful reactions.

Reference to a particular project will perhaps illustrate the types of questions that should be raised in guiding class discussion. In an eighth-grade reading unit centering on teen-age problems in city living, two pupils reviewed the book *The Latchkey Club* (McKay, 1949). This story, written with a sixth- to eighth-

grade interest level but an easier reading level, deals with a family that moved into an apartment building in a densely populated neighborhood, where all the young people carried latchkeys because the parents worked. The book treats concretely of matters quite relevant to students in the class—problems of adjusting to new surroundings among the various age-level groups, of being unsupervised throughout the day, of the difficulties children get into—and describes how the problems were solved through the formation of a community club. Although the solutions presented in the story are perhaps too pat, the book provoked fervent argumentation.

The teacher was able to focus attention on salient features of the story that would enable the students to interpret situations in terms of their own experiences and feelings, by raising such questions as, "How would you have acted in this particular situation?" "Do you agree with a certain individual's attitude toward the newly arrived family? Why, or why not?" "In what ways do you think this individual has changed by the end of the story?" "In your opinion, what caused such change?" By dealing forthrightly with real problems of the early adolescent, such discussions can assist students in grappling with their developmental tasks—in the case just cited, the tasks concerned with adjusting to new social relationships, extending interests in the social environment, and fostering democratic practices.

Other effective techniques in making the reading program more meaningful are familiar. Round-table book reviews, in which three or four students present a particular selection, are useful in getting different points of view. Dramatization and role-playing involving characterization and incidents in stories are recommended, especially when the dramatization permits spontaneity and creativity of interpretation.

EVALUATING GROWTH THROUGH READING

The test of whether the reading program is promoting personal and social growth is the extent to which each student inculcates reading experiences into his pattern of behavior—thinking, feelings, actions—in a way that enables him to cope with his developmental tasks. This is a difficult area to measure objectively. The most promising method seems to be the close observation of behavior throughout the year and the recording of such observations on some form of check list or anecdotal record. At that, we may not be sure to what degree the changes in behavior result from reading or from the totality of curricular, community, family, and peer influences. Yet, by noting spontaneous reactions to material read and the manner in which reading sources are utilized, we get indications of development.

Encouraging the early adolescent to develop techniques of self-evaluation in his reading, for example, by a guided list of questions, further aids teacher-student evaluation of the meaningfulness of the reading. Even so, one must constantly realize that reading is essentially a vicarious experience, which per se is not going to solve personal and social problems. As has often been stated, the students' acceptance of reading and their responses to situations are conditioned by factors such as background, prejudices, and preconceived ideas. This is especially significant at the emotionally charged level of early adolescence. The teacher can be reasonably assured that he is providing for personal and social development when students are applying their reading experiences to concrete problems of daily living in a manner consistent with the democratic precepts of our nation.

* * *

IN GRADES TEN THROUGH FOURTEEN

HELEN C. CASKEY

*

WE ARE committed to the proposition that reading can be a useful means of achieving a higher level of personal and social development. The members of the Commission on the English Curriculum have indicated the acquisition of personal values and social insight as a major purpose for reading and conclude:

The literature of the past and present can give students that sense of the continuity of human experience without which life has neither significance nor direction. It can, at the same time, help them to understand the motivations and the attitudes, the strengths and the weaknesses of the many racial, social, and national groups with which they must live and work today.[1]

The difficulties encountered in achieving these goals are perplexing to all teachers. There are no blueprints to show exactly how to enlarge the narrow mind or how to phrase the precise question which

[1] Commission on the English Curriculum of the National Council of Teachers of English, *The English Language Arts*, p. 10. New York: Appleton-Century-Crofts, Inc., 1952.

will lead an unhappy adolescent to face a problem wisely and bravely. Herein lies our troubling challenge, and our ennobling hope. While there can be no exact prescriptions, an analysis of some aspects ·of the problem may be helpful. The remainder of this paper will be concerned with three areas: (1) realizing more clearly the nature of students' present needs in personal and social development, (2) providing for contacts with reading materials, and (3) guiding students' reactions to materials read.

STUDENTS' PRESENT NEEDS IN PERSONAL AND SOCIAL DEVELOPMENT

We may have failed to view today's students in today's social setting and may need to inquire whether there are not some factors in their situation which merit particular attention. As I have observed persons in this age group, it appears that adult responsibilities, for example, come somewhat sooner than they did to young people of a decade or so ago. A check on current vital statistics confirms the supposition. The United States Public Health Service reports that approximately 13 per cent of the children born in 1952 were born to mothers nineteen years of age or younger. In 1940 about 10 per cent of the children were born to mothers in this age group.[2] The median age of first marriage has dropped from 24.3 years for men in 1940 to 22.7 in 1950. The median age for women was 21.5 in 1940, and 20.3 in 1950.[3] Boys of eighteen remind us that persons old enough to go into the armed forces are

[2] As cited in *Information Please Almanac 1956*, p. 112. New York: Macmillan Co., 1955.

[3] J. Frederic Dewhurst and Associates, *America's Needs and Resources: A New Survey*, p. 57. New York: Twentieth Century Fund, 1955.

old enough to vote, and there are many persons in public life who would agree with them.

It is also true that the pressure to succeed, to earn enough money to stay in school, to choose and prepare for a vocation, to achieve financial independence, all assume increased importance to these young people as they come closer to taking a place in the world of adults. Furthermore, it is of great importance to persons in this age group that they achieve a satisfactory understanding of themselves as human beings. They cannot afford to wait to discover who they are; they must make that decision soon, building some satisfactory philosophy, deciding by what they can live. They cannot comfortably drift along on a sea of indecision, as was possible for young persons in less troubled times. Today may offer our last chance to bring the right book and the right person together and so to structure the meeting of the book and the reader that the contact results in desirable and positive changes for the individual concerned.

PROVIDING FOR CONTACTS WITH READING MATERIALS

The task of providing the right book and the appropriate experience with it requires a somewhat different approach in each situation. However, the following questions may give some helpful indications of possible courses of action.

Can you plan with the school librarian in the use of reading materials? Co-operative planning for the purchase of books, for the library experiences of students, and for the kind of guidance needed by students is helpful to all concerned. The librarian has opportunities for observing the reading activities of students that the teacher in the classroom may not have and can draw helpful conclusions therefrom.

Can you make use of the students themselves in planning for greater usefulness of the library facilities? Perhaps an "advisory board" for your school library can be formed, with students and teachers as members, which can bring out many helpful suggestions for increasing the effectiveness of the library resources of your school and community. Students in such a group may also bring to other students a greater understanding of the resources for study and recreational reading which have great potential value but which have not been hitherto used.

Can you make better use of reading materials in areas where Negro boys and girls are attending desegregated schools for the first time? As complex problems relating to the desegregation of schools are worked out in many communities, their experiences serve as guides for others. A recent report from a southwestern community notes the need for placing in the library magazines and newspapers published by Negroes. These publications are of unique service to Negro young people in telling of the daily lives, hopes, successes, and aspirations of Negro people, and they are good for non-Negroes as well, who "also need to learn that Negroes are a very human people, with talents, hopes and dreams, human weaknesses, and noteworthy achievements and successes in numerous widely dispersed fields of human endeavor."[4]

Can you stimulate young people to read more critically the kinds of materials they are likely to read anyway? Day-by-day consumption of newspapers and magazines will be a regular pattern of reading for many young adults, and it seems reasonable to devote some effort to these materials. I have, for example, seen a tenth grade analyzing the content of newspaper advertisements, a twelfth grade seeking information about the kind of magazines available to them, a college class trying to discover the basic assumptions regarding people and their relationships which were implied in current magazine fiction. These students were concerned with the kinds of reading materials that they will find around them all their adult lives.

Can you improve the environment for reading? A well-lighted, comfortable, cheerful library in which the reader feels welcome and books are easily available is highly desirable. A special "reading room," featuring recordings, pictures, and filmstrips, as well as an abundance of attractively displayed books, may be a possibility. The potential reader should be able to reach this spot with ease, for, if the opportunities for reading are favorable, the student is much more likely to find books a helpful means of approaching his own personal problems.

Can you acquire a continually wider knowledge of books? Help on which books to suggest to individuals and which to provide for class groups may be found in the useful book, *Reading Ladders for Human Relations*.[5] The compilers have listed books at all levels of difficulty, from the easiest books for the elementary-school child to novels for the mature reader. These listing are by theme, each relating to some aspect of human relationships, and brief annotations are particularly useful. In addition, there are

[4] W. A. Robinson, "The Functions of Libraries in Newly Integrated Schools," *School Review*, LXIII (October, 1955), 390.

[5] Margaret M. Heaton and Helen B. Lewis, *Reading Ladders for Human Relations*. Washington: American Council on Education, 1955 (revised).

suggestions for guiding the discussion of questions based on students' reading.

Other helpful sources of information include the *Standard Catalog*,[6] which is an invaluable aid in locating materials dealing with a wide range of topics. A more specialized aid is the revision of Rollins' bibliography of books for and about Negroes.[7] Issues of the *Wilson Library Bulletin, Elementary English,* and the *English Journal*, appearing within the past five or six years, have presented twenty or more book lists on subjects of interest to young readers, from science fiction to stories of romance for the adolescent girl.

GUIDING STUDENTS' CONTACTS WITH READING MATERIALS

Maturity in the interpretation of materials read does not appear automatically. The students in senior high schools and in the first years of college are likely to need specific guidance in making the best use of what they read if they are to achieve a higher level of social sensitivity and of understanding of the world in which they live. For example, a group of college Sophomores were made more sharply aware of the insidious effects of the stereotype in fiction by a re-examination of the characters portrayed in some of the series books which they had read with such uncritical delight only a few years before. Even in the senior high school a reader will need help in order to read from an adult point of view.

He may still cling to a childlike insistence that the "story end right" or may be baffled by complexities in the characters portrayed which make it impossible for him to recognize the "good" and the "bad" people as he had seen them in the sharp blacks and whites of his earlier reading.

Classroom doors opened in September to thousands of young people who during this year will have their last contact with instruction in English. Many of them are in Grades XI and XII in programs which do not lead to college. They tend to be impatient with anything in print which is not "true" and deeply concerned about the realities of earning a living. We are fortunate indeed in having a gratifying number of well-illustrated and well-written factual books on every topic of interest to young people. There are excellent biographies, historical reference materials, scientific and how-to-do-it books which are of interest to them.[8]

Although much of the growth in understanding that ensues for the student from his reading will come as he reads on his own, independently, it is through guided discussion and shared experiences with books that maximum development in personal growth and social understanding may occur. If he is to find through his reading a more mature and more satisfying outlook upon the world around him, the reader must put himself in the position occupied by the personages in the story, seeing himself faced with like problems, meeting similar triumphs and defeats. Provocative questions may stimulate thinking along these lines and serve to help the reader use books as a means of becoming a wiser and

[6] *Standard Catalog for High School Libraries.* New York: H. W. Wilson Co. (published at five-year intervals).

[7] Charlemae Rollins, *We Build Together: A Reader's Guide to Negro Life and Literature for Elementary and High School Use.* Pamphlet Publication No. 2. Champaign, Illinois: National Council of Teachers of English, 1948 (revised).

[8] E. G. Ryan, "How-To-Do-It Books: A Hit with Slow Readers," *Clearing House*, XXIX (March, 1955), 434–35.

more tolerant person. For example, such questions as, "How did the person in the story feel?" "Why did the people around him treat him as they did?" may be a means of developing sensitiveness to the feelings of others. Sometimes the responses to these questions may be wordless but highly charged with feeling, as in the case of a group of adolescents who cringed visibly as one of the class was commenting on the rejection felt by the hero of *Johnny Tremain* as he struggled to reconcile himself to his crippled hand.

Knowing how it feels to be in the situation implies doing something about it. "What would you have done had you been in this situation?" "What have you seen or experienced that was similar to the experience described?" are questions which help the reader to relate happenings in the story, novel, or play to his own experience and to perceive the probable consequences of an action described.

Like any endeavor involving complexities of human relationships, the difficulties involved in the procedures described are numerous. Wrong conclusions will be drawn by students, and questions calling for penetrating analysis will be answered with comments based upon the usual stereotypes. Some pupils will be extremely verbal; others will sit day after day without uttering a word. All these situations call for patience, forbearance, and a persistent and hardy hope. We must realize that growth is not always rapid, that sometimes the young people who remain silent are thinking, wondering, reacting deeply, perhaps recognizing for the first time the depth and significance of an idea they had previously given only the most casual consideration.

SUMMARY

The importance of guiding the reading activities of students in order that they may thereby be aided in reaching a higher level of personal and social development is unquestioned. There remains the problem of how best to aid young people in this endeavor. Although there are no specific prescriptions, we may be aided by studying the situations in which youth now find themselves, by making every effort to provide suitable material, and by giving specific guidance to pupils in their reactions to situations presented in their reading.

CHAPTER VIII

RELATIONSHIP OF MASS MEDIA TO READING INTERESTS

✷

PAUL A. WAGNER

✷

THE phrase "mass media" is so awe-inspiring in its connotations that only those who delight in being known as mass-media specialists ever attempt to discuss such a subject. I would like to drop any pretense of being a specialist in either the field of mass communication or the field of reading, and to approach the subject of the relationship of the two from a very simple and direct point of view. As a teacher, I am interested in all media of communication, from reading to lecturing, from field trips to television. As one who is interested in the sociological aspects of education, I am concerned with the communication of ideas, no matter the size of the audience or the medium employed.

It is from the vantage point of the classroom that one can understand the dilemma facing the average teacher in the performance of his duties. It is a dilemma that can be stated best in four terms: (1) Society expects the school to educate young Americans in the abstract values of American society. (2) Reading is the medium best suited for carrying the individual to the ultimate abstractions embodied in the concepts of American liberty and justice. (3) Reading of serious and significant writing is an activity engaged in by a pitifully small percentage of our population, at any age level. (4) Democracy, to be successful and crea-tive, must be based on intercommunication among *all* citizens. (I dislike the phrase, but "mass" intercommunication is an important American concept.)

READING AND "OTHER LANGUAGES"

What does society demand of a teacher? "Prepare our children for life." Prepare them for fatherhood, motherhood, brotherhood; for statesmanship and ethical dealings in business, labor, and politics. Prepare them to vote intelligently on the problems of segregation, atomic-energy control, use of public lands, the admission of Red China to the United Nations. In almost every case the unit objectives would have to be stated in abstractions of a high order.

In communicating the abstract ideals of our society during the past several centuries, the teacher has relied mainly, in fact almost completely, on books. This is quite natural, for the book still remains the finest tool for the absorption of ideas and ideals by the individual. Democracy is an individual phenomenon, and reading is a medium allowing for the widest variety of individual differences of mind and heart.

But the sharp horn of the dilemma is first felt in the fact that the language of books has always been the province of the elite. In past eras, only the most wealthy or the most dedicated had access to books. Later, only those who could afford college were allowed the luxury of thoughtful reading. And now, as Lester Asheim reminds us (chapter iv), fewer than 10 per cent of our adult population are reading books of any stature or profundity.

At the same time that the language of books is largely ignored by the "masses" (strike that word and use "90 per cent of the American voters"), other languages are being called into play for the communication of attitudes and opinions on the Bricker Amendment, the government control of network telecasting, or the sending of arms to Israel. Each of these issues requires the most careful study, often the delicate balancing of other abstract ideas. And each of these issues is determined by the vote of every adult American—not just those who can or will read—but *every* American.

The "other languages" used by the 90 per cent of Americans who are not interested in books include the language of radio; the language of the cartoon; the language of the bold, black, condensed Gothic headline; the language of the motion picture; and the language of television.

The word "language" is repeated for one reason only. It has more validity in an educational discussion than the term "mass medium." For one can read a book, listen to the radio, see a film, or watch television, all in the privacy of his own den. The old distinction of mass media requiring the auditor to be part of a large crowd no longer holds. Unless you wish to give a numerical definition to "mass," the book is as much a medium for communicating with the masses as is a kinescope. Those who understand the language of books are called "readers." But those who cannot read books often

are very adept at "reading" these other languages. Indeed, we can teach our students to read these other languages. Just as we teach them to read between the lines and beyond them, so too can we teach them to read behind and beyond the scenes. When we teach these other languages, we will succeed in winning converts, among a majority of the American population, for the most important language of all, that of books.

FILMS AND RECORDINGS TO DEVELOP INTEREST

Making the shift in thinking from "mass media" to "languages" is not easy. Since we teach as we were taught, and since I was taught for eighteen years almost entirely by textbooks, I did not realize the true significance of these other languages until after two, for me, rather dramatic teaching experiences.

During the depression of the thirties, I became an apprentice teacher in a metropolitan high school. Most of the students were still in school only because they could find no employment elsewhere. Although they exhibited none of the viciousness of the class in the *Blackboard Jungle*, they did share with that group a complete antipathy for anything intellectual, especially in English class—and most particularly in American poetry.

With this group my first assignment was to teach the beauties and philosophic serenities of "Thanatopsis." To say I failed is to put it mildly. And each succeeding assignment found the class gaining the upper hand in its battle against reading books. I decided to catch their interest with a novel that no literary critic would put very high on the list of American classics, but certainly one that had all the elements that might appeal to such a group of nonreaders: the opening of a new territory in the Southwest, a slam-bang story of oilmen fighting with the earth and with each other, and a rip-snorting finale in which the main male figure dies in an act of heroism. Edna Ferber's *Cimarron* had all of this, but I could not sell even that.

And then a friend of mine suggested I obtain a short film entitled *Men and Oil.* Perhaps it would tie in with the lessons of the moment. The next day I showed it to the class. For the first time, these antagonistic nonreaders sat on the edges of their seats and attended to something at the front of the room. They asked questions; they argued; they wanted to see the film again. They were even ready to listen to passages from *Cimarron,* and, most important of all, they began to read, *really read,* a book whose covers they had previously refused to crack. For the first time, I was able to communicate with the class, because the language of the film was a language they understood, a language they could read. Once I contacted them in *their* language, I could begin the transition to communication in *my* language.

Lest you think that I have taken an extreme case and attempted a Pygmalion-like moral, let me remind you that these other languages are read by many students who are, by our standards, excellent readers of the printed page also.

The most literate students I ever had the pleasure of teaching were in a Sophomore English class in a Wisconsin secondary school. The principal had invited me to give a demonstration class, "to show how to use movies." I had agreed, provided he allowed me to visit the class every day for a week and then take the regular teacher's place on the fifth day,

carrying on the normal work of the week. The class was studying Shakespeare. The teacher was an attractive woman, physically, mentally, emotionally. And the class was devoted to her. They were studying *Julius Caesar* that week and were enjoying it. In short, this was an ideal teaching situation. I would like to stress this point since it is so important to an understanding of the relations of all the languages used by modern youth.

On the fifth day I became the substitute teacher. The class was about to discuss Act III, Scene 2, the immortal Forum scene. By way of introduction, I asked them to characterize each of the principal figures. Cassius was dismissed as a "bad man," and Brutus as one who was just a cut above. Caesar—there was a man they admired. He had refused the crown; he was a man of the people. And Antony—there was a man who could talk to people, talk from the heart. Having established their beliefs in general terms, I then asked them to record the scene by means of a tape recorder. The student who played Brutus made him sound like a cheap, regional politician, while Mark came out a younger version of Clark Gable.

It was appropriate to remark that Shakespeare lent himself to various interpretations down through the ages and that it might be interesting to hear other versions. Did they know of Orson Welles's production of *Julius Caesar?* None of them had (this was a decade later). They guessed what part Orson Welles had elected to play. Most of them voted for Antony; some, for Caesar; none, for Brutus. And then we played the recording. The sonorous lines forged by a master-actor: "Not that I loved Caesar less. . . ." (Their teacher had attempted a reading of some of the great lines, but no soprano, even a beloved one, can do justice to the rolling, biting, cruel male lines of this greatest of tragedies.) The class was no longer so certain of its original interpretation.

Then we showed a ten-minute excerpt from a British film, *The Forum Scene*. Here we had not only the voices but the costumes, the background, the swaying mob against which the rhetoric pounded.

Then, and only then, could we discuss such things as dictatorship, and the courage it takes to stand up against the mob, to be an individual in a conforming society. Then, and only then, could I teach the abstractions these students needed for an understanding of an individual in modern society. Only then could they begin to *read* the greatest play ever penned.

This anecdote is not so immodest as it might seem on the surface. The regular teacher was a master-teacher; I was not. But I had tools with which to teach, and she had only a textbook and her voice. She could reach the students with only one language; I could employ three or four.

I wonder what would happen to the status of Shakespeare in American high schools if all English teachers were equipped with the proper tools? (Not long ago a school superintendent took a poll of students in his school system and reported that 87 per cent of them voted Shakespeare "the subject they hated most to study.")

From these experiences I learned that what we educators condescendingly call "audio-visual aids" or "the mass media in the classroom" are not mere *aids* in the teaching of reading, but tools that are as integral a part of the teaching process as books themselves. Unless I as

a teacher learn to use the idiom of my students, I will continue to be a teacher to the elite.

Perhaps a tired analogy may be forgiven if it serves to spotlight this concept of the inevitable interrelationship of reading and the other language arts. Communication may be likened to a loom, the warp of which is the child's experiential background. The reality of his life is joined by the near-reality created by vivid electronic and mechanical screens, and on this combined "reality" he builds all future understandings. The term "near-reality" is added because it is the peculiar power of the radio, the film, or the televised image to draw the student into situations that make him feel as if he were *really* involved. Rightly or wrongly, he sees this warp of personal experience as LIFE, real life.

Coupled with the warp is the woof of reading. You and I know it as the best method of weaving life-experiences into a meaningful pattern, an ordering of the parts, a maturing. But to the hardheaded youngster, bred of pragmatic parents, the woof seems gossamer, and he will have none of it. It is true that this young American who will not accept reading is settling for a life in which experience remains a series of disjointed threads, providing no covering from the elements, no beauty for the wearer. But let us not castigate him too severely. What have we, as teachers of reading, done to show him the relation of the warp and the woof? Have we worked in his idiom, or have we ignored it? Have we taken the best of radio and Hollywood and television and captured "reality" for him, before leading him on to the higher and more abstract planes of that reality?

The answer is a resounding "No." Less than 10 per cent of the school systems of America have professional audio-visual co-ordinators; less than 10 per cent of our teachers use audio-visual aids with any regularity at all; and less than 30 per cent of our teacher-training institutions are willing to acknowledge the fast that teachers need to learn about languages other than the language of books. We teach as we were taught.

So is it any wonder that, when the subject is discussed at general educational conferences, the consensus seems to be, "Nice, but not necessary"? Occasionally, someone will even ask the rhetorical question, "Are the mass media conflicting with reading?"

A professor for whom I have always had the profoundest respect once described literature as "a window to the world." That happens to be the slogan of a Chicago television station, WTTW. It is an apt phrase for both windows, located as they are in a tower—ivory, granite, flame, whatever stuff we build into our individual towers. The view from the window is essentially the same. He who raises the shade at WTTW has the same landscape in mind as you who raise it in the classroom—the same abstract understandings and appreciations. It is a prejudice of mine that the book represents a window higher up in the tower. It affords a wider view; both the immediate scenery and the distant hills are in better perspective.

But (and this is an important but) the window at WTTW, or the window in Ed Murrow's studio, has far more interested viewers than has your window. It is fulfilling the task of mass intercommunication better than you and I. We can continue to ignore it and teach reading by books alone to one, two, or a few. Or we can harness that energy and that interest, and take a majority of our classes to higher planes of learning.

FUTURE RELATIONSHIPS

The teaching profession may be forced to recognize these other languages sooner than we think, for within a score of years the world will see international television, and it will see tape-recorded television programs, playable on any set in the land. These records will be book-size, book-weight, book-cost. They will be sold in bookstores and carried by libraries and be as available as any book is today. Whatever the subject, there will be a video recording available.

Is this a threat? No, I don't think so. It is, rather, a thrilling opportunity. Once a man becomes engrossed in the history of his country through vivid video, he will be led inevitably to the vivid volumes that extend his horizon even more. Imagine, if by 1980, you and I could give good books a status they have never before enjoyed in recorded history: the status of being *wanted* and *used* by a majority of the citizens of a great democracy.

With this challenge in mind, and as you discuss the topic in your sectional meetings, refer to the following questions:

1. Do I have an adequate understanding of the function and power of these other languages?
2. Do I have a professional audio-visual co-ordinator to help me obtain the best material?
3. Do I, an administrator, understand the grave need for an integration of these various language skills?

CHAPTER IX

USING RADIO AND TELEVISION TO INCITE
INTEREST IN READING

*

IN KINDERGARTEN THROUGH GRADE THREE

CLARIBEL M. NAYDER

*

MANY teachers throughout the nation have availed themselves of the help that well-planned, dramatic, intimate, and inspiring radio and television programs, commercial or educational, can give them in their teaching. One way to determine whether a program is functioning as an educational device is to observe pupils' reactions following the program. Did the listener attempt an experiment or a project such as the one discussed? Did the listener so enjoy what he saw or heard that he wanted to know more about the stories or the people and, of his own volition, found picture- or story-books on the same subjects? If not yet able to read, did he ask someone to read to him a story similar to the one heard or seen?

If there is to be a kinship between entertainment and education, the teacher will need to be the stimulus through which children's inquisitiveness will be further satisfied. The primary-grade teacher must enlist the aid of parents in the effort to get from the radio or television program more than the entertainment that children seek. A note to the parent telling the title, the day, the time, the station or channel of desirable programs is the first step in furthering the teacher's motive.

A UNIVERSAL APPEAL

Since nearly all little children like animals, it is safe to suggest the use of the nationwide broadcast of "Disneyland" as a means of integrating the entertainment hour with the education that can, and should, follow it. Discussion of an animal's playful or foolish antics, its struggle for existence, its peculiar habits, its use to man, and its many and varied experiences supplies opportunities for showing pictures, reading stories to the children, and urging them to obtain, for themselves, picture-books and simple story-books about animals. A well-liked book is *Dumbo* (Simon & Schuster, 1946), the delightful story of a baby elephant who, like the ugly duckling, was frowned upon because of his looks but finally is victorious over his trials and disappointments.

Radio and television bring circus animals to the child's experience too. *Little-or-Nothing from Nottingham* by Marguerite Henry (Whittlesey, 1949) is the tale of an inquisitive dog that gets under a circus tent and into many

95

troubles. The facts of this pup's undoing came out of an item in the *National Geographic Magazine* telling about a real dog that belonged to a circus. Animal-lovers will also want to hear the story *Rufus* by Dorothy Childs Hogner (Lippincott, 1955). Rufus, a red fox, gets into a chicken-house, where he instigates much trouble.

Radio and television presentations of animals and birds provide many primary-grade children with experiences in the field of scientific discovery. Again, Disney's programs on birds may be the impetus for reading many of the excellent stories which are available. *Thistle B* by Tasha Tudor (Oxford, 1949), a little book with delightful pictures showing two children and their canary, should be read to a small group so that the pictures may be shown as the story progresses.

Various farm programs broadcast or telecast throughout the nation provide children with knowledge of farm animals. *Danny and the Dog Doctor* by Jerrold Beim (Morrow, 1950) acquaints the child with the work of the veterinarian and teaches kindness to animals and birds.

The cow, an animal to which children are introduced early because it is the source of the milk they drink, provides excellent story material. To correlate further, the teacher might read *Friendly Animals* by Karl Patterson Schmidt (Donohue, 1947), *Animal Babies* by Margaret Jean Bauer (Donohue, 1949), and *Susannah, the Pioneer Cow* by Miriam E. Mason (Macmillan, 1941).

Program-planners realize the appeal that animals make to children. Many programs consistently present stories in answer to this appeal. "Zoo Parade" is another national hook-up program worthy of note. The alert teacher will en-courage interest in animals through reading to the children and placing at their disposal books which they can enjoy.

Space does not permit further discussion of the multitude of stories and radio or television programs, available to children of the primary grades, which use animals for their themes. Here, then, is a topic which teachers may use as a springboard for leading children, through reading, to learn more than was presented on the radio or television program.

ROUTINE AND REGULARITY NEEDED FOR PROGRESS

All teachers, but particularly primary-grade teachers, recognize the importance of doing things regularly. If children are to learn to associate entertainment through radio or television with learning through reading, a routine of discussion of programs and associated reading must be established. When it becomes known that the majority of the class is listening to, or watching, a particular program, it is wise to set aside a period on the day following that program, or directly following the program if it is heard in school, to discuss what was learned and to read books or to show pictures associated with the ideas presented on the program. The teacher must be familiar with what was presented. Educational stations frequently issue handbooks of suggestions to the teacher in advance of the program. In the case of out-of-school listening or viewing, it is not wise to discuss programs that the teacher has not witnessed.

The habit of listening to or watching a particular program can be instilled. Some pupils who may not at first have participated will join in the listening and the reading of books because they want to belong and to do what others are doing and enjoying. The teacher must establish this habit if the children are to learn to think of books and programs synonymously.

To help establish this habit of program and book association further, the teacher may appeal next to the child's interest in himself and other people, particularly persons close to him. Many popular programs, such as "Father Knows Best," "Ozzie and Harriet," and other family-type stories, while not on the child's level and not always exerting the best influence on him, interest him because he has experienced similar adventures. Teachers can help correct undesirable impressions by reading stories associated with happy home experiences, such as *Mr. Apple's Family* by Jean McDevitt (Doubleday, 1950). This delightful book of six chapters describes lively, likable experiences, the first of which tells of naming the Apple children after different varieties of apples, such as McIntosh, Delicious, and other. Another family story is told in *Kid Brother* by Jerrold Beim (Morrow, 1952). Here is a story of family conflict, in which all eventually ends well.

The improvement of human relations is the worthy motive of *Pierre Comes to P.S. 20* by Helen Train Hilles (Messner, 1952). This story, if presented as a dramatization, requires that the teacher give a vocabulary lesson to acquaint the children with French words used in the story. Pierre had difficulty with English pronunciations. The class can appreciate problems of foreign children if the teacher will have them try to pronounce some of the easier French words in the story. Even kindergarten children, through books, radio, or television programs, can

be given a better understanding of people of strange lands. In Chicago the educational radio station WBEZ presents "Hand in Hand," a program for primary-grade children which attempts to instil better human relations and a stronger feeling of brotherhood.

Programs concerning workers—delivery men, bus operators, telephone operators, policemen, dentists, doctors, and hosts of others—furnish an unending source of ideas for discussion of pictures and for books that the teacher can read aloud to give the children a better acquaintance with the world about them. The presentation on radio or television may not have been specifically concerned with that worker, but his part in the story may promote discussion which the teacher can use to introduce specific books on the subject. *Who Blew That Whistle?* by Leone Adelson (W. R. Scott, 1946) is a book which illustrates, as well as it tells, the many problems of a traffic policeman.

Frequently it is advisable to read to the children before the radio or television presentation of a story, especially in the case of holiday stories or stories of fantasy. The fascinating story of *Cinderella*, an ever popular favorite, intrigues children to such an extent that it is not uncommon for them to look at pictures of the story, not once, but several times. If such intense interest is noted, the teacher might read Kingsley's *Water Babies* with its similar theme. Inexpensive tableau books of the Cinderella story are available and should be placed at the children's disposal.

Stories for particular holidays are interesting to children. One such story is *The Country Bunny and the Little Gold Shoes* by Flack and Heyward (Houghton, 1939). This book is full of beautiful pictures of bunnies all dressed up like boys and girls and doing things boys and girls do. The story tells that there is not just one Easter bunny, but five of them, all of whom hope to be chosen as Easter bunnies. One double-page spread shows a sleeping child receiving an Easter egg, with just a few words on the page. Primary-grade children love beautiful pictures and not too many words to read.

PARENTS AND LIBRARIANS

Teachers must be ready to suggest to parents the good practice of purchasing books as gifts for children. In a note to the parent, a prescribed list of books to accompany radio and television programs recommended for listening or watching might well be included.

Through the increased demand for a particular title, librarians are aware of the enthusiasm and interest in books aroused by certain radio or television programs. Even in the primary departments of the library there are bulletin boards displaying jackets of books associated with current programs.

CONCLUDING STATEMENT

The parents' and librarians' contributions are valuable aids, but the teacher is the important stimulus in making an entertainment device pay greater dividends by inciting interest in reading. An alert teacher who becomes acquainted with the content of a series of radio or television programs so that motivation for the program can be prepared in advance, who enlists the aid of the parents and informs them of the school's purposes, who regularly sets aside a period for reading before or after the audio-visual aid is presented, who establishes a routine and recognizes the tremendous potentiality of these mass media, and who places at the disposal of the inquisitive minds of children quantities of beautiful, easy books—such a teacher exerts an influence like that of a pebble thrown into the water, whose circles of influence spread wider and wider.

Unfavorable criticism of the effects of radio and television serves little or no purpose. However, with purposeful planning by parents and resourceful teachers, these media become invaluable aids in the process of learning.

＊　＊　＊

IN GRADES FOUR THROUGH SIX

VIOLA S. SODERSTROM

＊

EXPERIMENTATION in the use of radio and television has established many values for the educational program. Three areas are discussed in this paper.

DIRECT INSTRUCTION

The approach to the direct lesson through radio and television is compara-

tively new. Information received over the air has, in the child's mind, an authenticity on the same level as that conveyed by a book. Children have learned how to cook, sew, build birdhouses, perform experiments, and handle animals as a result of watching television. A post card to the broadcasting station brings written directions, plans, or recipes to the viewer. Boys proudly show their skill in cooking since they have seen François Pope do a masterly job.

A radio program, "Play It Safe," catches the interest of the pupil by using familiar characters from comic strips. Mr. Magoo learns safety by enjoying a common-sense Halloween. Tarzan teaches first aid and playground safety. Jack Armstrong, Brenda Starr, and Joe Palooka add their bit to make children safety-conscious. After this series the children rush to the library for safety materials.

Another favorite radio program, "The Tip-Top Twins," teaches how to stay well and to live fuller and happier lives. The children read to learn how to plant a vegetable garden, how the body regulates its temperature, and how to plan for a summer vacation. They use books, magazines, charts, graphs, and diagrams in this series of lessons.

An object lesson in the operation of a democratic government was brought to boys and girls in Chicago schools when President Eisenhower's inaugural ceremonies were carried into the classrooms through the miracle of television. This program correlated with the social studies by showing on-the-spot news. Broadcasts of this type serve as a springboard for wider reading in the field of history. The "Landmark Series" of books (Random) have become very popular because of the television program "You Are There."

Many specialists in their fields and persons of public interest make valuable contributions by sharing with pupils over the air waves their knowledge and understandings. They serve as master-teachers to promote interest and research in every field of endeavor.

"Sounds of Science" radio programs have excited young minds by acquainting them with thousands of wonderful things going on about them every day. "How the World Began," "From a Trip to Saturn to a Trip Five Miles below Sea Level," and "From the Universe to the Atom" have kept pupils constantly seeking answers. The pupils' impression of the earth's beginning was greatly broadened by following up the handbook's reference to an artist's conception of it.[1]

The program on "The Weather All around Us" helps create a lively interest in reading the weather maps and forecasts printed in daily papers and in almanacs. The libraries find the calls on the section devoted to weather are growing in number. "The Story of Machines," in which simple machines are demonstrated, gives impetus to interest in a new field. A simple experiment in aerodynamics sends the class to encyclopedias and technical books for more complete information.

ENRICHMENT TO CLASSROOM EXPERIENCE

Many of these direct teaching programs are also used for supplementary purposes when the class has previously covered the area or when the program provides an isolated incident in a larger unit for study. The direct teaching of how to make a telescope employed in the program "Sounds of Science" could well provide a beginning for the study of the stars and aid in contributing much information to the class in the development of the unit.

Some of the greater values of radio and

[1] George Jennings, *Sounds of Science*. Chicago Board of Education Bulletin, Division of Radio and Television Bulletin. Chicago: Board of Education, 1955–56.

television are that they broaden the child's experiential background, introduce new worlds of thought, and thus stimulate the desire for more extensive reading. As a result of discussion with a sixth-grade class, one teacher reported that she was surprised to learn to what extent radio and television programs stimulated an interest in reading. The pupils mentioned "Science Fiction Theater," "Disneyland," "Warner Brothers Presents," "Mr. Wizard," "Dr. Hudson's Secret Journal," "Wide, Wide World," and "Let's Take a Trip" as favorite programs. Asked why they read a book after seeing the program, they remarked that the book was more detailed and that it was fun to compare the two. Many children said that they wanted more information about things they had seen and heard. A majority of the stories presented on television are found in books that are in the school library, and these books are in popular demand.

A fifth-grade class reported reading books on science, social studies, fiction, and fine arts as a result of listening to radio and television. Another fifth-grade class listens to the "Magic of Books." This program has encouraged good reading tastes through good radio listening. Pupils have learned to use the library by exploring books in similar categories, thus augmenting their supplementary reading. One program on a sport in France was taken from a book written by Clair Huchet Bishop. This book was not in the library, so the pupils took out the author's other books to read. The class selected three books by other authors that were given on the supplementary list. After reading them, the class became interested in all sports in France and other countries. The dictionary and encyclopedias were used. The public library

had a book on games of many nations. The interest then shifted to good sportsmanship. Sports in France led the pupils to *Time, Life, Saturday Evening Post, Holiday,* and *Newsweek*. A bulletin board of clippings, a products map, and a booklet on French industries grew out of this activity. One pupil became concerned about the value of health and its relation to sports and later reported in class on her findings. Two children found a book on making puppets, from which they learned to make wire figures of athletes. Thus, from one program many subjects were touched upon and many activities resulted.

Josephine Wetzler of WLS asks teachers in her "News of the Week" program schedule: "What is your approach? Do you have a chalk editor to put key names on the board; a map editor to locate important places mentioned; a news bulletin board; a class newspaper; a scrapbook on current events?" These are all good techniques, and each activity points up the need for reading in newspapers, magazines, pamphlets, and books.

"The Magic Harp," a radio musical series, opens up many new fields for exploration. The idea of brotherhood is presented through songs of ethnic and religious groups. The events depicted in "Pioneer Days," "The History of Our Country," "Hiawatha," and "Paul Revere's Ride" (with background music) are all part of our great American heritage. Music programs for Easter and St. Patrick's Day are impressive and delightful. American inventors are extolled. "Oil, the Black Magic" and "The Laying of the Atlantic Cable" add to a wonderful series for young people interested in social studies. Their reading connected with these programs is done in encyclopedias and in books on biography, music, poetry, religion—in short, in almost every field of knowledge. A wealth of material is offered to arouse every child's interest in some of these fields.

In one school the reading selections were related to programs familiar to the pupils. The librarian discussed books which would supplement the children's favorite programs. Books based on space navigation, on opera, on musical instruments, on dancing, and on marionettes were listed. The librarian's relating the books to the programs is a technique which not only helps to guide the tastes and interests of the pupils' out-of-school listening program but also affords an opportunity to get pupil evaluations of programs. These in turn can lead to interest in criticisms written by professional critics. "Book Box" on WLS and "Cavalcade of Books" acquaint the audience with good books that children can find in libraries or in bookstores.

PARTICIPATION, A STIMULUS TO FURTHER READING

Radio and television offer an opportunity for children to participate in professional broadcasts. In addition, mock broadcasts are held in classrooms and on assembly programs. Many of these follow the format of professional productions. A favorite is the quiz type, such as the one called "Animal, Vegetable, or Mineral."

"How It Works" and a "Lady Make Believe" series have been used by some groups. The "Twenty Questions" game is very popular with a library group for guessing book titles. Pupils become very adept in following an orderly pattern to help them guess the title of the book. Perhaps the most generally used program is "Battle of Books." A great deal of reading is required to enable the pupils to pose good questions. The teams must remember a great many books to identify them from the questions. This program is good fun as well as a wonderful incentive for reading.

CONCLUDING STATEMENT

We are justified in assuming that radio and television are inescapable parts of our educational program. Their potentialities are boundless in scope and exciting to anticipate. Not only do the magic box and video screen sell products, but they change the habits and lives of the nation. If we as educators seize the opportunity to use these media and do our job well, television and radio will serve as a motivating force to create interests which will overcome the apathy of many pupils toward reading. Ideas will be sold that will help children discover new fields of interest leading them to turn more and more to the printed page.

IN GRADES SEVEN THROUGH NINE

DAVID V. CURTIS

*

THIS paper deals with the use of radio and television in the classroom of a Chicago public school. It will tell first about the over-all city program and then about an experiment in an eighth-grade classroom of a crowded area where the teacher is making a definite contribution to inciting reading interest through the use of these media.

THE RADIO COUNCIL OF CHICAGO

The Radio Council, Division of Radio and Television of the Chicago public schools, offers many interesting series of programs which can be used as spring-boards for preparation and follow-up activities in reading. The radio station is on the air seven hours each day. It presents series of programs from the kindergarten through the college level. Some of the major networks in the Chicago area permit some of these programs to be broadcast over their stations. These programs are carefully rehearsed in the radio and television workshops. The Division of Radio maintains two student workshops for training young people who are interested in radio acting, writing, or engineering.

Each week a bulletin listing the programs for the following week is sent to the schools. The programs include "Skyways of Science," prepared by the staff of the Adler Planetarium, which is a series of science programs designed for upper-elementary and high-school study. A social-science series called "The Plains to the Pacific" tells of the trail that Lewis and Clark took to the Pacific Ocean. The "Elizabethan Theater" presents Elizabethan and Shakespearean tragedies. "Exploring Music" is designed to help young people develop an ear for classics, as well as for good modern music. The series "Background in Government" acquaints the student with the working structure of government agencies. "How It Began" is a series on "first" things, such as baseball, electric lights, moving pictures, etc., that make our American life enjoyable today. "Books in Review" is designed to encourage better reading. Many more programs are prepared for every grade level, including material related to art, history, geography, literature, social studies, music, and reading.

These programs are used in the classroom to help meet a specific educational need. The teacher must prepare the children for listening. The teacher must also initiate the children's interest in the program to be heard. On the other hand, the program must relate to the content of what is being studied in the classroom. The students should engage in discussion before the program starts and after it is finished. The teacher should use any method that he can to encourage the children to give their undivided attention to what is being said over the air.

USING PROGRAMS TO INCREASE READING

It is apparent that follow-up activity is an essential part of classroom listening or viewing. For example, a class may be

102

studying a unit on electricity and may see a television program which demonstrates the usefulness of carbon. In order to understand the carbon rod in the dry cell, several boys read about it in one of the supplementary books on electricity. As a result of this extra reading they are able to understand that carbon is needed in order to start the flow of electricity in the dry cell. These boys also perform many other experiments with the carbon rod. This is one example in which the television broadcast is used as a stimulus for reading activity.

Many of the bulletins suggest supplementary reading materials which are related to the radio or television programs. Through observation of the children during free-reading periods in the classroom, the teacher can evaluate the effectiveness of his preparation and follow-up program. The radio and television programs chosen for classroom use should be those that fit into the basic course of study and not those which help to relieve boredom.

Many of the children in my classroom have read books in the public library because they saw television programs which were beyond their comprehension and they wanted to increase their understanding. They have recommended these books to me. I in turn have recommended the books to the school librarian for possible purchase for our school. As a result of this interest our school librarian has met with me on many occasions and has sent books for the entire class to examine. We have a room library, from which students take books to read for the unit they are engaged in or the recreational reading that they are doing. We also keep a shelf of magazines.

Radio and television have been accepted by many educators today as media for stimulating children to do serious thinking, to increase understanding, and to stimulate children to read. For example, children who have seen pictures on television or heard stories about guided missiles, atom bombs, and the like are motivated to read scientific literature on these subjects because they become interested in this material. We cannot measure the extent of this reading accurately because it is not a part of the course of study but is done on a voluntary basis. If, however, the children express themselves in classroom discussions, we can measure, to a certain degree, their knowledge on these subjects.

AN EIGHTH-GRADE EXPERIMENT

The neighborhood in which our school is located is crowded, and the people are in a low-income bracket. A recent survey of the homes of our students revealed that most of them have a radio or a television. But most of the homes have no books and do not subscribe to magazines, except a few who subscribe to a Polish magazine. Hence the school must provide these children with reading materials to satisfy their interests.

As part of the current-events assignments, the upper-grade children are required to listen every morning to the news broadcasts presented by the Chicago Board of Education. We have discovered that those who listen read the newspaper more than they did before they became avid listeners to the newscasts. Some children say that they have talked about the programs with their parents. There are some who bring the newspaper to class every morning and lead in the daily classroom discussions. As part of the homework assignment, they have a choice of listening to the radio or looking at television news broadcasts. These aids seem to increase their understanding of the world about them and help to promote critical thought and participation in classroom discussions. Some students who are not interested in reading may listen to the radio or watch a television broadcast. It is much better that they get this limited amount of information than none at all. Those children who are interested in further details will be stimulated by the radio and television to read the newspaper.

Thirty eighth-grade students wrote compositions on the effect of radio and television on their reading. Some said that the radio did not make them want to read because the announcers talked too fast. Others, however, were stimulated to read. One student wrote: "I think television makes me want to read more because I can see what is happening and if I do not understand I can read for details." This girl has an interest in the stars. As a result of a trip to the Adler Planetarium, she read *When the Stars Come Out* (Viking, 1942). Another student claimed that he did not get much stimulation for reading from viewing programs. He wrote: "As a matter of fact, I haven't read a really good book in almost a year. I do watch a lot of TV. The reason I got a high reading average is from reading comic books. They are very interesting to me. Radio and TV are helpful in my education, for I remember most of what I see, but they do not make me want to read more." Asked if he had read *Tom Sawyer*, he said, "I have seen it on television." A few passages from the book were read to him, and he was asked to take it home and examine it. He finished the book in a week and gave a report on it to the class, in which he said that he had missed a lot of action in the television program. Comments from other students follow:

Television helps me to read. When I am watching "Science Fiction Theater," I always get interested in their experiments. One picture that interested me a lot was about the moon. A photographer developed a camera that could photograph the stars and moon very close. He decided to try it on the moon. When he developed the film, he saw big streaks on the print. When he studied it closely, he saw a rocket ship doing something on the other side of the moon. After the picture was finished, I took my encyclopedia and looked up the moon and learned a lot about it. Sunday I watched "You Are There." They had a program on the Chicago fire, how it started and how much destruction it did. After that I looked up the Chicago fire, the date it happened and why they could not put the fire out. The "Quiz Kids" is a good show because I try to answer the questions they ask and, if I'm wrong, I find out the right answer and look up more information about it. When I listen to the news and I want to find more information about something, I take the newspaper and read about it.

I do think radio and television help in encouraging you to read. I think television more so than the radio. The radio does a little, but I think the television does more, because it gives you the whole picture. It shows you pictures of where the things are happening and pictures of the people. If you see a science show in which they do an experiment and you want to know why the experiment turned out that way, you find books and read about it and some of these books give you an interest to read more books.

Some people think that radio and television are just for pleasure, but in a sense they are educational too. To get anything out of a program, you have to listen or watch carefully to see what is happening. Radio has many fine programs that make you want to read. The news broadcasts tell of interesting things, but I think the broadcasters talk too fast, so the people who try to catch up with what they are saying read the newspaper to get more details. Television also makes people want to read more. Some programs are about history which you have already read, so when you watch the program it makes you want to read that particular part of history over again.

There are two programs which I like. They are "Medic" and "Dr. Hudson's Secret Journal." I chose these two programs because I am interested in what goes on in a hospital. About a year ago I turned on our TV, and I saw "Medic." I thought it was very interesting. A few days later my friend suggested a book for me to read, and I did. The name of the book was *Sue Barton, Neighborhood Nurse*. Then I discovered "Dr. Hudson's Secret Journal," and I began watching it regularly. I went back to our library and found some more books about Sue Barton. Then I found that I had read all her books about nursing. Gradually I began to read more books as a result of watching television.

One student stated that he enjoyed reading but could not find books that he could read: "They are all baby books." This particular student had a low reading-achievement score. He was introduced to the "Landmark" series of books, and the good readers in the class helped him with difficult vocabulary. On the last reading test his achievement had increased from Grade 5.0 to Grade 5.8 in six months.

CONCLUDING STATEMENT

In utilizing any radio or television program related to art, music, geography, science, social studies, and history for study in the classroom, the techniques must vary with each broadcast. They should be related to the children's thought, reactions, and personal experiences. Any spark of interest in reading that children get from listening or viewing television helps to meet some of the educational needs.

✳ ✳ ✳

IN GRADES TEN THROUGH FOURTEEN

HOMER B. GOLDBERG

✳

SINCE December, 1955, audiences in the Chicago area have enjoyed the facilities of a noncommercial television station devoted to educational broadcasting. Supported by public subscription, WTTW, or Channel 11, has co-operated in the production of programs developed by various cultural and educational institutions of this area which are its participating members.

In co-operation with WTTW, members of the faculty of the College of the University of Chicago, from December, 1955, to June, 1956, presented a series of twenty-six programs under the general title "The Humanities." These programs were concerned with the critical exploration of a variety of works of literature, music, and graphic art. Although the initial conception of the series derived from an introductory course offered to students in Grades XI, XII, and XIII at the University of Chicago, the programs themselves were not intended to be a course of study, but rather a series of stimulants to increased awareness of, and interest, in the arts. Presented at a time when the younger children might reasonably be expected to be in bed, the broadcasts were aimed at a broad adult audience, which included some high-school and college students as well as secretaries, housewives, and business-men.

THE AIM OF THE HUMANITIES SERIES

This series was intended to give an introduction to the arts, but it was not designed to provide the viewer with an accumulation of background informa-tion, historical generalization, or ready-made formulations of art. Instead, we tried to sharpen the average viewer's awareness of what he or she could per-ceive in literature, music, painting, and sculpture and to encourage his interest and his confidence in his own capacity for aesthetic appreciation and enjoyment. Underlying this conception of the pro-grams was the idea that the fundamental equipment for aesthetic understanding and appreciation—the ability to see, to hear, and to read—is not the exclusive property of a few specially endowed, sensitive souls but that it is possessed, unrecognized, in varying degrees by most adults.

We made this point in our first pro-gram by showing how aesthetic responses and judgments are involved in such everyday experiences as the decision about where to hang a picture or the re-action to a singing commercial. It was even suggested that aesthetic enjoyment has a good deal to do with the catchy appeal of a simple political slogan like "I like Ike." Our aim was to suggest ways in which the average viewer might apply this unconscious capacity in a more self-conscious fashion to increase his enjoyment and understanding of art. Thus it can be said that the literature programs were intended to arouse inter-est in reading, interest in a *kind* of read-ing and kinds of works which some of the viewers might be currently studying in school, but which other members of the audience might not have thought about since they left high school or college, and which still others might never have known about before.

THE WORK AND ITS EXTERNAL CONTEXT

What were the means used to arouse and sustain this interest? We elected on principle to dispense with a major source of interest; there was no exploitation of the reader's curiosity about the circum-stances surrounding the book, its ma-terials, its historical epoch, or the life of its author. These are fascinating and im-portant aspects of the subject, and the teacher of literature cannot feel that he has treated his subject adequately with-out considering them. Each of us, in the classroom and out of it, draws upon this material in trying to arouse interest in a book. The romance of the Brownings is in its own way as exciting as much of their poetry. But no amount of discussion of the Barretts of Wimpole Street, fact or fiction, is an adequate alternative to the careful consideration of Browning's poems themselves, and the extensive use of these "external" sources of interest would be clearly inappropriate to a series of programs committed to developing the idea that the real source of interest, the reason for reading (or looking or listen-ing), lies in the unique experience of the work of art itself.

PROBLEMS IN PRESENTING THE WORK OF LITERATURE

One possible conclusion to be drawn is that our programs should be devoted to presenting the work of art as fully and effectively as possible, letting the sonata, the painting, or the poem speak for itself. As one professor suggested at an educational television conference, we should present oral readings of Robert Frost's poems while the television camera focuses on a series of appropriate New England scenes. Something like this, without the visual aids, is the principal device used on the only commercial radio program I know which is intended to arouse children's interest in reading. N.B.C.'s "Carnival of Books" relies heavily on the dramatic reading of portions of the books being promoted.

While we recognize that the teacher cannot supplant the experience of the work of art, it is apparent that something more is needed than confronting the viewer with the poem or painting and suggesting that he should find this a moving experience. Even avoiding especially difficult or obscure works, it is obvious that the sharpening of insight and enlarging of perspective which we seek can be achieved more easily with some assistance from persons trained in "knowing what to look for." As we have found in our teaching, this kind of assistance can be provided most effectively when the teacher and the student are operating as directly and particularly as possible on the work itself. Accordingly, we tried to have the works of art present during the broadcast whenever possible. This was considerably easier to do in the graphic arts and even in music than it was in the literature programs.

The time required to read aloud even a very short story or a moderately long poem makes a considerable inroad on the half-hour at the teacher's disposal. It is clearly impossible to present a play or novel, except through brief excerpts, and this practice involves the danger that the viewer will lose sight of the understanding of the work as a whole. Moreover, the effectiveness of an oral presentation of a text which is to be subjected to analytical or critical reading is limited by the viewer's ability to retain the material in his mind clearly while it is being discussed. Nor is there much hope for "visual aid." Poems cannot be reproduced on the screen in their original format, because the proportions of the television screen make it impossible to present readably lines of more than five or six words, and no cameraman has succeeded in scanning lines of print so that the viewers can follow. A teacher discussing a statue can ask the camera to focus on the piece or on any part of it at any time in his talk; a musician seated at the piano can "recall" passages whenever he chooses; the teacher of literature does not have such flexibility.

After confining the opening literature programs to short works, we decided to acknowledge this difficulty and meet it by making a special demand upon the audience. The subjects of forthcoming programs were announced in advance, and the viewers were asked to read them in preparation for the program. The programs themselves contained readings of portions of the work chosen to bring out points made in the discussion. There is an apparent circularity in the procedure of assigning reading. The audience was asked to read a work in preparation for a program which was intended to arouse their interest in reading this or similar works. This is not as paradoxical as it seems. We were not teaching these few poems, stories, and plays as such; the program on Shakespeare's *Romeo and Juliet*, for instance, was not intended to "explain" that play, once and for all. Emerging from all the literature programs were two related points: (1) that there is more to reading serious literature than—literally—"meets the eye" and (2) that the kinds of questions and problems raised in reading these works might be applied in reading other poems or stories or novels.

Ideally, under this conception, the successful program would provoke the viewer to reread the work examined with new insight and to discuss it with others. Thus by assigning readings in advance, we hoped to engage the viewers' more active participation before, during, and after the program. Since, however, we could not assume a constant audience from week to week, it was necessary to compromise by attempting to give some minimal summary of the work for those persons unacquainted with it. Although the viewer who had read the work would be likely to benefit more from the discussion, we were hopeful that the discussion might arouse others to read it for the first time.

"TEACHING" ON TELEVISION

It would be inappropriate and impracticable here to discuss at any length the conception of literature and of how it should be studied and taught which underlay this series of programs. The general approach is perhaps by now a familiar one. It is based on the idea that analysis of a poem or a story increases our appreciation and enjoyment of it. Running through the inquiry into the various literary works were two broad questions: "What is the particular effect or expressive character of the work as a whole?" and "How do the various elements of the work contribute to the whole experience?" In pursuing this inquiry, it was inevitable that the viewer would become acquainted with some of the analytic concepts frequently applied

to literature, that he would become familiar with such terms as "plot," "character," "imagery," "metaphor," and so on. While our approach to each work was in this sense systematic, there was no attempt to develop these analytic principles systematically in successive programs. Our focus was on the individual poem or play, not on literary doctrine.

The particular pedagogical techniques employed are perhaps of more immediate interest. The initial format was a kind of lecture-demonstration, in which the professor talked about the poem, with readings and occasional reference to blackboard diagrams or printed lines. This has the obvious advantage of insuring a coherent organization imposed by the instructor, but it also puts a great demand upon the speaker's capacity to arouse and sustain the viewer's interest and greatly reduces the sources of variety. This is the method employed by Mr. Frank Baxter in his celebrated Shakespeare programs, which have been so popular on commercial television. Since, however, the teachers engaged in the "Humanities" series were all accustomed to teaching principally by the discussion method, it was natural that we should experiment with the possibility of adapting this method to the circumstances of broadcasting.

Several teachers took part in our discussions on the air. They could not achieve the most desirable effect of the discussion method as it is employed in the classroom, namely, the active participation of the student in the process of inquiry and problem-solving. But this format does offer several advantages over the lecture or informal talk. Most immediately and superficially, it engages the viewer in a little drama, the interaction of several persons with similar, different, or sometimes sharply conflicting ideas. By confining the "script" to an agreed outline of topics or problems, and limiting "rehearsal" to one or two "runthroughs," it was possible to achieve a spontaneous and vigorous discussion. In each of the programs, one or more of the participants contributed something which had not been anticipated in rehearsal. As a result the viewers had the sense of being present while the teachers themselves were thinking through the problem. They saw the discussants asking questions and facing problems which they encountered in reading the poem or the play. We hope that by this means they may have been incited to read in this questioning and scrutinizing way with similar enthusiasm and energy. In this sense the actual structure of the program provided a model which the viewer might imitate in his own reading.

THE LIMITATIONS OF EDUCATION BY TELEVISION

I wish that it were possible to report on the success of these programs. I cannot do so for a reason which makes clear the exact limits of television (or radio) as an educational medium. Broadcasting is a one-way communication. There is no way for the student to ask questions, to show that he has understood, or to express his puzzlement. There is no way for the teacher to determine whether he has been understood before moving on to his next point. In *The Aims of Education*, Whitehead analyzes the process of education into three phases or stages which succeed each other cyclically throughout one's learning life. He calls the first "the stage of romance"; the second, "the stage of precision"; and the third, "the stage of generalization." It is only in the

first of these stages that educational broadcasting can properly be effective. The teacher in the picture tube has no way of measuring the precision of his viewer's thinking, and it is not really educational, in the sense that real learning is taking place, to make generalizations about facts or materials through which the audience itself has not worked directly. What one can do on a radio or television program is to capture the interest of the viewer in a subject with which he may have been unfamiliar. Whitehead describes the stage of romance as "the stage of first apprehension" in which "the subject matter has the vividness of novelty." He continues: "Romantic emotion is essentially the excitement consequent on the transition from the bare facts to the first realizations of the import of their unexplored relationships."[1]

It was with the transition from the "bare facts" of the printed words and the ideas and feelings behind them to their "unexplored relationships" in works of art that the "Humanities" programs were concerned. That they brought about this transition in at least one case is suggested by one viewer's experience. After seeing a program in which the teacher analyzed Shakespeare's "Sonnet 73," a fourteen-year-old boy who had not previously shown any great interest in poetry proceeded to search out all the sonnets he could find. As he told his father, he was looking for one that could equal the poem he had heard discussed on television. The awakening of this young critic's interest is perhaps sufficient justification for calling the programs a success.

[1] Alfred North Whitehead, *The Aims of Education and Other Essays*, pp. 27–40. New York: Macmillan Co., 1929. Used with permission of The Macmillan Company.

CHAPTER X

METHODS AND MATERIALS FOR CLASSROOM INSTRUCTION

✳

BASIC INSTRUCTION IN READING AND THE PROMOTION OF READING INTERESTS

HELEN HUUS

✳

How can basic reading instruction— the teacher's regular, day-by-day teaching—help promote the reading interests of children and youth? In answering this question, let us first look at six aspects of basic instruction, then at some illustrative selections of different types of content and style, at different levels, and see the possibilities for promoting reading interests.

DEVELOPING ATTITUDES

First of all, basic instruction in reading introduces the child to his first participation in the reading act. If his first experiences are satisfying, he will approach each day's reading with anticipation and keen delight. If his experiences are unhappy, he will evade, or bluff, or just quit trying. The primary-grade teacher faces a real challenge in devising assignments which are within the child's grasp, which he can do without undue strain, which he knows he can do, and which the teacher knows she can teach him to do. The confidence of the teacher is catching, and it does much to build the child's security in facing a new task.

Teachers in grades above the primary, even through college, often have in their classes students who have never had a good start in reading and consequently have accumulated difficulties ever since. Their need for satisfying experiences is no less, is perhaps greater, than that of the beginner in Grade I.

EMPHASIZING MEANING

Second, basic instruction emphasizes reading as a meaningful process. Through their first experience stories, children are shown how reading and speaking are related; that, as Marion Monroe says, reading is "just *talk* wrote down."[1] Then as the story characters in the first pre-primer are met, children accept them as real friends. Current methods of teaching beginning reading by having children acquire a basic sight vocabulary (words they know at sight) allow for this emphasis on meaning from the very beginning.

There are, however, levels of meaning with different depths of penetration and analysis. At the lowest level is simple comprehension, repeating "what the book says," but in one's own words. Some children find this difficult, for it presupposes a familiarity with the vocabulary, both recognizing the word and recalling an appropriate meaning from their back-

[1] Marion Monroe, *Growing into Reading*, p. 68. Chicago: Scott, Foresman & Co., 1951.

110

ground of experience. Content areas, with their technical vocabularies, complicate the situation further.

Deeper and fuller meanings must be explored, analyzed, compared, and evaluated. Underlying shades and tones must be recognized, allusions related to their referents, and figures of speech understood and appreciated. "As slow as molasses in January" means little to one who has never lived in a cold climate; "as mad as a hatter" has no context if Lewis Carroll's classic is unfamiliar. Proverbs, cartoons, and jokes have no point at all unless what is behind the print is understood; a varied background of information and experience lends meaning to otherwise unintelligible phrases.

PROMOTING INDEPENDENCE

The third aspect of basic reading instruction to be considered here relates to promoting independence on the part of the child so that he is able to read without having a teacher or other adult constantly at his side. This entails helping him figure out new words for himself. Good teachers have always given children skills in this area: using context to see if the word makes sense in the sentence, using the sounds of letters or groups of letters to aid recognition, using prefixes or suffixes to help with unknown words, and using the glossary or dictionary to check when he is not sure.

Another phase of independence in reading is that of the study skills. Basic to any real problem-solving is the understanding of how to effect a solution. Study skills, whether at Grade I or XII, include first of all the ability to grasp the main idea and the supporting details. Given this ability, the relationship among the ideas can be analyzed, and the foundation is laid for outlining.

Locating information, taking notes, summarizing material, and synthesizing ideas from various sources are other important study skills.

USING READING

A fourth aspect of basic instruction deals with helping children acquire the habit of reading and of turning to reading for help in the solution of problems they face, whether personal or professional, trivial or serious, real or imagined.

Well-written stories offer children opportunities to identify themselves with the characters and their problems and to see how these people solved their difficulties. This identification leads the child to get ideas for solving his problems or to acquire a standard of behavior for situations he is likely to meet. Many of the sports stories show the importance of losing as well as winning gracefully, of showing good sportsmanship, of playing fairly, and of doing one's best even in the face of defeat. Stephen Meader's books for boys include many problems of adolescent adjustment, as do books for girls by Mary Stolz and Betty Cavanna.

PROVIDING A STANDARD OF TASTE

Fifth, and best of all perhaps, basic reading instruction introduces children to the whole realm of enjoyment which is theirs when they have acquired the requisite skills. The reading they do in a basic textbook sets a standard against which other materials are judged. That reading textbooks include selections which are truly literary is the goal of publishers, and the array of books today is testimony to that objective. The analysis of style, mood, plot, and characterization that forms an essential part of basic teaching provides children with a critical background for their own analysis of individual selections. Granted that a child will not mechanically analyze every book he reads, still the emphasis placed on quality in school will sharpen his awareness of quality as he reads on his own.

EXTENDING HORIZONS

The sixth aspect of basic instruction is the opportunity it offers to extend the child's horizon by contact with various topics and with various styles of writing. Since reading as a school subject has no content of its own, what is read in a regular reading period can be, and is, drawn from a variety of content areas. The ideas in the selections read can be the springboard to further reading on the same or a related topic. Perhaps the most obvious way in which a teacher can stimulate additional reading is to call attention to the total work from which an episode the children liked was taken. Children who have enjoyed a chapter such as "The River Bank" from *Wind in the Willows* (Scribner, 1953) will want to find out what else happens to the self-sufficient Rat, the shy Mole, the pompous Toad, and the worried Badger.

The experiences with variety in style which children get through basic instruction help them approach poetry, drama, and assorted types of prose, from essays to humorous sketches, with confidence and security.

Learning to read poetry, for example, takes real skill, and many children are surprised to discover that there are ideas and moods in poems as well as rhyme. Even in lower grades there is a wealth of suitable material. Poetry has many possibilities; there is a wide variety of types and rhyme schemes; and there are many different subjects—humorous ditties, down-to-earth couplets, free verse, smooth lyrical poems, gay light verse, and the deeply emotional dirge. Each has a contribution, and children should be helped to realize that poems need to be understood and interpreted in relation to their type and content.

Drama, short stories, biography, scientific reports, essays, and fiction are other types of materials represented in basic textbooks, and each provides a stimulus for further reading.

ILLUSTRATIVE SELECTIONS

The first illustration is a simple realistic story at the second-grade level. Suppose the children are reading *The New Friendly Village* (Row, Peterson, 1948) in their reading period. They are enjoying a story entitled "A Feeling in Your Bones," which has five parts. What possibilities does this story hold for extending the reading interests of second-graders? Perhaps the most obvious one is the goat. What kinds of things do goats do? If there are some good readers in the group, the teacher might suggest that they would like to read a book called *Eddie and Gardenia* by Carolyn Haywood (Morrow, 1951) or *Eddie and the Fire Engine* (Morrow, 1949), which tells about the same boy.

The children in a fifth-grade class are reading a story entitled "Jonathan's Buffalo" from *New Days and Deeds* (Scott, Foresman, 1955). What possibilities are there here to lead children to read further and to extend their interests? They may want to know more about buffaloes or wagon trains. Some might find out what the encyclopedia says about buffaloes and their importance in the opening of the West. Someone may mention Buffalo Bill and wonder how he got his name. This could lead directly into reading biographies about him, including the beautifully illustrated one by Ingri and Edgar Parin d'Aulaire or perhaps the easier story in the "Childhood of Famous Americans Series" edited by Augusta Stevenson (Bobbs-Merrill, 1948). Other children may be interested in finding out more about the wagons and wagon trains. Some may be interested in the Oregon Trail, and the teacher could suggest such books as *The Treasure in the Covered Wagon* by Vera M. Graham (Lippincott, 1952) or *Tree Wagon* by Evelyn Lampman (Doubleday, 1953).

For better readers the teacher might suggest the book by James Daugherty called *Of Courage Undaunted* (Viking, 1951), which describes the Lewis and Clark Expedition and includes quotations from the original report made by Meriwether Lewis to President Jefferson. Such reading might lead to other aspects of the opening of the West—the exciting stories about the Pony Express, the California gold rush, the Santa Fe Trail, and so on. There are poems, too, which children could locate—poems about journeys, or Indians, or the sky at night as the dauntless pioneers must have seen it, or poems of courage, and fortitude, and thankfulness.

A similar procedure could be used with an eighth-grade class reading "Before Its Time" from *Tales of Today* (Macmillan, 1951). This kind of magical story can lead children to reading many other similar stories. One amusing book of this type is called *Take It Easy* by Thelma Harrington Bell (Viking, 1953). In this story Margie is helping her mother clean the living-room when she is given the task of polishing the brass elephant from India. As she is rubbing, she conjures up Mr. Askew, who is the servant of the

elephant and will do her bidding when they are alone. This story has the same bridging-the-gap-between-centuries as the reader selection.

If children have not read the series by C. S. Lewis about the magical land of Narnia, they will be interested in *The Lion, the Witch, and the Wardrobe* (Macmillan, 1950), *Prince Caspian* (Macmillan, 1951), and *The Voyage of the Dawn Treader* (Macmillan, 1952), to mention just the first three. In fact, the story of Mendi might lead to a complete study of magic and magical creatures the world around. If children do not know *The Little Witch* by Anna Bennett (Lippincott, 1953), they will chuckle as they read how Minx learns from her mother about being a witch. She causes havoc in school when she brings her flying broomstick and lets the children have turns at recess time. A similar study of wizardry could be carried on at the high-school or even college level.

Perhaps a high-school class has been reading a radio play written in 1942 and first introduced over the air in 1944 by Norman Corwin. It is called "The Lonesome Train" by Millard Lampell and is found in *People in Literature* (Harcourt, 1948). The play describes "a slow train, a quiet train, carrying Lincoln home again." In different places in the play, Lincoln is described as being in Kansas, in a hospital ward, and in crowded Springfield, Illinois. The pictures that are given of him there represent different aspects of his character, and the last chorus presents a summary of the kind of man he was. Students who have read this play might want to read the beautiful biography written by Carl Sandburg, if they already have not done so. Students who do not read quite so well will enjoy the illustrated biography of Abraham Lincoln written by James Daugherty. They will be impressed by the way in which the Gettysburg Address is presented in this book, in blank-verse form, and may be surprised to realize that this immortal document contains but ten sentences. So at the high-school level, too, a selection in a textbook can lead to extended interests on the part of the students.

A college class that may be reading essays by Ralph Waldo Emerson on "Self-Reliance" or "A Declaration of Intellectual Independence," for example, might become interested in the whole group of New Englanders of whom Emerson was a member—Thoreau, Hawthorne, Alcott, and other early American writers and philosophers. Students might pursue their interest in *The Flowering of New England* by Van Wyck Brooks (Dutton, 1936), or *The Peabody Sisters of Salem* by Louise Hall Tharp (Little, 1950). The essays might send some students to other essays of freedom, such as those written by the fiery Tom Paine or the talented Thomas Jefferson.

Thus stories of various types—realistic, historical, fanciful—radio plays, and essays, all offer possibilities for the extension of reading interests.

SUMMARY

In summary, basic reading instruction offers at least six opportunities for promoting reading interests.

1. It develops positive attitudes toward reading.

2. It places emphasis on meaning, not just superficial meaning, but deeper interpretation and evaluation.

3. It promotes independence in reading and in locating materials so that reading becomes a real avenue to learning and a source of enjoyment and pleasure.

4. It develops the habit of reading and of turning to reading for help in the solution of personal problems, in meeting individual needs, and in providing fun and laughter.

5. It provides a standard of taste against which to compare and evaluate individual reading. The vivid language, the apt turn of a phrase, the careful consistent character delineation, the exciting plots and amusing incidents included in textbooks in reading and discussed in a reading period provide a background for developing an increasingly higher level of taste.

6. It offers experience with a wide range of subject matter, which lends new meanings to ideas already held, which whets the appetite for more information, and which stimulates the search for related materials.

It also offers experience with a wide variety of types of writing: prose, poetry, drama; factual or fictional, humorous or serious, reportorial or descriptive. Indeed, basic instruction *does* promote reading interests—if the teacher will but use it thus!

INTEREST AS A CRITERION FOR SELECTING MATERIALS FOR READING TEXTBOOKS

DOROTHY M. HORTON

✳

TODAY more people are busy preparing more reading textbooks for more children than ever before in the history of our country. In *Textbooks in Print* for 1956, ten pages are needed to list basal reading materials. Old and new, widely used and relatively unknown series are listed, but all are being used by some children in some classrooms under the guidance of teachers.

A glance at the advertising from publishers of reading textbooks and at teachers' manuals reveals the importance we attach to selecting materials that will capture and cultivate children's interests. Then, too, publishers are making every effort to help teachers stimulate children's interest in reading all kinds of contemporary and classical writing as well as the selections in reading textbooks.

Perhaps the present emphasis on interest as a criterion comes from our need to make printed language as vital to the child as television, radio, and movies, and all the other media of learning with which he is surrounded. Perhaps, like Old Man Kangaroo and Yellow-Dog Dingo in Kipling's classic tale, we run because we have to! But looking back over the last century, we can see why interest has become the important criterion it is today.

CRITERIA OF THE PAST

A hundred years ago the United States was an essentially rural society, and McGuffey was its midwestern school-master. In his earnestly compiled readers, primary-grade children were given stern sermons in conduct. The *McGuffey Readers* included stories concerned with morals and manners and made up a treasury of literary masterpieces for an "era of bookless millions." The interests of the pupil had little bearing on the selection of the readers' contents.

By the turn of the century it was apparent that the era of "bookless millions" was on the wane, for people in all walks of life were developing an interest in reading. New book titles and printings multiplied annually, until in 1925 over twenty-five million children's books were printed.[1]

Meanwhile, leading scholars were engaging in scientific studies of the nature of the reading act, the differences between oral and silent reading, the influence on reading habits of different purposes of reading, to name but a few. Of equal importance were studies of reading interests and of child growth and development, which revealed the need for reading materials that were of vital concern to children at each level of their growth.

These stirrings in the social and educational scene created sympathetic vibrations in textbooks. The first part of the twentieth century was marked by exploration in the publishing field as well as in the classroom. Primary textbooks,

[1] Paul Hazard, *Books, Children and Men*, p. 87. Boston: Horn Book, Inc., 1944.

115

known as "phonic" or "word-method" readers, emphasized word recognition and provided little content other than sentences designed to give practice on words. Other textbooks, known as "literary" or "story-method" readers, based their content on folk literature, in the belief that skills should be developed in connection with material of literary merit. Until about 1920, even as "phonic" and "literary" readers vied for ascendancy at primary-grade levels, the literary ideal prevailed above third grade. Here publishers competed on the basis of which literary masterworks were most meaningful to children.

By 1920, however, the proponents of the cultural values of literature were being seriously challenged by pragmatists, who insisted that, if reading were to become an essential means of meeting the needs of daily life, silent reading was more important than oral reading, practical study skills more important than literary appreciation. Popular new "study" or "work-type" readers based on informational content emerged from the controversy. Many schools, seeing the merit of each, used both a literary and a work-type reader.

Whereas the first quarter of this century may be characterized as a period in which schools used different textbooks for different purposes, the next twenty-five years were to be characterized by the emergence of basal reading programs with workbooks and teachers' manuals closely related to the textbook, and with content based on the interests of children rather than on the adult literary ideal of the nineteenth century.

EMERGENCE OF INTEREST AS
A CRITERION

Perhaps the most important single influence in bringing about rapid changes in

textbooks and in establishing interest as a criterion was the Twenty-fourth Yearbook of the National Society for the Study of Education.[2] The committee that prepared this volume listed three major objectives for instruction in reading: (1) rich and varied experience through reading; (2) strong motives for, and permanent interests in, reading; and (3) desirable attitudes and skills.

Since 1925, publishers have vied with each other to produce readers that would give teachers practical help in achieving the three major objectives listed in the Twenty-fourth Yearbook. Gradually, however, has come the realization that, if we are to establish permanent interests, children of all ages must engage in wide reading. Today the six- and the sixteen-year-old alike are developing fundamental reading skills and abilities, engaging in wide reading, establishing wholesome attitudes, and refining their tastes in reading.

Among the many changes and improvements made in reading textbooks during the last three decades, perhaps the most significant in terms of interest is the development of child-centered materials. During the 1930's many of the selections in new primary-grade readers were based on the activities and interests of children. By the late 1940's this principle reached the middle grades, and today it is reflected in textbooks for junior and senior high schools.

APPLICATION OF INTEREST AS
A CRITERION

All major improvements in reading textbooks during the last thirty years

[2] *Report of the National Committee on Reading.* Twenty-fourth Yearbook of the National Society for the Study of Education, Part I. Chicago: Distributed by the University of Chicago Press, 1925.

have come from the practical search for ways and means of establishing and maintaining children's success and interest in reading. There can no longer be any doubt that interest is a valid and crucial criterion in making reading textbooks.

What, then, does the application of this criterion mean to the publisher? What is involved in its use?

In any classroom and certainly within the national group at any given reading level, there are differences in age, mental ability, and reading achievement. Then, too, in a country as vast as ours, children bring to their reading different backgrounds, experiences, talents, natural bents, language patterns, and personalities. Finding common denominators of interest among such differences is the first task of authors and editors in making reading textbooks. So they ask themselves how they can satisfy current interests, create new ones, and promote such strong motives for, and permanent interests in, reading that each child will turn to books to satisfy his personal needs, both now and in later life.

The success of publishers in meeting these challenges lies in (1) the degree to which they can hit the bull's-eye of interest at each maturity level; (2) their ability to encompass a wide variety and range of interest; (3) the extent to which they can keep abreast of children's current interests; (4) their skill in organizing material; and (5) the degree to which they can help teachers capitalize on interests and stimulate wide reading. There are many evidences that authors and editors are keenly aware of these five facets of the interest criterion.

1. First let us look for evidence that publishers are hitting the bull's-eye of interest for most children in the middle ranges of age, mental ability, and experience at each maturity level in such a way

that neither the lowest nor the highest range will be penalized. Authors and editors can best hit the middle range of any maturity level by utilizing universal interests, values, and ideals. For example, children of all ages, from six to sixty-six, are interested in themselves, in their contemporaries, and in their families. All basal readers use these interests as major themes at primary-grade levels. Among adolescents there is universal interest in sports, and there are good sports stories in all reading textbooks for this age level. Equally universal are the emotions of love, fear, anger, hate, and the qualities of courage and loyalty, with their opposites, cowardice and betrayal.

2. An examination of the 316 selections in six popular fourth readers indicates the range of interests covered at that level. Sixty-two, which deal with the world of nature, include thrilling adventures in caves, jungles, and forests. Stories, poems, and articles about animals, from ants to zebras, take the child from his backyard to the Arctic.

Another sixty-two meet the child's need for humor and fantasy and are divided equally between traditional literature and the best of modern humorous and fanciful writing. Sixty-one selections center in regional life or life in foreign lands. Their content ranges from the present to the past, from the desert to snow-capped mountains. Sixty selections of historical fiction, fact, or biography include exciting stories and authentic accounts of life in the past.

Forty-seven stories and poems are concerned with the games, hobbies, pets, friendships, and rivalries of characters who are counterparts of youngsters who are using fourth readers. Twenty-four selections are addressed to the interest of the potential mechanic or engineer. In these a problem is solved or a task accomplished through the use of a modern machine.

An examination of junior high school textbooks reveals that much of their content is youth-centered and that they cover as wide a range of interest as do representative fourth readers. Most tenth-grade textbooks, however, shift toward traditional literature in their attempts to prepare students for the more scholarly study of American and British authors in the eleventh and twelfth grades.

3. Analysis of the contents of current fourth readers has revealed a weakness in publishers' use of the interest criterion. The knowledge that only twenty-four selections, or less than 9 per cent of the total, deal specifically with the machine and its place in life today, raises serious questions: "Is that weight in harmony with the interests of modern children?" "Are publishers keeping abreast of children's current interests?"

4. The fourth facet of our criterion focuses upon the organization of material. The common practice of grouping selections by theme or topic enables the teacher to explore specific areas of interest with children. As youngsters talk over stories in the reader and informational material in the workbook, the enthusiastic child sparks the interest of his friends. In the fourth-grade books analyzed, the 316 selections were grouped under such titles as "In the Long Ago," "Neighbors 'round the World," "Fun and- Nonsense," "Animals We Like," "Young Citizens of Today," "Famous Americans of Other Times," "Eskimo and Indian Trails," and "Tales of Make-believe."

At the junior high school level and in the tenth grade, modern literature is grouped under such titles as "Everyday Experiences," "Family Living," "The World of Nature," and "The World of Sport." The older, heritage-type material is presented under such titles as "famous Tales from Many Lands" and "Treasures from Our Heritage."

At tenth-grade level and above, however, the prevailing content is still traditional literature, which is organized by type or chronology as well as by theme.

5. Finally, the criterion of interest challenges the publisher to suggest books for wide voluntary reading so that teachers can capitalize on interests aroused by the basal materials. Conscientious reading editors rarely prepare a selection for a textbook unless they can find related books of acceptable literary quality for children who want to read more. All publishers and educators feel that teachers should be familiar with good juvenile books, but, when we stop to think that in 1954 alone 1,193 new juvenile books were published, we realize that no teacher can keep up with them and be ready at all times with the right book for the right child.

Bibliographies of carefully selected books for wide reading are an integral part of all modern reading textbooks. Some teachers' manuals offer suggestions for introducing such books and for discussing them. Some suggest ways of motivating children to turn naturally to reference materials for answers to questions arising from the text. The bibliographies in basal readers, if used in light of suggestions in the teachers' manuals, offer invaluable aid in finding the right book for a child at the moment he wants or needs to read it.

In their search for interesting materials, authors and editors always give weight to literary quality. If I may say so, they "listen" to each selection carefully and with a sensitive ear. Quality of writing has an impact upon interest, and for evidence one has only to hear delighted youngsters reading, "Not by the hair of my chinny-chin-chin"; or listen to a verse choir of ten-year-olds romp through the rollicking lines of T. S. Eliot's "McCavity, the Mystery Cat"; or watch the absorption of more mature readers as they savor the words of Thomas Wolfe. Informational material that is direct in style, from which extraneous ideas have been eliminated and in which every word or sentence contributes to an idea a child can grasp, is more interesting to children than is indifferently written material. In selecting any and all kinds of material, then, the textbook maker considers that not easily definable but very real mark of taste which distinguishes the excellent from the shoddy.

CONCLUDING STATEMENT

Both publishers and teachers may well ask, "How are we doing? Are children of today interested in reading?" In the past twenty-five years the number of juvenile books sold annually has increased 157 per cent, the number of adult books only 57 per cent. The American Library Association tells us that more than half of the users of public libraries today are under the age of twenty-one. From such evidences as these we may assume that both publishers and teachers are doing a good job in establishing interest in reading.

CHAPTER XI

CLASSROOM METHODS FOR DEVELOPING READING INTERESTS

✳

IN KINDERGARTEN THROUGH GRADE THREE

BETTY BELL

✳

IN THE promotion of reading interests, three essentials must be considered. First, children must be systematically taught to recognize words and to understand what is read. Second, it is essential to provide materials to appeal to children's interests. Third, the teacher must use every means at his command to help children experience the joy of reading.

Our school system, which encourages heterogeneous grouping in the classroom, employs a developmental reading program in the primary grades. Each day reading skills are taught in a sequential manner to small groups of from five to ten pupils. When the first-graders are ready to read, they start recognizing words which are part of their oral vocabulary. The word-recognition skills are more fully developed as the children's capacity increases in Grades II and III. During this reading period the reading vocabulary is being steadily enlarged. Thus the children are taught to recognize words and to understand what is read.

To enlarge upon the reading skills which are taught in a skill period and to enable the child to experience the joy of reading, it is essential for the teacher to provide materials that interest the child. In order to locate these materials, the teacher must use many devices in discovering and developing the child's interests in reading.

DISCOVERING INTERESTS

The various interests of children from the kindergarten through Grade III have been located by our teachers in several different manners One of the first methods used was the three-wishes test, which asks: "Suppose you could have three wishes which might come true; what would be your first wish? Your second wish? Your third wish?" Previously the teacher had established a considerable amount of rapport with her pupils in order to obtain sincere answers. In Grade III the answers were written by the pupils, while in the other grades the children dictated their answers individually to their respective teachers.

In the kindergarten the answers fell into three main categories: toys, pets, and play equipment such as swings. The first-grade children expressed the wish to be specific persons, such as a fireman or a policeman, and wished for toys, for play equipment, and for pets. In Grade II the pupils wished for sports equipment, pets, toys like toy soldiers, and expressed the desire to be specific persons. In Grade III the children wanted things for their immediate family, wished for pets, and

120

wanted to participate in sporting events as spectators or as participants. Even though there was some similarity in the wishes, each pupil expressed unique wishes.

In capitalizing, in the reading program, upon these expressed interests of the children, many different projects were devised. Books were chosen by the teachers for individuals according to the results of the three-wishes test. For example, for a second-grader who wanted a horse and wished to be a cowboy, the book *Cowboy Sam and the Rodeo* (Beckley-Cardy, 1951) was chosen. The books selected were read by the pupils, with the teacher's aid, in a free-reading period. Some of the children enjoyed their books tremendously, while others did not. Many individuals wished to read more books in the same areas. In many cases, reading related to their own interests started a leisure-time reading program for children, especially in the last semester of Grade II and in the whole of Grade III.

Another device which was used in all primary grades was for the teacher to collect books pertaining to the interests identified by the test and to allow the children to make their own choices. Before the children chose their books from the library table, the teacher previewed each book, discussing a small section of the book, to enable the pupils to predict what was in the material.

Throughout the kindergarten and Grades I–III, observational records were kept of the children's undirected play periods. It was discovered that, in the kindergarten and first-grade rooms, pupils played in small groups and participated in such activities as jumping rope, roller skating, and revolving on the merry-go-round; while in the second-grade rooms they started more competitive games in small groups, such as marbles and ball; and in Grade III the pupils started forming large group games, such as baseball.

After the children's undirected play period, the children and teacher discussed the activities in which each child had participated. A record of the different activities was kept in the form of a scrapbook, and the children were able to read selections from it during their leisure time. This device seemed exceptionally effective in Grade I and the early part of Grade II.

In addition to the group record of play experiences, there were individual experience stories, which were illustrated by the children. The children also brought pictures of activities similar to their play experiences. Interpretations of these pictures were made by the pupils, and the teacher inscribed the interpretations beneath each picture. After several such pictures were collected, a bound book was made in which the children read each other's interpretations with enthusiasm. In the kindergarten, pictures alone were assembled into a booklet and, as the grade level increased, the inscription beneath the picture lengthened.

In many of the basic reading series, stories of children's activities were located for the pupils. Books and parts of books were selected by the pupils and read in order that the pupils, in the sharing time, might be able to report on play activities, associating them with their own recent activities. In these various ways, play was used as a learning experience, as an experience to further silent-reading interests.

The teachers also discovered many interests of the children through parent-teacher conferences. In one conference, for example, a teacher discovered that the child enjoyed working with carpenter tools. Immediately the teacher located books on tools, such as *How Things Work* by Peet (E. M. Hale, 1950). This book greatly interested the third-grader so that he presented parts of it to the class. The pupil did not stop after reading one book which was concerned with tools but, with the encouragement of the teacher, read others pertaining to a mechanical science. Many things can be discovered about a child in a tactful parent-teacher conference, enabling the teacher to locate appealing reading material for that pupil.

One day a teacher may say to the pupils, after giving them crayons and paper, "Now draw anything that you have done recently or would like to do." In the primary grades the pupils may express many different things in answer to this challenge. After he has expressed himself, each child explains his picture. The explanation is written into a short story by the teacher. Thus the teacher not only has silent-reading material which will interest others but also discovers some interests of the pupils. The pictures may also be used as a criterion for choosing further reading material.

In addition to having the children express themselves through their own drawings, the art teacher drew black-and-white pictures representing types of work in the school curriculum, such as a unit about trains, pets, and toys. The children chose the pictures they preferred, thus giving the teacher some idea of the types of units they might enjoy. This device for discovering a child's preference in the case of a given selection of materials was somewhat limited in its usefulness for locating the child's interests, for he could have been attracted to the drawing itself or might not have preferred any of the pictures. This system, however, did aid the teacher in selecting material for certain pupils, especially children who were not free in expressing themselves verbally. The choices of the pictures coincided with the results of the three-wishes test even though the two devices were used at separate times in the primary grades.

Today television seems to be one of the main after-school recreations of the primary-grade child. Therefore the child becomes greatly interested in what the television set has to present and in activities pertaining to the programs, such as joining clubs, discussing a program, participating in a "do-it-yourself" program, and so on. A teacher may utilize television programs for some ideas in the classroom. For instance, a clever teacher may rewrite the television stories which the children narrate in a sharing period and use them for leisure-time reading material within the room. The favorite television program among the primary-grade children was "Disneyland." For one third-grade girl who showed interest in this program, the teacher found the book *The Little Pig's Picnic* (Heath, 1939). The girl immediately read the story, "The Old Mill," which had been on the television program that week and then shared it with the class. She then branched into other areas, such as fairy tales.

A sharing period is used for the children to share their own specific interests or events within their immediate lives. Many teachers have kept a record of items which have been talked about by the pupils and have used the information to select interesting materials for them. In Grades I, II, and III the teacher wrote experience stories concerning some of the activities that a child discussed during the sharing period. In some cases this reading was the starting point of a work project for the pupil or of a leisure-time reading program for him.

In summary, then, one way of encouraging children to read silently is to choose reading materials that will appeal to their immediate interests. The teacher must try several ways of locating the individual child's interests and must use various types of materials in capitalizing upon the interests.

TEACHER CREATES INTEREST

Even though the children's interests may be discovered, the teacher must create interest within the room. There should be opportunities for carrying on many activities within the room itself; for in a vacuum nothing occurs nor does a pupil learn.

One effective way by which the teacher is able to create interest within the room is the use of unit study. Through questions which are developed by the pupils upon one area of work, such as the farm, the teacher is able to select suitable materials. Many farm books may be collected in the room, and the pupils will read parts or all of a book to locate answers to the questions. Then the questions will be answered by the pupils in a group discussion.

A variety of materials may be used to elaborate upon the main ideas of the unit, including commercial items, free materials, and materials made by the teacher and pupils. Both the teacher and the pupils will be able to create materials within the unit because they will have a great resource of experiences to use. A visit to a duck farm and hatchery was included in a farm unit in order that the first-grade pupils might see the hatching and development of ducks. This trip created such interest that the children wrote their own stories, drew pictures of

their own stories, and wrote experience charts about the trip. The teacher made several different booklets concerning her own research work on ducks and also wrote about their trip for the children to read. All this material was stimulated by one trip within a farm unit, and most of the children were interested in the reading material.

Even in the primary grades, much free material can be used successfully in the unit of work. If the teacher has the pupil send for his own material, the child usually is greatly interested in what he will receive. When the material is received, the teacher should have the pupil present it to the class immediately in order for him to retain his interest. By rewriting the free material to meet immediate needs, the teacher will be able to locate useful silent-reading material for some pupils.

Although books are largely used as research tools in a unit, they may also stimulate reading interests. For instance, a third-grade pupil was reading a certain part of a book about transportation for a report he was to make in class, but he found the book so interesting that he decided to read the whole book. After he had finished one book on transportation, he continued to read others.

A teacher may also create interest in reading in other ways. For example, one day there was a heavy snowstorm, which fascinated most of the first-grade children. The teacher had a group discussion concerning the storm in order to discover what interests the children had in it. Some children wanted to talk about fairies because the snow on the bushes reminded them of fairies; others wanted to play in the snow; and others wanted to know what made snow. After the discussion the children went to the library to locate books which pertained to the sudden interest.

The teacher is able to establish many new interests among the pupils through the room atmosphere, unit of work, projects, and his own attitude. After the teacher has created interest within the room, he then must quickly capitalize on the interest in order to obtain a successful silent-reading program.

SUMMARY

To locate a child's interests, the teacher must use many devices. After discovering a particular interest of the child or several different interests, the teacher may choose reading material that coincides with the child's immediate interest. In this manner, suitable reading materials may be provided for many children.

A combination of many methods must be used within the classroom to locate material that will interest children in silent reading. It is a continuous process in the primary-grade classroom to discover, create, and maintain interest within each individual child.

✳ ✳ ✳

IN GRADES FOUR THROUGH SIX

EMERY P. BLIESMER

✳

POSSIBILITIES for developing reading interests in intermediate grades are many and varied. The success of any one method or technique is, to a considerable extent, dependent upon the teacher, the particular children or particular group of children, the particular classroom or school situation, and other factors. The ideas and suggestions presented in this paper represent an assimilation, in part, of my personal experiences, my observations in classrooms, the ideas and methods reported in periodical literature, frequent discussions with teachers, and the like. Within the confines of this paper, only a relatively few possibilities can be briefly discussed.

PROVIDE MATERIALS

Materials with which to feed and stimulate interests are necessary. Consequently one important consideration in promoting reading interests is to make reading materials readily available to children. Since interests of any group will vary, and since we also wish to promote variation in interests, materials on numerous topics will be needed. Some children will prefer fictional types, while others will prefer factual; some, the fanciful; others, the more realistic. Sometimes materials more commonly regarded as study or content-area resource materials will be the types that some children will choose for recreational reading. Since a range in reading ability levels is typical, books of varying levels of difficulty are also essential. Even though interest in a given book or topic is extremely high, we cannot expect a child to continue reading that book and to experience enjoyment if his reading is a constant struggle with one obstacle after another.

There is also much to be said for short books, or booklets. These seem to merit special attention when the reluctant reader or the retarded reader is the object of our concern. (These two types are not necessarily synonymous.) Completing a regular book often impresses such a reader as an impossible task; initial interest frequently is not strong enough to carry him through the book, or he is stymied by the seeming hopelessness of the task. He has a better chance of finishing a smaller book; if he does finish it, he has "read a book"—sometimes a novel experience for him and one which can provide motivation for reading other books. For similar reasons, children's magazines and books or collections of short stories or selections also merit special consideration.

In addition to having available a variety of materials, teachers also need considerable familiarity with materials so that they will know where to direct children when following through on interest cues, know what children are reading so that further interest cues may be obtained and what similar books might be suggested, and know more definitely what needed materials to request. (The frequent problem of paucity of materials and the extent of teachers' familiarity with materials often seem to be related.)

USE CURRENT INTERESTS

In developing interests in reading, teachers will need to utilize the interests already possessed by their pupils. This entails knowledge of the typical interests of children, but teachers will also need to be on the lookout for departures or deviations from the typical. Specific or particular interests cannot always be assumed. Teachers may find that they have a pupil like Jack, who in Grade V became interested in fairy tales for the first time; or one like Price, the eight-year-old, who wanted to read only about "dinosaurs, prehistoric man, and discovering strange diseases" and who thought animal and cowboy stories were "dumb"; or like

Nelly, the fourth-grade girl, who found exciting reading in the cowboy and mystery stories that the boys liked; or like Bobby, who thought all fiction and humor were "just plain silly."

Many teachers have employed to good advantage the more or less formal methods for obtaining or detecting indications of interests; but continual use will also need to be made of the more informal techniques, such as noting favorable reactions of children while listening to selections being read aloud, children's browsing habits, particular subjects about which children read voluntarily, reactions in informal discussions which might indicate particular interests, favorite books brought from home, and the like. Information concerning children's out-of-school activities and interests, such as hobbies, recreatory pursuits, clubs, and favorite radio or television programs, often provides significant clues to actual or potential reading interests.

Adequate consideration of the interest factor involves more than looking for interests or waiting for interests to be evidenced. Interests are also learned, and we might consider the teaching of interests as one of the more important aspects of a teacher's job. The practice of reading stories aloud to children, a frequent one in primary grades, should not be discontinued in the intermediate grades. Teachers frequently read interesting selections to their classes and then make available similar types of selections or stories for pupils to read. Reading a part of a selection up to an exciting part and then making the story available for children to finish by themselves is also a fairly common practice. Pupils might also participate in reading stories aloud.

Class correspondence with an author of stories that children have liked especially well has often prompted and furthered reading interests. Where children have had the good fortune to have writers of children's stories visit their schools to talk with them and to discuss some of their stories, reading interests have usually been given quite a boost.

A teacher's own interest in, and enthusiasm for, books can also be reflected to children and be rather contagious. The teacher will need to avoid being artificial and "gushy" or emotional and imposing his own adult standards and interests. He will also need to have varied interests (or develop them) and considerable knowledge of the interests and reading habits and abilities of his pupils.

ENCOURAGE SHARING

Individual pupils' enjoyment in, and enthusiasm for, books has often proved to be a potent force. Peers can influence one another very effectively. Teachers need to provide opportunities for, and to encourage, discussions and sharing experiences. Discussions should be informal so that children will not view them as formal, required, structured periods. Discussions should not be quizzing periods or tests of retention, and children should not be made to feel that they will be held accountable for everything they have read. Remarks should be spontaneous and not be expected to meet class standards of formal speech. Sometimes a group of children might dramatize suitable portions of a book which has given them common pleasure, or a group might read orally chosen portions of a book.

Sometimes individual children can be encouraged to share books owned personally, assuming willingness and agreement on the part of the home. Book reports have come to be frowned upon by a number of teachers. Required reports,

viewed by children as rigid and difficult tasks, can be deadly; but judicious use of book reports can affect and stimulate positive reading interests. If we have to have reports, they should be brief and should be concerned with something which the child has had some part in choosing and which he has actually enjoyed. When giving reports, children frequently give all the details of a story—and then some. If the whole story is revealed, there is little reason for the listeners to read the story, which should be one of the main purposes of a report. Children will need to be guided in selecting and reporting some exciting and interesting parts, in giving reasons for enjoying the story, or in giving a summary or résumé in such a way that other children will want to read the story.

There has been rather definite evidence of the way in which some television programs have stimulated reading, the most notable of which has perhaps been the Davy Crockett epidemic. Many teachers have built up interest in, and anticipation and preparation for, specific programs by finding and making available reading materials related to the topics of those forthcoming programs. Many have also followed through by finding and providing materials pertinent to interests initiated or generated by specific programs. A number of teachers have also tried to make a positive use of comic books to stimulate an interest in other reading. In attempts which seem to have had some success, children have been led to make comparisons of comic-book versions and regular-book sources, to discuss differences between versions, to note points of agreement and points of discrepancy or distortion, to note omissions in the comic-book versions, and so on. Comic-book reading habits might also be studied for indications of the types of content which might appeal to particular children.

Bulletin boards are frequently used to call attention to books and to provoke interest in them. Jackets of new books are often displayed and may be of some help, but this is not enough. A display might be built around a topic or unit of current interest or a unit currently being studied, or it might be set up to prepare for, or to introduce, a topic to be studied. Bulletin-board displays or exhibits should arouse curiosity and interest. Intriguing or puzzle-like questions concerning a story might be presented. Pictures and informational notes concerning authors often stimulate interest. Appropriate illustrations for given books can also be used advantageously. Children can also help in arranging displays. If encouraged, pupils often come up with good ideas, and some can share enjoyable reading experiences in this way instead of through oral reports or discussions.

The subject matter of content areas in which children are particularly interested is often used to strengthen interests and to stimulate further reading. If this avenue is tried, the teacher will need to find and make provisions for availability of a variety of books beforehand. This approach seems to work especially well with books treating science topics and with biographical materials.

PROCEED SYSTEMATICALLY

It is also important that children have a definite time when they can read just for enjoyment. This should be a period which is devoted exclusively to such reading, not a time for catching up on homework or other assigned work or for studying. This time needs to be planned for, not decided upon hurriedly because the teacher did not have time to plan for something else or because he ran out of things for the children to do. Pupils need to be helped in forming habits of reading for enjoyment, and some will need considerable direction and guidance. Children should also have an attractive place which invites and encourages reading for enjoyment. This could be provided in the classroom or in the school library, or both. In many places it may have to be in the library because of space limitations. Tables and chairs would be desirable; if desks must be used, those should be kept relatively clear. Reasonable quiet should obtain, and children should have sufficient room and be generally comfortable.

As is true in nearly all teaching, we need to "start where the child is" if we are to help him develop and extend his reading interests. A child will need to experience actual "fun" in reading before he can "read for fun," and we cannot dictate or legislate it. I do not mean to say that it does not matter what a child reads as long as he reads something. But he needs to start with something, and, before we can do much to improve the quality of his reading tastes, he will need to be able to, and want to, read something he can actually enjoy. Paradoxically, we occasionally, perhaps all too frequently, cut off reading interests before they really have a chance to be started.

IN GRADES SEVEN THROUGH NINE

J. T. HUNT

✳

STIMULATING children's interests in reading is obviously a continuous process and unfortunately cannot be accomplished once and for all at the beginning of a school year or by enticing a pupil to read one book or a dozen books (although getting him to read is a necessary beginning). Children and books may be brought together by scheduling visits to the library; by having free-reading and library periods; by establishing classroom libraries; by utilizing bookmobiles; by having the librarian bring books to class and talk about them; and by co-sponsoring, with booksellers, book fairs, exhibits, or bazaars. Frequently changed displays of book jackets, blurbs, reviews, and lists of best sellers also make pupils aware of the world of books. To stimulate interest in a particular selection, read portions to the class, or sketch a scene or character or the setting or plot, leaving the pupils to finish the story or book.

Although a number of selections probably should be "studied," the pupil should not be allowed to equate pleasure reading with detailed reading or the library with reference-type reading only. We have typically labored over individual selections too long, taking them apart line by line and even word by word until all the life and fun were squeezed out.

Pupils should be given time to read— in class, in the library, and at home. They should be encouraged to browse and to withdraw books for the week end and vacations. Also, they should be given opportunities to talk about what they have read.

Further suggestions for stimulating interest will be considered under the broad topics of the pupil, materials, present interests, class discussions, and records.

KNOW THE PUPILS

Knowing the pupils as individuals is, admittedly, a big order, for it implies knowing reading-achievement levels, reading interests, types and amounts of reading done, attitudes toward reading, and also out-of-school interests, hobbies, and activities. The cumulative folder should supply much of this information, at least mental ages and reading-test scores. In some schools the folder includes lists of books read and a personal-data sheet. Pupil autobiographies and interest questionnaires supply additional practical information. The interest questionnaire should include not only the names of books and magazines read and enjoyed but also information about the student's habits and interests (including approximate time spent per week) in movies, television, radio, sports, hobbies and other leisure activities, and in homework and other related school activities.

PROVIDE A VARIETY OF MATERIALS

Arousing interest in reading serves little purpose unless children and books are brought together. Ideally, the pupil will have access to a wide variety of books and materials on many levels of interest and difficulty through a school library and a supplementary classroom library. Since the prospect of reading a whole book frightens some junior high school students, it is desirable also to have a large number of magazines, newspapers, and pamphlets. Interesting short stories or articles clipped from magazines, newspapers, or discarded anthologies and bound in attractive folders make good additions to a classroom library.

Expense is always a problem, but enterprising teachers and students usually find some way to get the essential materials. Most community libraries, if given a little time, will supply a quantity of books, changing them periodically. Since people seldom reread a book voluntarily, students may be encouraged to contribute books that they have read and enjoyed. Many classics and best sellers are available in paperback and other inexpensive editions. The fall, 1955, edition of *Paperbound Books in Print* (Bowker) is an index to forty-five hundred reprints and original editions, listed by subject and author. Teen-agers are buying approximately three million paperback books annually through the Teen Age Book Club alone. A wealth of material awaits the teacher with a little time, fifty or so postal cards (although school stationery is better and sometimes required for free publications), and a copy of *Free and Inexpensive Learning Materials* (George Peabody College for Teachers, 1956) or *Elementary Teachers' Guide to Free Curriculum Materials* (Educators' Progress Service, 1955). Although all such materials should be checked for suitability, they are frequently more authentic and up to date than some of the current textbooks in social studies and science, where they have their nearest parallel.

Several guides, in addition to the standard library catalogues published by H. W. Wilson Company, have been useful: Roos's *Patterns in Reading* (American Library Association, 1954), an annotated list by interest groups; Strang's *Gateways to Readable Books* (Wilson, 1952), an annotated list by subject matter and readability; and other lists published by the American Library Association, the Association for Childhood Education International, and the National Council of Teachers of English. Blair's "Reading Materials for Pupils with Reading Disabilities"[1] suggests several types of materials and includes a list of eighty simplified classics. Hunt[2] has compiled lists of easy suitable books for the handicapped reader in junior and senior high school, giving both readability and interest levels.

MAKE USE OF PRESENT INTERESTS

Few pupils will ever learn to love books and literature and to develop a continuing interest in books unless they *read* and like to read. The avid reader is already "on his way" and is likely to select books at a level which pleases the teacher. If not, he has at least taken the first step toward better and more mature reading tastes. In the case of the poor reader or the nonreader, however, interests cannot be upgraded or reading ability improved until he is given books he wants to read and can read with enjoyment. A good

[1] Glenn M. Blair, "Reading Materials for Pupils with Reading Disabilities," *High School Journal*, XXXIX (October, 1955), 14–21.

[2] *a)* J. T. Hunt, "Easy Non-fictional Materials for the Handicapped Reader," *High School Journal*, XXXIX (March, 1956), 322–32.

b) J. T. Hunt, "Easy and Interesting Fiction for the Handicapped Reader," *High School Journal*, XXXIX (April, 1956), 378–85.

idea, whenever possible, is to supply him with books or materials with a reading difficulty about a year below his achievement level. Certainly no teacher wants the student to remain at the level of the dog story or the cowboy story or the fairy story or the comics or the pulps, but trying to push him too fast into the adult reading interests and tastes of the teacher may turn him farther away from reading. The important thing is to get him to read by providing him with understanding and encouraging guidance and by allowing him to read at his own level. Space will permit only a glimpse into teenagers' reading interests.

Although several of the classics are represented in the Teen Age Book Club's list of one hundred best sellers, only five are represented in the top fifty. The most popular classic, Stevenson's *The Black Arrow*, was in twentieth place, with 55,000 copies sold between 1949 and 1954 as against 185,000 copies for the first-place *Boy Dates Girl*. Among the top fifteen books are *Junior Miss; Your Own Joke Book; Dennis the Menace; Hot Rod; Silver; Tawny; Mystery of the Empty Room; Hi There, High School; The Spanish Cave;* and *Sue Barton, Student Nurse*. These may not represent the best of our literary heritage, but they are what teenagers buy and enjoy.

LET PUPILS TALK ABOUT THEIR READING

Probably one of the best ways to curtail interest in watching movies or television programs is to require students to take tests on them or to write a report on each one viewed. So it is with reading. Excessive testing or writing may serve as a basis for assigning marks, but probably at the expense of a real interest or enjoy-

ment in books. Let students *talk* about their books, not necessarily as a formal report which simply takes the place of a written report for marking purposes, but informally through small-group discussions, dramatizations, panels, skits, mock radio or television programs, and in other ways in which large numbers participate. Students are frequently more influenced by what others are reading than by what the teacher recommends.

One teacher[3] has reported a successful activity called "Hit Parade of Books," a poll taken every two weeks of books read. The purpose is to determine the most popular books and those which, although not hits, are to be listed as "Books To Be Boosted." Posters or charts of the results are displayed, and discussions bring out the reasons for popularity of the various books. A big demand usually follows for these books, which may be separated and put on specially marked shelves.

Variations on the popular "Twenty Questions" and "What's My Line?" are used by Romano[4] to stimulate discussion and interest in selected characters and books. Additional procedures suggested by Romano are student and parent panels on problems relating to literature and reading, discussions of movies and television plays, and courtroom procedures to debate moral or ethical issues raised in selections studied.

Class book or literary clubs in which several students purchase the same selections each month give additional impetus to talk over common experiences.

[3] Charles M. DeWitt, "Stimulating Leisure Reading," *Elementary English*, XXX (December, 1953), 514–15.

[4] Michael J. Romano, "Stimulating Pupils' Reading Interests," *High Points in the Work of the High Schools of New York City*, XXXV (October, 1953), 21–24.

It is desirable to know not only the kind and amount of reading the group is doing but also what and how much the individual students are reading. Some teachers prefer a card file in which each student keeps his own card up to date by recording each book read, the date, and possibly a simple rating similar to our standard letter grades of A, B, C. Others prefer a short review or a standard book-report form filed in a folder which includes all the pupil's written work.

My Reading Design (North Manchester, Indiana: News Journal, 1946), with space for listing sixty books, is a convenient way of recording books read. A feature of this record-guide is the circle graph which shows the concentration of reading around major interests and helps to challenge the reader to develop a well-balanced program by exploring new fields.

The English teachers in one junior high school agreed on the type of reading information which would be most helpful to them at the beginning of a new year and worked out two or three simple forms which were to be passed along to subsequent teachers. Each student kept both the card file and the *Reading Design* up to date, and the latter was forwarded with his other records at the close of the year.

Annotated lists giving a clue to the nature of each book may be posted on the bulletin board. On his personal copy the teacher may wish to add a further note as to the book's character-training or human-relations value and its difficulty level.

One suggestion I wish to stress especially, both in record-keeping and in the entire reading-for-interest program, is this: *Let the students help.* Not only are their suggestions and ideas surprisingly good, but their interest in reading seems to increase in direct proportion to the extent of their planning and participation.

If we are to make maximal use of the classroom to promote reading interests, teachers must know their students and must provide materials which have interest appeal and which are readable. Furthermore, teachers will find that time is well spent in talking about books informally. Records of reading done assist in diagnosing individual and group needs and also serve as a basis for guidance in reading.

* * *

IN GRADES TEN THROUGH FOURTEEN

IRWIN J. SULOWAY

*

YOU will note that the subject of this paper is *developing* reading interests rather than *creating* them. That is as it should be. It is well that we realize at the outset that as teachers of literature we do not *create* reading interests in our students; we merely cultivate, stimulate, and to some degree shelter and protect these interests. Sometimes, alas, in a foolish effort to keep these interests neat and tidy, we prune them too closely and kill them entirely.

Too many teachers have thrown away their time and their dispositions laboring in vain to create in adolescents certain desirable interests. The creative process by which interests arise is of course sensitive to, and affected by, experience and environment; yet individuals do not react in exactly the same way to particular stimuli. The adolescent is not a blank tablet; he comes into our classrooms with a set of previously acquired interests. We have the power to enhance these interests, to advance them toward maturity, and possibly the power to eradicate some of them. But we can create new interests only in the sense that we can create an environment conducive to such interests. Whether the individual student will so respond as actually to create a new interest is primarily up to him, not to us.

We shall concern ourselves primarily, then, with the *development* rather than the *creation* of reading interests. And if we are careful and wise, we shall see the already present reading interests develop and flower until they spill over, seemingly of themselves, into new areas of thought and experience.

We must avoid setting up arbitrary and unnatural goals for our students. It is not reasonable to expect that students, even after having been given the benefit of our fine teaching, have acquired the aesthetic sensitivities and literary standards which we ourselves have attained. We cannot even insist that they like or respect Shakespeare. Perhaps the best we can do for many, or even most, of our students is to help them acquire broadened interests and whetted appetites for reading. For many, the standards of taste and discernment, the preference for "literature" rather than journalism or "trash," will come, if at all, long after the students have stopped reading under the guidance of a teacher.

DETERMINING WHICH MATERIALS TO USE

What shall constitute the reading diet in the literature class? The answers given to this question are many and varied. Considerable disagreement exists between the advocates of the great works of literature, at one extreme, and the mass-communication specialists, at the other, who would settle for learning how to read a newspaper or the "educational" edition of the *Reader's Digest*.

If we bear in mind what was said a few moments ago, it is obvious that the choice of reading materials will depend on the present interests and reading achievements of a given group. This may possibly mean the popular magazines, after all, as a start, although we must bear in mind that our long-range goals go far beyond such reading and that we must work toward a more mature *development* of interests.

We must give the students liberty in reading, setting up a procedure whereby they can follow their own interests and sample many kinds of reading. There should be available a wide variety of books, real literature whenever possible, but other reading materials as well, particularly if our students cannot yet handle real literature.

The ideal literature class would of course deal with the great works, with the imperishables of poetry and prose, but unfortunately few of us teach in ideal situations. We would like to teach *War and Peace*, but we shall probably have to settle for the *Caine Mutiny* (Doubleday, 1951) or possibly even *Mr. Roberts* (Houghton, 1946). We shall have to realize that we are living in an age of prose and that poetry is, and I fear will remain, of limited appeal to most of our students. I mention this, not because I feel that we should give up on poetry, but because I would caution you that the fragile strand of typical student interest in poetry will not normally bear the weight of Tennyson's "In Memoriam," Whitman's "Passage to India," or Eliot's "Waste Land."

We cannot ignore in our classrooms the fact that the vast bulk of America's current reading is from newspapers and magazines, that one magazine sells more copies annually than do all regular books in a single year. We cannot turn our backs on this fact or point Cassandra-like to the shortcomings of such "journalism." We must work with these materials, using them as means of sharpening the critical faculties and literary standards of our students in the hope that they may some day through surfeit and through further maturity, discover the satisfactions of real literature.

SELECTING AN APPROACH

In our classroom procedure, success or failure in teaching will frequently depend upon the way in which a particular work is approached. There are seven ways in which we can approach literature. We may settle, if we are not ambitious, for simple comprehension, the ability to retell the story. At the opposite end of the scale there is the analytical approach, which would probe so deeply into technique and hidden meanings as to be accused sometimes of performing autopsies on living literature. There is the aesthetic approach, which seeks to plumb the emotional depths, as well as the moralistic approach, which seeks "lessons" from the literary word. Still another would press each work of art into a historical frame. Very popular recently have been the social and the psychological approaches. The former relates literature closely to the society that produced it and looks for *social* significance as its particular brand

of didacticism. The latter measures both authors and characters by means of Freudian and other psychological yardsticks.

As teachers we must avoid what is often a natural predilection for one or another of these approaches. No single approach will suit all the diverse selections we use; no single approach will consistently appeal to students. We must become perceptive enough to recognize and select that approach appropriate both to the specific work and to the interests of the students. We must, for each essay, poem, or novel we teach, ask ourselves which approach or approaches will be most successful given (1) the selection at hand, (2) the present reading interests of our students, and (3) the objectives of the specific lesson. And we had better be sure that our objectives are reasonable ones for the selection and the students involved.

Wilbur Schramm[1] has set up a "fraction of selection," which should be useful to teachers interested in choosing reading materials that require students to work at the very peak of their abilities. This fraction is formed by placing the "expectation of reward" over the "effort required." By increasing the former (that is, making the reward seem more worth while) or decreasing the latter (making the effort appear less taxing), the teacher can increase the fraction and thus make a given selection more appealing to students. Successful teaching of difficult works of literature depends upon the skill of the teacher either to motivate students so effectively that the difficulty will not deter them or to anticipate and

[1] Wilbur Schramm, "Why Adults Read," *Adult Reading*, chap. iii. Fifty-fifth Yearbook of the National Society for the Study of Education, Part II. Chicago: Distributed by the University of Chicago Press, 1956.

to dissipate difficulties to such a degree that they will not prove overwhelming. Unless the teacher can do one or both of these, he would be wiser not to attempt to teach the "difficult" works.

Regardless of the quality or the difficulty of reading materials used, the teacher always has, as one of his important though unannounced objectives, the development of standards of excellence by which to measure literary merit. It is far more important that we provide students with criteria to apply when forming opinions about what they read as adults than it is to acquaint them with given works of literature. Fortunately the more basic of these standards can be evolved pragmatically and almost incidentally from selections which are neither particularly difficult nor of limited appeal, from *Huckleberry Finn*, for example.

EVOLVING SPECIFIC TECHNIQUES

Here I will merely sketch briefly some specific techniques which illustrate the general methods just discussed. The resourceful teacher evolves his own techniques; the less imaginative ones go to the pages of the *English Journal, College English*, or the recently revived *Exercise Exchange* for reports of effective lessons in particular situations.

One technique worth your attention is that of using magazines as sources of classroom and individual reading assignments. Most of us still have the rather American and irrational notion that "good" reading is most likely to be found *only* between hard covers and that trash appears in the periodicals. Thoughtful comparison of the best-selling books with the contents of our better magazines ought to be sufficient to disabuse us in this regard. Since for some reason our students assume that the contents of magazines can be grasped with less effort than the contents of books, we automatically decrease students' resistance when we use selections from periodicals even though the selections may be "difficult" and weighty. I suspect the same reduced resistance applies to paper-bound or pocket books and is an element in their popularity. We would do well to make wider use of paper books in our classrooms.

Another technique involves making use of student interest in radio, television, and the movies. Librarians and booksellers have learned that presenting a story over the air or on the screen enhances, rather than detracts from, sales of that story in book form. We should cater to the whetted appetites created by these mass media and, without denying the potential of electronics, lead students to see the peculiar values of the printed word. This may involved taking classes to see professional performances of plays or the assignment of class listening projects. In our teaching of poetry, where the appeal is so largely to the ear, we should make wider use of recordings by poets or gifted readers. The good teacher of poetry throughout the years has relied on his own voice rather than the printed words to "sell" a poem to his classes. In one sense a printed version of a poem is as poor a substitute for the heard poem as is a description of a painting for the actual canvas.

There remains another approach to reading interests of high-school and junior-college students which deserves attention: the problem approach. Our students have their problems; the more important of these are rarely out of their thoughts. Their problems often govern their interests, as indeed their interests often create their problems. Without attempting to do more than scratch the surface, we can call to mind problems of achieving emancipation from parents, making appropriate sexual adjustments, evolving a code of conduct which can stand the stress of adult reality, choosing a career, and seeking the acceptance of one's peers. Certainly here is a fertile field for the teacher. Properly introduced and related to a problem which "hits home," almost any comprehensible work will receive the respectful attention of our students. But I must add that such attention will continue to be afforded only if the relationship to a present problem is genuine and the author's treatment of the problem is honest. Here the writings of the twentieth-century realists are extremely useful. Eugene O'Neill's *Ah, Wilderness*, Salinger's *Catcher in the Rye* (Little, 1951), and *The Great Gatsby*, to name a few which come easily to mind, strike the adolescent where he actually lives and are compelling reading. The student who has learned that reading helps or at least comforts him on his essentially lonely path through life has been won over. He will read as long as he has sight, and from his reading he will acquire vision.

CHAPTER XII

THE ROLE OF THE CONTENT AREAS IN
EXTENDING READING INTERESTS

✳

MILDRED C. LETTON

✳

THE responsibility for developing in an individual a permanent interest in reading is a heavy obligation which no teacher can bear alone. To make reading a habitual activity, one must understand and appreciate its usefulness in a variety of situations. It is at this point that teachers interested in one or more of the content areas can make a significant contribution.

Examine your own reading habits. Consider the subject area of major interest to you at present. To what extent are *you* using reading to further this interest? Can you name the last book you read on the subject? How long ago was that? The teacher's own reading interests are reflected in his teaching, his conversation, his enthusiasm for his own and other subject areas. Especially in terms of developing permanent reading interests, our children and young people need to discover for themselves that mathematics teachers *do* read novels, that history teachers may know something about atomic energy, and that it is not impossible for industrial-arts teachers to be well-informed geographers.

A DUAL ROLE

The teacher in a content area seems to play a dual role in the process of extending reading interests. Here he may begin by creating initial interest in the particular subject. Once this is accomplished, while the pupil's desire to read is at its crest, the teacher identifies possible vocabulary problems and considers the reading skills demanded by the materials. These skills are taught where necessary, whether the class is one in arithmetic, geography, civics, or chemistry. There are few experiences more discouraging than to be unable to read an article or book because, although the subject interests you, the author's style, vocabulary, and presentation of concepts are too complex. Interest soon lags when reading becomes too difficult. So the teacher uses whatever aids are available to develop reading skills in the content area in order that the child may explore the particular subject with satisfaction and success. The better one reads, the more likely he is to want to continue to read.

Once the student is motivated and can use the reading techniques appropriate for a given content area, the second part of the teacher's role becomes apparent. By beginning with present interest, the teacher of that subject can expand the student's interest to include related literature in the field.

136

The subject matter of the content areas is really the basis of all reading materials except literature. At first, the teacher may need to use simple materials to teach the child how to read in the particular content area. Later he promotes reading to expand interests, widen horizons. The content areas offer almost endless experiences to the reader. He may dabble in the water with his hands; he may wade about if he wishes; he may swim in the deep water if his teachers have taught him how to swim and have given him confidence in his own ability.

DEVELOPING A PERMANENT INTEREST IN READING

Content-area teachers in general tend to be encouraged when students develop reading interests related to the particular subjects they teach. However, we must realize that to develop interest in a content area is not always the same as extending permanent reading interests in that particular area. Certainly the teacher in the elementary school is *not* trying to develop a permanent interest in any *one* subject. Rather, his job is to show the child how he may use reading to pursue a variety of personal interests. Content-area interests change frequently and last for indefinite periods. Some live but briefly, others last for years. These changes continue as the student's school experiences broaden, and adults, too, frequently move from one area of interest to another.

What factors contribute to the development of a permanent interest in reading? First, if an interest is to become permanent, it must be a pleasurable pursuit. If reading is to be pleasurable, the reader must possess the skills needed to handle the materials with some degree of ease. Most of us who work with chil-

dren can cite isolated examples of young readers whose self-motivation was so high that they "waded through" content-area materials that were really too difficult because they wanted to find out how something worked, how to make something, or how to do something. Reading can make the reader a vicarious part of a scientific team as it makes an important discovery; it can make the reader an observer of life in other places and at other times in the history of the world; it can become a companion in the reader's solitary hours; it can challenge the reader to search out the answers for problems yet unsolved. Yes, reading should be a pleasurable pursuit.

One does not always find the reading materials of the content areas easy. Skills different from those needed in reading fiction must be called into use. I say again that these skills must be learned and that the teacher of the content area must teach them, whether the lesson is about stars in Grade II, the constellations in Grade V, the planet earth in Grade VIII, or astronomy at the college level.

Recreational reading tends to give the reader vicarious experience. In the content areas, reading often does this, but it also goes beyond to direct the child to personal experience which challenges his thinking and extends his interests. In reading light fiction, the demands on the reader are relatively few. If one can follow the plot and keep the characters in mind, he can usually say he has "read" the book. Reading in a content area is somewhat different. The reader must do some thinking too. He must understand the vocabulary of the subject. He cannot get even the author's general meaning if he knows little or none of the technical vocabulary. He must understand the sentence structure that may be commonly used in such writing.

As has been known for some time, both through research and through observation, most nonreaders appear among the boys. Much of the reading done in high school occurs in the English class. If this is confined to the reading of outmoded literary selections, it is unlikely that we shall be able to capture the reading interests of the boys, much less make such reading interests permanent. To reach the boys, Grambs[1] suggests we expand our idea of reading to include all subjects. This, in a sense, makes all teachers partners in the venture of building permanent reading interests. In glancing over some favorite poems, I was surprised to notice how many could be used appropriately with classes or groups that are interested in particular content areas. There is the world of natural science which the young child explores—the snails, the butterflies, the caterpillars. The sea, the mountains, the heavens above are of interest to all ages.

PROVIDING FOR INDIVIDUAL DIFFERENCES

In the content areas, teachers have one of their best opportunities to provide materials that cover a wide range of reading abilities. An examination of the books now being published in the fields of natural science, history, or art shows a wide range of materials to capture the interest of readers of varying skill.

For example, in general science and physics courses, some attention is usually given to machines. But young readers, too, often are interested in this subject.

[1] Jean D. Grambs, *The Development of Lifetime Reading Habits.* New York: National Book Committee, Inc. (24 West Fortieth Street), [1954].

Even for preschool and early primary grades there is Browning's *The Busy Bulldozer* (Rand McNally, 1952). This may be followed by Zaffo's *The Big Book of Real Building and Wrecking Machines* (Grosset, 1951) for Grades II through IV. Colby's *Earthmovers* (Coward-McCann, 1955) and *The Tractor Book* by Otto (Morrow, 1953) are for middle- and upper-grade readers and Burlingame's *Machines That Built America* (Harcourt, 1953) may appeal to junior high school readers. College engineering students will read at other levels about machines.

Whether the subject is astronomy, or prehistoric animals, or atomic energy, the teacher in the content areas can find materials suited to the present reading levels of members of the class. In the content areas in particular, we have an opportunity to see that every class member does not *have* to read what every other pupil reads. Here the reader may begin anywhere along the line and be interested in more than one subject at a time. This is easily evident in high school, where students are pursuing a number of courses concurrently.

The content areas point up the need for a variety of reading materials, the need for reading materials of high quality, and the need for easy access to these materials. Research consistently has shown that the availability of reading materials influences appreciably the use readers make of such materials. The administrator must be aware of these facts.

GUIDING PRINCIPLES

H. Neil Hardy, chairman of the science and mathematics department in Lincoln-Way Community High School, New Lenox, Illinois, has given a considerable amount of time and thought to the development of reading interests in the field of science. In a letter to me, he has defined some guiding principles that seem applicable to any content area and at any grade level.

First, locate the interests of your students. This includes their hobbies, extra-school activities, career interests, extra-curriculum activities, favorite school subject, vocational interests, especially if related to the vocation of some member of the family.

Second, provide reading materials. Select general books for the library. Keep a complete pamphlet file up to date. In two years Hardy has developed a four-drawer file. After two years he removes materials that have had little or no use. Current magazines should be available at all times. He lists a dozen in the field of science, ranging in readability from the rather easy *Science Digest* to the difficult *Chemistry* and *Engineering News* and *Journal of American Physicists*. Specialized books and materials should be purchased by the librarian as students develop interest.

Third, teach your students to read efficiently and effectively. This includes building readiness through concrete experiences where possible, presenting the technical vocabulary in an organized fashion, developing concepts with great care, teaching students how to read and follow directions accurately, helping students to have clearly in mind their own purpose or purposes for reading any given piece of scientific writing.

Fourth, lead your students to read. Suggest materials related to their particular interests. Provide materials for project work. Point out special articles from time to time in class discussion. Usually students ask to borrow such articles to read for themselves. Comment to students about materials you have read and suggest that they read them, or ask some of them to read certain materials and report to you since your time as a teacher is limited. If students are to read in a science course, the materials must be readily available in the classroom where the young people can pick up a magazine or book, inspect it, and borrow it if it looks interesting.

At Lincoln-Way Community High School an unusual plan for encouraging reading is in use. It might not be practical in many places, yet others should know about it. Students here may take all magazines and most of the books without signing out for them. Books on special demand must be returned the following morning, and two sets, because of extensive use, cannot be checked out. During the last school year the school lost about ten dollars worth of books and magazines. But who knows how many students discovered a new field of interest, how many improved in their ability to read in a content area, how many found a new interest in reading?

The fifth step is to evaluate the program. This may be done in part through reports received from students on what they have read. Some of these reports are made to the class and some to other students concerned with particular subject matter. Performance in reading natural-science material can be measured by standardized tests. Students working on Senior Science projects can be judged on their ability to read and interpret professional materials which they must use.

CO-OPERATING WITH PARENTS

Larrick recently reported the results of a study in New York State, in which a selected group of parents was interviewed concerning the reading done by their children of intermediate-grade level. Sixty per cent of the responses expressed interest in questions related to the development of their children's interest in, and enjoyment of, reading and choice of reading materials. Forty per cent of the responses were concerned with the development of reading skills.

Asked what books the parents recommend to their children, 79 replied that they were dependent upon the teacher and librarian for suggestions, 46 indicated they could suggest only the books they had read as children, and 26 recommended titles they had read about in some book or magazine. Interestingly enough not one parent interviewed in the pilot study had received any suggestions from the teacher or librarian as to the books that might well be recommended to children. In fact, several volunteered the wish that occasionally teachers and librarians would send home brief lists of books that parents might recommend to their youngsters.[2]

Many schools and libraries do prepare such lists, particularly for summer reading, but Larrick's report indicates that much remains to be done. The content areas are rich resources for such lists. Those parents who must rely on suggesting only books they have read as children are likely to miss selections in the content areas entirely. Twenty years ago there was much less general interest in the sciences, for example, and far fewer attractive, challenging materials for the young reader in the content areas than there are today.

Parents, teachers, and librarians should make a concerted effort to encourage children to own and keep books. We need to know more about the effect of book ownership on developing permanent reading interests. The librarians who have been meeting with the Grades VII through IX section of this conference have agreed that the teen-age book clubs have done much to stimulate interest in reading. They find that students who read these books are unaware, in some cases, that the library editions of the same titles have been gathering dust on the shelves throughout the school year. What is there about owning a book that makes its words more treasured, its meaning more personal?

One's obligation as a teacher, librarian, or parent does not end with helping the young reader find or own books about things in which he is interested. There is a mutual sharing of ideas that ought to follow. The reader should have a chance to talk about what he reads. Particularly is this important at home. Ashley Montagu has suggested:

We teach the three R's, but we teach them as techniques for the achievement of limited objectives. Our educational attitudes are not directed toward "drawing out" but toward "pumping in."[3]

When one has been exploring a content area, there is often much that is new, challenging, and thought-provoking to the reader. One needs the opportunity for this "drawing-out" experience.

Discussion following reading in the content areas is one of the best ways to develop lasting reading interests. If the reader has no opportunity to discuss the new ideas, to challenge the author's opinions, to weigh the facts, to argue about the presentation, then an important personal and social experience

[2] Nancy Larrick, "What Parents Think about Children's Reading," *Elementary English,* XXXIII (April, 1956), 208.

[3] Ashley Montagu, "The Annihilation of Privacy," *Saturday Review,* XXXIX (March 31, 1956), 9.

has been lost. At the same time, the teacher needs to realize that staying too long with one book creates, after a while, a kind of intellectual vacuum in which interest in further reading may perish as the book is "talked to death."

SUMMARY AND CONCLUSIONS

The content-area teacher plays a dual role in extending reading interest. First, he gets his pupils interested in reading, and prepared to read, material on the particular subject. Second, he uses the content area to give depth and breadth to the original reading interest so that growth of reading interest may be thought of as a spiral in pattern.

For one to develop a permanent interest in reading through the content areas, one must (1) find reading a pleasurable pursuit; (2) have the reading skills needed to handle the material efficiently and effectively; (3) be motivated to the extent that he participates actively in the reading process; (4) have easily accessible appropriate materials for whetting his appetite for reading; (5) have an opportunity for discussion following reading in the content area so that he may participate in the "drawing-out" process. The young reader profits, too, if those adults about him, both parents and teachers, have already acquired a permanent interest in reading. Book ownership seems to promote reading, although we need further research on this point.

Guiding principles have been suggested for the teacher, and he has been encouraged to explore for himself, as well as for his students, the exciting world of reading materials related to the content areas.

CHAPTER XIII

USING THE CONTENT SUBJECTS TO PROMOTE
READING INTERESTS

✳

IN KINDERGARTEN THROUGH GRADE THREE

ELIZABETH P. DAVEY

✳

THE content subjects give the child a chance to put to use the skills and habits that are being developed in the reading classes. While the basic readers make use of content in teaching the skills and habits, the content subjects should place the child in "situations that lead him to have such an inner urge to read that he aggressively and diligently attacks the problem of learning to read."[1]

CONTENT MUST BE INTERESTING

The content we teach must be interesting and significant to the child. Whatever it is, social studies, science, or arithmetic, the child must want to know about it. He must have questions that he wants answered.

Last year I taught a unit on the zoo. The children wanted to know where the animals came from, how much they cost, and how they were obtained. Marlin Perkins, director of the Lincoln Park Zoo, had just returned from a trip to Africa, where he had collected animals. His television show, "Zoo Parade," during the fall and winter dealt with accounts of how the animals were captured. Also the

[1] W. A. Saucier, *Theory and Practice in the Elementary School*, p. 214. New York: Macmillan Co., 1941.

children were helped by Glenn O. Blough and M. H. Campbell's book, *When You Go to the Zoo* (Whittlesey, 1955). On a visit to the zoo the pupils discovered that a card on each cage identified the animal and told its origin. Reading these cards proved as interesting as watching the animals. Through television, books, and a trip, these children were able to find answers to their questions. Their interest continued after the unit was completed, and they brought to class many articles from newspapers and magazines about animals that were purchased for, or born in, zoos.

We must make sure that children have a continuing interest because that is what promotes reading. To stimulate this interest, I keep finished units in labeled folders available to the children. Whenever they find pictures, books, or relevant material, it is filed in the folder. Then once a week we have a period in which the children present this new material.

CONTENT MUST USE READING

When the content has continuing interest for the children, they will want to learn more about it. They can do this in many ways: through movies, television, radio, and excursions. Our job is to pre-

142

sent reading as the most satisfying and enduring way.

In kindergarten the units taught should stimulate reading readiness. Much background and the desire to read can be built through experience. Not long ago I visited a kindergarten where the pupils were studying the care of pets. The children had been given a rabbit for Easter and were busy taking care of it. They had enlisted the aid of two upper-grade boys to build a cage, which was under construction while I was there. It was being built according to plans and pictures in a *Popular Mechanics Magazine.* One of the kindergarten children said to me, "I'm the helper. That book tells them how to make the house. There's the picture." Several charts hung on the wall, one of which pictured the foods that rabbits like. Another named the children who were to feed the rabbit on different days of the week. A third had printed at the top, "Names for Our Rabbit," and on this were listed twelve suggestions. One little girl told me that they were going to vote the next day, and she showed me which name she preferred. On the library table were picture-books about rabbits. A girl was studying a picture, and she said to me, "The rabbit in this book is called 'Marshmallow.' Do you think he looks like ours?" Certainly these children were learning how to care for a pet, but, more important, they were going to be ready and anxious to read.

In Grade I the children have limited reading skill, but they can read pictures, experience charts, and their own stories. The teacher can strengthen their desire to read by reading to them. In Grades II and III the children will be reading independently in the content fields if the teacher supplies them with appropriate materials. Often children will read things of greater difficulty than their readers if the material is concerned with a subject that is intensely interesting.

Much preparation should precede reading at this level. Each subject presents new words and new concepts, which should be clarified by movies, filmstrips, excursions, and conversations. I have had success with picture dictionaries. Before starting the farm unit, I printed such new words as *silo, tractor,* and *cultivate* on a large piece of cardboard, and then the children found pictures to illustrate the words. When they had finished this chart, they were familiar with the words, but the chart was available if they came across a word they had forgotten.

To gain information is the purpose of content reading. A second-grade class planned to make a model airport, and one of the boys was reading a book on the subject. He came to the word *hangar,* which he did not recognize. When he asked the teacher for help, she went to the blackboard and wrote the word *sang,* which he recognized. Then she changed the *s* to *h,* and he said, "Hang." She then wrote *car,* which he recognized, so she erased the *c* and he said, "ar." She wrote the two syllables together, and he said, "Hangar." The teacher, very pleased, said, "Now you know the word." The boy said, "But what is a hangar?" Word recognition was not enough for him. He had to understand what he was reading if he was going to build an airport. Children must get meaning from their reading in the content fields. They will acquire and use word-attack skills, not as ends in themselves, but as tools to be used in reading for understanding.

EACH CONTENT FIELD REQUIRES SPECIFIC SKILLS

Certain fundamental skills and habits are necessary in all reading. We are best able to teach them if the children are ready to learn them. We can teach the special skills and unique vocabulary necessary for reading in specific content areas if the children are ready. It is our job in the primary grades to begin the development of the special reading skills used in the content areas.

Although the units of study we use in the primary grades combine different subject matters, they provide opportunity for teaching some of the special reading skills which will be used later in the subject matters studied separately in the middle and upper grades. Each subject matter demands special reading skills. One reads an arithmetic book in an entirely different way from the way in which he reads a story-book. Painstaking attention must be given to detail in arithmetic. One cannot depend on contextual clues. In science-reading, facts must be weighed and evaluated, and generalizations must not be made until much evidence has been studied. In the social studies, one must read critically, for relevancy, suitability, and reliability.

We must build also experiential background in our units of study. Each subject field has a unique vocabulary and, in the primary grades, the children should become familiar with some of these words. The desire to read, the background and the skill for reading in the content fields, must begin in the primary grades.

STUDY SKILLS MUST BE ACQUIRED

To utilize fully the content subjects, we must help children acquire study skills. Ernest Horn has summarized these skills:

1. *Location.*—The student must be able to find materials which bear upon the problem.
2. *Comprehension.*—He must be able to understand and appraise material.
3. *Organization.*—He must be able to organ-

ize ideas gained from his reading.
4. *Utilization.*—He must put to use what he has read.[2]

My first-grade pupils learned about locating material through the room library. First a simple classification of materials was made: books, magazines, and newspapers. Then the books were divided into subject areas, such as farm, zoo, and plants. Then each subject area was subdivided. The farm books were arranged into stories about farms and information about farms. The children could read some of the books, while other books were marked by them so that I could read to them the parts which they wanted to hear. Books that contained a variety of material were marked for the farm sections. Illustrations and tables of contents were consulted.

Children must understand and appraise what they read. Checks can often be made by oral reports and class discussions and by reading difficult sections with the children. Some second-graders were discussing firemen, when one girl reported that firemen volunteer their services. Another child challenged this statement because the book she had read said they were paid. In the ensuing discussion the pupils discovered that there is more than one kind of fire department, and they learned that books do not always agree and that several sources must be checked and evaluated.

Children must be given considerable help in organizing ideas gained from reading. When material is read by the class, or when an excursion is taken, the teacher may write on the board what the main ideas are. Start the habit of note-taking

[2] Ernest Horn, "Current Issues Relating to Reading in the Various Curriculum Fields," *Recent Trends in Reading*, p. 199. Supplementary Educational Monographs, No. 49. Chicago: University of Chicago Press, 1939.

and outlining. A boy in my room, giving a report about cows, spoke from the following notes: "(1) Cows are big. (2) Cows eat all the time. (3) Cows give milk. (4) After they die, we eat them." Another boy, less advanced in written language, spoke about sheep. His notes included pictures of a sheep, shears, a wool coat, and a lamb chop.

Keeping ideas and events in sequential order seems difficult for children, but order is an important part of organization. Concrete experiences, such as following directions for making an aquarium or planting a bulb, give practice in seeing order.

Utilization is probably the most important study skill. In the primary grades, where most of the content fields are studied in units, the culminating activities are practical tests of retention. The pupils study the zoo, then make a zoo. In addition, separate units should be reviewed and related to other units. We must take time for synthesizing what the child has read with what he is reading.

ALL CHILDREN CAN PARTICIPATE

The range of reading abilities is great in any group. The content subjects provide suitable materials for each level of reading ability in the group. Every pupil can find some material that he can read and enjoy. The child who makes a chart of safety pictures is contributing as much in relation to his ability and reading level as is the child who can do the more difficult reading. The job of the teacher is to provide reading materials for various levels. This is not as difficult as it once was, since much more material is now available. Most publishing houses now have textbooks in social studies, science, arithmetic, and health for the primary-grade level and are publishing more and more informational and story-books for these grades. Magazines, newspapers, and pamphlets are also good source materials.

CONCLUDING STATEMENT

If we present subjects that are interesting to children, if we use reading as a means of finding out about these interesting subjects, if we develop the reading skills necessary for reading content, if we help children acquire study skills, if all children participate in content study, we shall be making fullest use of the content subjects to promote reading interests.

✳ ✳ ✳

IN GRADES FOUR THROUGH SIX

HELEN BLACKLEDGE

✳

WHEN children come to school, they have many interests. They are naturally curious and have innumerable questions for which they would like to find answers. Teachers need to be alert to possibilities for guiding children's questions into worth-while activities. It is our responsibility to extend the interests of children into areas beyond their own immediate environment. Pupils have no way of knowing how many fascinating areas there are to explore unless we provide leadership and guidance. The content subjects permit many opportunities to stimulate children into wide reading. We should make use of these interests.

EXTENDING INTERESTS

A teacher can never know just how far the interests of a class will extend because of the stimulation of the content subjects. When a certain class was studying the Maritime Provinces of Canada, one member read in the newspaper about the proposed St. Lawrence seaway. As others in the class became interested, one group decided to work together to see what they could find out on the topic. They were curious to know why some congressmen were greatly opposed to the project, while others seemed just as decidedly in favor of it. Some members of the group wrote for information; others went to the public library and brought back pamphlets and newspaper clippings. They made lists of arguments for the seaway and lists of objections to it. They wrote a history of the project and told of the many times that this same topic had been brought up for discussion and decision in Congress. To present their findings to the class as a whole, they made a map of the Great Lakes region and the St. Lawrence River and used the opaque projector to view the accurate map. Then they placed this map in a metal map table and, using clay, made a relief map of the area. They even used blue-colored water to represent the Great Lakes and the St. Lawrence River. They located not only cities that might be affected by the project but also sources of iron and minerals. They gave their report to the class and pointed up their arguments by using the relief map in their demonstration. The teacher had not planned such an intensive study of this project; it served, however, to connect the study of Canada with another project that was under consideration at that time. It not only gave the pupils valuable basic training in research techniques but

also showed them how various factors affect a person's attitudes.

SETTING UP GOALS

Research techniques are well suited to children of the intermediate grades. When boys and girls have had a part in setting up goals and in deciding what steps shall be taken in achieving these goals, they are very willing to assume responsibility for getting information to solve a problem. Children will read widely if they feel that their reading will serve a real purpose. The first step, after recognition of the problem, is to help children set up their purposes for reading. These purposes may be listed on the board, in the form of topics or questions, as children talk about the things they would like to know. Later these questions or topics can be organized and placed on a chart as a guide to further study.

This problem-solving technique gives us a wonderful opportunity to provide for the individual differences in reading ability and in interests that are to be found in any class. We need in the classroom a wealth of books on all grade levels so that each child may choose the books that suit his interests and ability level. He should also have access to a library so that he may become familiar with the information available and learn how to use the library effectively.

DEVELOPING RESEARCH TECHNIQUES

Since many skills are essential to solving problems, it is the responsibility of the teacher to see that children learn these skills as they are needed. One important reading skill is the ability to adjust the rate of reading to the purpose for reading. Sometimes a common background for discussion is provided by a basic textbook, a film, a filmstrip, a news item, or a radio or television program. For getting the most important ideas from a selection, the pupil will need a slow rate of reading. His reading should be carefully guided by the teacher, and the new vocabulary must be presented before the reading is attempted. One of the ways of providing a common background for a discussion of a problem is wide exploratory reading, which requires a rapid rate of reading. As one skims down a page to look for a specific bit of information or as one looks through the index to locate information, the most rapid rate is required.

We must not overlook the rich opportunities for problem-solving that are sometimes found close at hand in the community. When one class became intensely interested in the building of a new wing to the school, a lively class discussion produced a list of questions that needed answering. The contractor was a very willing and helpful resource person. A visit from the contractor to the room and a trip through the new wing under his direction brought a lot of answers to questions and also raised many new questions. The contractor supplied samples of materials that were being used in the construction, and the children made an exhibit of these articles, labeling each with a description and a story explaining how it applied to the construction of the building. The children learned what was meant by "pan-slab" construction, how "bulldog clips" were used in attaching the flooring to the cement, and how the wiring was put into place. This study provided the class with definite purposes for wide reading and for art work. It also gave them much material for discussion and for writing. In addition, parents contributed to this study, for they were very much interested in the building of the new wing. Several parents came to give firsthand information to the class; others came simply to share the knowledge that the class had gathered.

The development of the research approach should be gradual. At first, the teacher should introduce each book that contains reference material pertaining to the problem. He should show the pupils where the information is located, put a marker in the book, and tell the children about the type of information it contains. Then gradually the teacher should help them develop techniques for locating material themselves. Children should become familiar with the specific skills that are needed in locating material, and each child should recognize his specific needs and work toward mastery of those skills. For effective use of the dictionary, children must develop skill in alphabetizing and in effective use of guide words. To find information in the encyclopedia, pupils need to identify the main idea of a selection. To find specific information in many books, pupils need to know the use of the index and the glossary. They should also learn that they may find much interesting background material about a country or a historical period in fiction. They will find that knowledge of the card catalogue and the *Readers' Guide* will help them locate the materials they want in the library.

Children should begin to judge material. They need to consider whether the contents of a book are related to the problem and whether they meet particular needs. Pupils should note the publication date to determine whether the information is obsolete. They need to think about the purpose of the author in writing the book and any evidence of bias in the writing. Children should identify the author of a book by name when quoting and should be able to question and discuss politely and courteously the authenticity of the information. They need to know whether the book is written as fact or fiction.

The recording of information is not an easy task for middle-graders. They tend to copy everything in the book, but they must gradually develop the important skill of learning to pick out the important idea from a paragraph and to put it in a few words.

Another source of information is observation. Children need the opportunity for going out into the community to obtain actual firsthand experiences. These field trips, however, are of little value unless they are well planned. Children need guidance in knowing what to look for and in summarizing their observations when they return from such trips.

The effectiveness of proper organization in research was demonstrated when one class began to wonder about the work of the weather bureau after they had read and experimented in learning about air and the weather. After they decided to visit the weather bureau, the class organized to prepare for the trip. One committee was responsible for transportation; another set up standards of behavior for the trip; and another group prepared a letter requesting the permission of parents. One group organized the class questions and took them to the weather bureau, so that the guide would know the interests of the children and could prepare a better learning experience for them. Significant learning resulted from the field trip, for each person knew his individual responsibility. Each child listened to the guide, observed, drew sketches to illustrate his report, asked questions of the guide, and took notes. After their return to the class-

room, a further discussion clarified their thinking and led them to set up a model weather station. They found it necessary to do much writing to explain each instrument and the work of the weather bureau. Very properly too, they wrote courteous "thank-you" letters to every person who had a part in the trip.

PLANNING WAYS TO SHARE INFORMATION

The desire to "do something" with the information gathered is a great motivating factor and often carries a reader through a difficult book. Children can share information in many ways. In the beginning of group work the teacher should suggest various methods of presenting a report to the class, such as dramatization, puppet shows, dioramas, roller movies, quiz programs, and radio and television shows. Other means to the same end are clay-modeling; using the opaque projector and felt board; arranging a bulletin board; making maps, murals, charts, graphs, and models; and composing original songs, dances, and poems. As the children grow in their ability to plan, the teacher must be careful not to limit the creativity of individuals. We often underestimate the ability of children and are amazed at the fertility of their imaginations. Some children will prefer working in committees, while others will enjoy making individual reports. It is important in the planning period that each person be sure of his responsibility and know how to proceed.

IMPROVING GROUP PROCEDURE

Organization into committees gives the class an opportunity to study their ways of working together and to improve group procedures. Every person must feel free to express himself even if his idea involves a misconception. Each person needs to have faith in his worth and in his ability to make a contribution to the class endeavor. He also needs to know that others have faith in him. The pupils grow as they continually evaluate, revise procedures and goals in the light of further evidence, and re-evaluate their efforts.

The members of one class, as they began to do committee work for the first time, organized one group and used it for demonstration. The children discussed procedures that the group used, noted methods of organization, and listed some criteria for good group procedure. They prepared a chart listing some responsibilities of a good group member, and each person kept his own evaluation of himself. Some of the responsibilities listed on the chart were as follows: "Contributes good ideas," "Encourages others to contribute," "Thinks as he listens," "Does not heckle," "Sticks to the point," "Summarizes ideas," "Takes his share of responsibility," "Tries to get along with others." As the group becomes more mature and more proficient in its use of the group process, the teacher becomes more

and more a resource person, and the responsibility for leadership is accepted by the group.

GAINING SOCIAL LEARNINGS

If we are to develop permanent interest in reading, children must be aware of the valuable information to be found in books; they must know where to look for information, how to record it, how to organize the material, and how to draw conclusions from many source materials. We are confronted with so much material to read that we too would be overwhelmed if we had not developed techniques that enable us quickly to sort out that which has value for us. We want children to develop understanding of basic concepts of interrelationship, cause and effect, time, space, and change. We want them to gain the social learnings that come from the dynamic process of working together on solving a problem. Above all else, we want them to develop truly effective, individual study techniques, to grow in their social development, and to feel the keen motivation for wide reading as their interests are stimulated through the content subjects.

✱ ✱ ✱

IN GRADES SEVEN THROUGH NINE

MARIE M. FOOTE

✱

MIDPOINT between the student and a department of curriculum stands the teacher, whose duty it is to introduce goals of achievement as well as to awaken and promote permanent reading interests through use of the content subjects. To the teacher falls the task of self-inventory with respect to his own teaching readi-

ness, of discovering whether he has a clear-cut understanding of the skills and attitudes, of the student interests and achievements, which indicate adolescent readiness for junior high school reading. Moreover, the teacher is faced with the reality that individuals vary in the avenues of approach by which their interest is aroused. The problem of capturing interests through use of the content subjects assumes dimensions of "Why, how, and what?"

WHY CONTENT AREAS CONTRIBUTE TO
READING INTERESTS

When presenting social studies, a handy technique for a teacher is that of showing the students how to dilute the concentrate of a whole period in history. For example, the writer of an American history textbook might condense the section devoted to the westward movement into a very few pages. In this case it is the teacher's responsibility to stimulate the students to read further. He must lead the young readers to appreciate history in terms of the participants of that time. Perhaps the teacher will choose to emphasize the role of the peddler, who was always welcomed by frontier people because he brought needles, trinkets, utensils, gossip, and news. His personal and economic importance grew with each trip so that he became a pivotal point in human-interest stories of this historical period.

Directing reading toward romance and trade of the river boats has a high motivating factor. One of the most exciting settings for further reading is the Louisiana Purchase. Interest in this one topic often develops into high-blood-pressure discussions in which the people, time, problems, and customs come to life for adolescent girls and boys.

Science offers a wealth of opportunity to read in magazines, pamphlets, science fiction, and the encyclopedia. Boys are interested in mystery and adventure of the woods; stories about avoiding dangers and learning how to tame nature have strong appeal. Boys like to read about forest rangers, camp life, and scouting.

Both girls and boys are enthusiastic about whales. Their chief complaint is that not enough has been written on this subject to satisfy their interests concerning the sleeping habits, dispositions, and sensory development of these immense mammals. Pamphlets and articles giving factual information on subjects related to plastics, medicine, glass, perfume, and dyes hold a strong fascination for both boys and girls.

A tri-level interest in the topic of color manifested itself within a classroom of forty-five seventh-grade students, ranging in reading ability from Grade 2.4 to 13.0. It is notable that the slow-reading group was desirous of learning about the discovery of color; the middle-ability group was concerned with skills and techniques for practical use in classroom art; and the top group had an insatiable curiosity about the functional use of color in relation to man and his environment. In short, when correctly discerned and applied, the directional drive provided by the content areas accelerates interests at the junior high school level and motivates broadening and deepening reading experiences.

HOW TO PROMOTE READING INTERESTS

"Science discerns the laws of nature—industry applies them to the needs of man." This quotation appearing around the table of the elements in the Museum of Science and Industry aptly fits the meaning of "fluid" and "packaged" interests.[1] When one realizes that not only

[1] "Fluid" and "packaged" are terms used by the writer to describe the operational difference between two sets of reading skills which unite to make a fruitful reading interest. Like the packaged cake-mix to which is added some type of liquid, so also packaged and fluid reading ingredients mix together to encourage interest

industry but also art, music, poetry, drama, history, geography, medicine, and religion may apply laws of nature to the reality of living, then his reading interests begin to broaden and deepen through an acquaintance with magazines, pamphlets, science fiction, biographies, and factual material which articulate contemporary progress through topics of the atomic age, such as space travel, precision tools, medical research, magnetism, radiosonde, signal systems, refrigeration, diesels, torque converters, refineries, and gravitation. When content-subject skills are classified as "packaged," they have definite dimensions and may be thought of in terms of *scientific measurements*, for example, how to recognize when an assignment is a fact-finding question, a topic, or a problem. It is interesting to note that reading interests have a correlation with packaged skills. Without an understanding of the quantitative skills associated with the reading tools for content subjects, the qualitative factors of desire and interest become stagnant and the developmental process of producing permanent reading interests is thwarted. Motivation is closely related to an intelligent understanding of these packaged skills in the light of know-how or efficient performance.

Fluid skills have no quantitative dimensions; they are characterized by *qualitative* expressions. The role of the fluid skills is not one of replacement. Rather, their function is that of *completion* of mechanical aims of the packaged subjects. It is through this aspect of fluidness that the soul of man soars to eternal heights; in this state of freedom

appetites. "Packaged" skills are similar to the mechanics of reading, while "fluid" skills refer to aesthetic or appreciative aspects.

the human spirit is touched by Eternal Truth and is engaged in contemplation; man's unfettered soul experiences the "thou-me" relationship, from which flows the wisdom of social culture. From the very heights of this qualitative state, a fluid quality flows down upon concrete measurements of the quantitative package, thereby conferring animation upon the stationary aspect of the content area or topic.

A teacher should be ready to serve students with the best teaching methods, devices, skills, and techniques which fit a given problem, subject, topic, or unit. He must be able to point out existing relations between one content subject and another and to act as guide in the process of helping students to integrate tools of research with factual information, skills, subject matter, and problems and thus to create a harmonious whole.

A very fine example of interaction between packaged and fluid skills is proper use of the encyclopedia. Most assignments which send students to an encyclopedia are not isolated topics. Usually they are part of a large unit or some specific problem which has many curriculum relationships. A *topic* entitled "The St. Lawrence–Great Lakes Waterway" illustrates how related content subjects were integrated while a junior high school class developed a problem in research. These content subjects included history, geography, science, English, mathematics, art, and music. The project involved use of the packaged skills. The fluid skills which had an active part in bringing about a unified *whole* involved qualitative kinds of thinking of an analytical and synthetic nature. It terminated in the construction of a very simple outline, used by students to point out relationship patterns discovered in the developmental process, namely, geography, history, science, and human relations.

The reading road in mathematics leads to the country of Greece, where, centuries before the Christian Era, a science of numbers and abstract ideas was developed. Interest in understanding constant and variable factors in relation to the denominators and numerators of everyday living adds zest to reading interests concerned with abstract as well as specific topics, such as tides, minutes and seconds in space, minutes and seconds in time, latitude, longitude, precision, origin of standards and methods of measurement (rule-of-thumb, cubit, barley corns, micrometer, interferometry, spectroscopy, and others), and mass production in terms of contemporary living.

A well-planned unit in American literature ought to include some general information on the life and environment of those who wrote the literature of a specific period. A good outline should promote depth reading while the student searches for an understanding of the meaning of our American heritage, the ideals of the people who founded our country, the courageous spirit of our leaders, and the developmental stages of cultural growth. This search could lead to hunting through personal records, diaries, letters, journals, essays, fiction, biographies, and poetry. Whether such an outline is planned to be handled through a parallel or an integrated method, the relations between the content areas of American history and American literature should be recognized in terms of daily living. This type of approach may culminate in many interesting activities, such as making a hornbook, or a picture map of the United States showing homes of American authors or settings for favorite American books. Others include selecting a favorite character, such as Evangeline, Rip van Winkle, or Ichabod Crane, and then writing a script of an original adventure to be used in a creative puppet show, or making a personalized New England primer using original linoleum prints in design and verse. Students may be motivated by comparing and contrasting some of the works of Mark Twain with those of James Fenimore Cooper, to show how they reflect historical and geographical settings; by defining and identifying contributions to American culture of historians, newspapermen, humorists, clergymen, essayists, novelists, poets, orators, and writers of short stories. Depth reading could lead to European roots. Familiarity in terms of chronological appropriateness with such works as *The Merchant of Venice*, *Ivanhoe*, *A Tale of Two Cities*, "A Dissertation on Roast Pig," *The Old Curiosity Shop*, and many other literary landmarks beckons students to vertical exploration of reading interests.

Taking "man" as a nucleus, the reader finds his interest circle enlarging in the field of social studies. In studying history, he should examine the activities of man and try to understand the control factors of his behavior, such as environment, climate, food, clothing, shelter, travel, communication, developmental stages, games, worship, and the like.

The areas of art, music, dance, and poetry may be viewed as communicative subjects. They speak a language through mood, rhythm, tempo, repetition, variation, radiation, and reaction. They express feelings of abandon, joy, sorrow, satisfaction, simplicity, achievement, discouragement, defeat, beauty, and patriotism. The feelings are evidenced in the dance of the gypsies, totem poles of the Indians, river music of the Mississippi, poetry of Acadia, and song of the cowboy.

WHAT IS TO BE READ

It is necessary for schools to have materials available to co-ordinate with units in the various content areas. But having materials is not enough. The materials must be functional and serve curriculum demands and student interests. The students, under teacher guidance, must be able to read the materials, understand them, explore them, interpret them, compare them, and share them. Publishers of fictional, factual, reference, periodical, and audio-visual materials have a responsibility, along with the teacher, to bring into focus the area of learning so that the teacher may capture the moment when the dynamic charge enkindles the students with the flame of truth. Through a keen understanding on the part of the teacher as to what is meant by teaching students to get meaning from the printed symbol, it is hoped that adolescents will receive a benediction of fruitful experience in fields of warmth and wonder.

CONCLUDING STATEMENT

Anyone writing so short a paper on so large a topic must of necessity omit something. In capsule form, my message reads: The purpose of using the content subjects to promote reading interests in Grades VII through IX should be to make the reader capable of coming into contact with reality.

✳ ✳ ✳

IN GRADES TEN THROUGH FOURTEEN

JAMES M. McCALLISTER

✳

WHEN one surveys the professional publications devoted to the promotion of interest in reading, he is impressed by the predominance of articles dealing with the development of interest in literature and the meagerness of reports of attempts to promote interest through other content subjects. Publications contain frequent allusions to the place of the content subjects in developing interest in reading, but the most direct references apply to popular books, fiction, the classics, and other forms of English literature. In preparing this paper, I have attempted to utilize suggestions that apply particularly to subjects other than English, but I have also used principles from the teaching of English.

If we ask individuals just what led them to develop habits of voluntary reading, a few persons may be able to pinpoint one experience, or a limited number of experiences, which enabled them to discover values in reading, but, in most cases, permanent interests are the outcomes of cumulative experiences from various sources. Without doubt, many of these experiences could be traced to contacts with content subjects because any good teaching develops interest and leads to voluntary reading whether or not the immediate purpose is to stimulate interest in reading. What, then, are some of the approaches which the content teacher may use to promote interest in reading?

INITIATING INTEREST IN VOLUNTARY READING

Many teachers of content subjects make an appraisal of the preparation and interests of students as a phase of the introductory work of each class or of each new unit of instruction. In this appraisal they attempt to discover the reading interests of students as a basis for selecting and using reading materials related to the course. They seek the answer to such questions as these:

1. Which students have well-established habits of voluntary reading?
2. Which students usually limit their reading to textbooks and other materials that all members of a class are expected to study?
3. Which students are being initiated into the subject and which students already have an interest in it?
4. What kinds of attitudes toward voluntary reading do the students exhibit?
5. What kinds of recreational reading, if any, do students do?

On the basis of the answers to these and similar questions, teachers may identify students who need to be prepared for new topics before reading is suggested or assigned, students who require relatively easy materials to initiate interest, and students who may enrich their own and the experiences of other members of the class by special reading. In general, the information ascertained by preliminary appraisals will be helpful in selecting reading material for the class and in adjusting assignments to individuals.

The effectiveness of such appraisals depends upon the ingenuity of each teacher. Formal inventories or teacher-made tests may be used, but, to a considerable extent, the teacher must rely upon his own informal observations and interviews to assemble information. In estimating the interests and degree of maturity of individuals and in selecting reading materials, the teacher must necessarily exercise his own judgments. Nevertheless, the number of adjustments that the intelligent teacher may make for individuals on the basis of a careful inventory is almost unlimited.

Once an appraisal has been made, the teacher has the problem of bringing the students and reading materials together in such a manner as to motivate the student to action. The alert teacher will discover numerous ways of initiating this contact. Following are suggestions that illustrate practices:

1. Introduce topics by means of films, visual aids, recordings, and other devices that will arouse interest and lead to voluntary reading.
2. Review or refer to books and articles that are relevant to the immediate assignment.
3. Display books, periodicals, and bulletins that are appropriate to the interests and reading levels of students.
4. Provide class time for reading from the room library, during which the teacher confers individually with students and guides their choices of reading through suggestions.
5. Compare the treatment of a subject by two or more authors to excite curiosity.
6. Permit one or more students to discuss books or other references that are not assigned to all members of the class.
7. Arrange for students to report reading experiences in panels or round-table discussions.
8. Permit friends to work together; sometimes better readers may help poorer readers.

These suggestions have been selected with the thought that interest in reading is contagious and that an enthusiastic teacher or interested students may encourage others to investigate new reading materials.

INTRODUCING NEW MATERIALS
TO STUDENTS

The degree of interest with which new materials are read depends to a large extent on the methods by which they are presented to the student. Required reading which is inappropriate to the reading ability and maturity level of a student may thwart interest instead of promoting it. Meanings are grounded in the experience of the reader. To assign reading without adequate preparation encourages mere memorization and verbalization. Before assigning new material, therefore, the effective teacher will satisfy himself that each student is ready to attack it with interest.

In introducing each unit or section of a course, there is usually a common body of informational background which will be useful to all members of the class. This information is ordinarily presented by lectures, class discussions, demonstrations, films, slides, recordings, or some other form of introductory experience. Sometimes it may be provided by a preliminary reading assignment. If it is effectively presented, these initial contacts should arouse a desire for further exploration of the subject and stimulate an interest in reading. The presentation offers an opportunity to define purposes, introduce essential concepts, and clear up difficulties which students are likely to encounter in reading.

The initial inventory of the reading ability and interests of students will usually reveal some students who require more preparation for new materials than do others. The reading of these students may need to be varied by suggesting extensive reading of materials suited to their interests and maturity levels in order to provide a more detailed introduction than is presented to the class as a whole.

Similarly, the inventory may reveal superior readers who may enrich the class discussions by bringing ideas and concepts that are not expected of the class as a whole. The superior reader may be directed to voluntary reading along the lines of his special interests. The alert teacher will attempt to assign reading responsibilities in such a manner that each student will experience the satisfaction of carrying them out successfully.

High-school and college students are interested primarily in what is familiar to them. Usually they do not realize that they may become interested in new things through experience with them. Only the exceptional student has the intellectual curiosity which motivates him to explore new fields of knowledge voluntarily. In introducing new units of learning, the teacher has excellent opportunities to expand the interests of students. Motivation of new interests is one of the most essential objectives when new subject matter is introduced.

PROVIDING READABLE MATERIALS

When we consider the wide range of reading interests and abilities in a class, it becomes evident that the room library and the school library must be well stocked with books and other reading materials to meet a wide variety of needs. The effective teacher will desire to assist in selecting reading materials that will meet all the criteria indicated by the needs of the students, as well as the materials required for the teacher's organization and treatment of the subject matter. The selection of readable materials is a somewhat unique problem in each class. However, a few suggestions may indicate how reading materials may be selected with the promotion of reading interests as an objective.

One essential purpose is to provide materials of varying levels of difficulty. Students who are taking their first course in a field are not as "ready" to read as those who have had preliminary courses. Some classes may require more introductory background than others. In some cases an easier textbook may be used to introduce students to concepts and vocabulary and to prepare the way for the reading of the regular text.

The variety of content should be great enough to provide for the study of special topics by individuals and groups. Superior readers may be challenged by materials that others do not read. Special assignments may be used for group reports to the class. To provide variation, some teachers may want to use more than one textbook.

The teacher should be sufficiently familiar with all materials to make intelligent recommendations to students. Sometimes teachers do not know materials well enough to match them with the interests of individuals. Furthermore, some supplementary materials may be so poorly written as to be of limited value in developing the essential concepts of a course. Reading recommendations lose much of their interest value if they are carelessly made.

ENCOURAGING PERMANENT ATTITUDES TOWARD READING

One of the chief reasons for stressing wide reading in the content fields is the encouragement of permanent attitudes which will persist into adult life. Unless the student learns to turn voluntarily to books and other reading materials to satisfy his curiosity, to solve his personal problems, and to utilize his leisure time, the reading program has fallen short of its possibilities. The development of permanent attitudes requires a long program of satisfying experience with many and varied types of reading. Any experience that helps the student to discover how reading can be satisfying and rewarding contributes its part to the reader's attitudes.

The concepts developed in the content subjects are particularly useful in building background for permanent attitudes because they will be used over and over again in voluntary reading. For example, the use of number concepts occurs repeatedly in the voluntary reading of individuals. Similarly, place-geography, social and economic concepts, science principles, and concepts from many other content fields are essential to the interpretation of modern reading materials. Such concepts not only aid in interpretation but also give assurance and motivation to the reader. Without such background, few persons will really want to read. The more clearly and precisely concepts are defined in the experience of the reader, the more useful they will be in interpretation. In some classes it may be desirable to introduce fewer concepts but to provide more materials to make each concept meaningful.

Permanent attitudes toward reading may be encouraged also by teaching useful techniques that may be developed into permanent habits. Many students in high school and college recognize only one technique of reading, which may be described as "reading and remembering." They have not learned to use purposefully many techniques which are valuable as permanent habits. The content subjects offer opportunities for developing such habits as varying rate of reading to suit the purpose of the reader, knowing when to skim and when to read more intensively, determining the validity of statements by comparing two or more authors, noting cause-and-effect relationships, identifying the principle or process to be learned from an example or illustration, recognizing emotionalized or prejudicial treatment of a subject, comparing textual materials with pictorial and other forms of illustration, etc. Such techniques promote attitudes which lead to the permanent use of reading as a useful tool.

CONCLUDING STATEMENT

Underlying the practices described in this paper, but not explicitly stated, is the necessity for favorable teacher-student relationships. The environment in the classroom must be conducive to free expression and must permit the free exchange of ideas obtained through reading. The teacher must have a sympathetic understanding of individual students, including those elements in the background of each student which explain his special interests or lack of interest in reading, his emotional and social handicaps which might inhibit reading, and his special difficulties with the subject, if any. This information is essential for the successful direction of reading interests, as well as the effective teaching of any course.

Throughout the paper I have purposefully avoided suggestions for the introduction of reading activities that are not related directly to the teaching of content courses. Ordinarily teachers of content courses do not respond favorably to the introduction of extraneous activities that do not contribute to the specific objectives of their courses. They consider that their first responsibility is to teach students the content of the courses. On the other hand, teachers are usually willing to promote activities which make a direct contribution to the learning objectives of the course. The procedures that are discussed in this paper are designed to promote reading without interfering with effective teaching of content.

CHAPTER XIV

READING INTERESTS DEVELOPED THROUGH THE HOME AND THE LIBRARY

✳

OPPORTUNITIES IN THE HOME FOR STIMULATING READING INTERESTS

NANCY LARRICK

✳

A QUICK look around the modern American home shows it to be a very different place from its counterpart of thirty or forty years ago. According to figures supplied me by the Columbia Broadcasting System, in 35.1 million of these homes —just over 73 per cent of the total—a television set is turned on for close to five hours a day, with one or more members of the family watching intently. Warmed-over Westerns, screaming murder mysteries, great symphonies, and high drama join puppet shows, science demonstrations, quiz programs, newscasts, and jazzed-up commercials in a varied parade on the magic screen.

And in 96 per cent of the homes of America there is at least one radio, often two or three. The average family spends 2.6 hours a day listening to radios at home or in automobiles. What they can hear is a grand conglomeration—soap operas, symphonies, sportscasts, quiz shows, news reports from around the world, and commercials that may slice listening time into split-second segments.

Into almost ten million of these homes come copies of *Look* or *Life* with unequaled pictorial material, from the most miserable "cheesecake" to really superb reproductions of famous paintings and detailed presentations of natural science.

In many ways the modern American home has become an audio-visual center pouring forth a bewildering assortment of sound and fury—some of it shockingly crude and sensational, some of it highly artistic and intellectually stimulating. But the variety is there, for every corner of the world is represented and every discipline. And the potential impact is there, for better or for worse.

From homes such as this, boys and girls come to school, where they spend approximately 16 per cent of their waking hours. Obviously their interests and attitudes in school are affected by experiences outside of school. In fact, what they learn and how they develop as individuals will depend in large measure on this out-of-school experience, which represents the largest segment of their lives.

Probably no part of a child's school program is more directly affected by the impact of his non-school world than his reading. How well he reads, what he reads, and how widely he reads will be influenced in part by the guidance he receives from his parents and the opportunities which are provided at home.

WHAT ARE PARENTS THINKING ABOUT CHILDREN'S READING?

With interest in television so high, it might seem that reading would be forgotten even by the parents. But the situation seems to be just the reverse. Today's parent is very much interested in his child's reading. The rise of the Flesch book[1] to best-seller rank and the popularity of the syndicated articles from that book give convincing proof. At the same time, several hundred thousand parents have shown further interest in children's reading by subscribing to children's book clubs, which deliver attractive titles to boys and girls in their homes. In a recent survey of parents in one community,[2] 60 per cent said their first interests regarding their children's reading are to help them enjoy reading more fully and to be able to recommend appropriate books to their children.

One of the most extensive studies concerning parents and their children's reading is that completed less than two years ago by J. Harlan Shores and Herbert C. Rudman at the University of Illinois.[3] In this study, questionnaires were returned by 6,313 pupils in Grades IV through VIII, 4,531 parents of those pupils, 212 teachers, and 169 librarians. The prime objective was to find out what children

are looking up in books, what they want to find out about, and what they want to read. A secondary objective was to find whether their parents, teachers, and librarians "had the same desires for children with respect to reading and informational needs as the children had for themselves and whether these adults were seeing children's reading and informational interests in the same way in which children saw these interests for themselves."[4] Adults and children were asked to comment on the things children are interested in reading about, the things they are interested in asking about, and those they will look up.

What this study tells us about children's interests is fascinating and frequently quite different from the findings of previous studies. But for our purposes here I will mention only those findings that have to do with the parents and what they are thinking about children's reading and reading interests. Let me give some of the high lights.

First, it seems clear that parents are attuned to their children's reading interests and informational needs. Asked about the areas in which children seek information, parents seem to agree more closely with their children than do either teachers or librarians. Children indicated that they believed their parents would provide a book more in keeping with their reading interests than would teachers.

Second, parents concern themselves with very serious topics when considering their children's reading. For example, parents, more than teachers and librarians, indicate a strong desire for children to read about ethics and religion. They seem to show, too, a keen sensitivity to some of the problems confronting our

[1] Rudolf Flesch, *Why Johnny Can't Read—And What You Can Do about It*. New York: Harper & Bros., 1955.

[2] Nancy Gray Larrick, "Your Child and His Reading: A Handbook for Parents." Unpublished dissertation, New York University, 1955.

[3] J. Harlan Shores and Herbert C. Rudman, "Reading Interests and Informational Needs of Children in Grades Four to Eight." Chicago: Spencer Press, Inc., 1954 (mimeographed).

[4] *Ibid.*, p. 1.

contemporary society. Parents of upper-grade pupils want their children to ask about problems of war, peace, segregation, housing, and conservation, for example. Of all the areas examined, science is the most persistent interest of pupils, parents, teachers, and librarians. Although both teachers and parents want children to ask about and read about their personal problems, parents are more concerned that children get information about vocations, while teachers are more concerned with the social skills.

In conclusion, the Shores-Rudman study seems to indicate that the adults working closely with children—parents, teachers, and librarians—perceive children's reading interests and informational needs much more accurately than is generally assumed. Further, the understandings that they have of each other with respect to their desires for children are generally good. However, one cannot read this report without realizing that even greater understanding can be achieved through closer co-operation between parents, teachers, and librarians, all working with the children.

HOW DO WE HELP PARENTS STIMULATE READING INTERESTS?

If we are to help parents stimulate reading interests in the home, we must help them first to understand the potential relationship between a child's interests and his reading. If one is already well acquainted with a subject, further reading is much easier for him than for someone who is not acquainted with the subject. So our interests, growing out of our experience, make reading easy because we bring meaning to the printed page, and make it pleasant because it fills a need we have built up.

The child who becomes fascinated with the period of westward expansion in America is building up a storehouse of information and queries that may become a dynamic, ongoing interest. As he reads adventure stories of Indians and pioneer life, his inner purposes are driving him on. But for the teen-ager who is trying to establish himself with his social group, Kit Carson and Wild Bill Hickok may not have the same appeal. His eagerness to gain acceptance and to behave as his peers would have him behave will create quite different reading interests in many cases.

The point that we must help parents recognize is that such interests are to be encouraged because to encourage a child's interests is to encourage his motivation for reading.

How can parents encourage children's interests?—It seems simple enough, yet we know that the busy schedule of today's parents frequently omits time for the development of children's interests. Certainly it is important to find time for family conversations that will encourage children to tell about their interests. What about Peter's garden? Did Janie's dancing teacher see the ballet on television too? Have the children noticed the jenny wrens that are building in the front porch? What did you see on television yesterday that you wish I could have seen?

When adults ask such questions as these in a warm, friendly fashion, they may encourage children to talk about their interests and next time to observe more closely and report more fully about their everyday lives and the world around them.

Still another way to encourage interests is to broaden the child's horizons—to meet new people, see new places, and face new situations. For the young child a trip to the fire department or a visit to the neighborhood bakery may be the beginning of new interests. For an eight-year-old a trip to the airport or planetarium may open new worlds. For the teen-ager it may be a big-league game or an overnight trip to some large metropolitan area.

Yet just going and coming is not enough. To be effective, such an excursion should be the cause for advance planning and research, for comments and queries, and for follow-up that will add meaning and richness to the child's experience.

In the proper setting, television often provides the basis for expanding interests. Alert parents are learning to scan the week's programs on Sunday and note those that sound promising. Here is one on snake cults, for example. Perhaps that will broaden horizons in natural history, in religion, in folklore, and in the cultures of other lands. Or this science program that is to deal with electricity might be interesting to Jimmie, who spent so much time yesterday pestering the electrician with questions. And that one on ballet is for Janie, of course. So by judicious suggestion the parent may encourage young television fans to dip into new subject-matter areas. And by interested queries he may be able to bring some idea into better focus or help some plan to crystallize.

Now how can we relate these interests to reading?—Not everything the child sees, hears, or does relates to his reading immediately. Many of these enriching experiences are being stored up as a kind of reserve that can someday give meaning to the printed page. But with most children new experiences stir curiosity. In the right atmosphere, questions pour forth: "Why did he do that? What did he mean when he said that? Where is Afghanistan? I bet the book didn't end like that." And so on. Some of these are questions to discuss on the spot. Some are the ones to look up. And some lead easily to further reading.

Here is where the parent can play an invaluable role. With some encouragement from him, the child may learn to use television as a springboard to further inquiry and further reading. Without such encouragement, he may sit with his eyes glued to the screen, raising no questions and gaining nothing beyond the sights and sounds that surge around him.

From the suggestions so far, one might think that all of children's reading could be classified as informational. To be sure, elementary-school youngsters are hounds for information. They seem to seek facts about everything they meet—facts and more facts. For some of them, finding information is high adventure, and the believe-it-or-not's of the world of science are indeed truth stranger than fiction.

It is a fairly simple thing to bring an informational book to a child who is seeking information. But what about those hundreds of books in which information is only incidental—the tall tales and folk tales, the modern adventure stories, the biographies, the poems and nursery rhymes, the fantasies and animal stories? How can parents relate children's interests to these kinds of books?

Sometimes the relation is immediately apparent, as with the horse enthusiast who is a natural for *Old Bones, the Wonder Horse* by Mildred Pace (Whittlesey, 1955), and the television fan who seems made for *Clarence, the TV Dog* by Patricia Lauber (Coward-McCann, 1955).

But for many, many books the relation between child and book must be established. Often parents can do this at home more easily than teachers can do it at school; for with the smaller, more intimate group at home, it is sometimes easier to talk about story-book people and to read aloud the tales of their escapades, their disappointments, and their triumphs. *The Borrowers Afield* by Mary Norton (Harcourt, 1955) may be just right for a small congenial circle at bedtime. And Sterling North's *Abe Lincoln: Log Cabin to White House* (Random, 1956) may be good family reading on vacation.

As I speak of a family's adventuring with books, I think of course of those two delightful books by Annis Duff, *"Bequest of Wings"* (Viking, 1944) and *"Longer Flight"* (Viking, 1955). They tell how Mrs. Duff and her husband introduced their two children to the world of books through reading aloud, talking about beloved book characters—in fact, by making books a part of their everyday lives. As one reads those two chronicles of the Duff family, one is deeply impressed by the familiarity which those two parents have with children's books. Few parents—in fact, few teachers or librarians—know books as Annis Duff knows them. For the rest of us it would take a little digging to be able to suggest a title as readily as Mrs. Duff does while she's washing dishes.

Such digging means we need to have book lists at hand so that we may consult them as we see interests developing in potential readers. One book written for parents contains many lists of books for children, with suggestions for introducing them. This book, entitled *Your Child's*

Reading Today (Doubleday, 1954), was written by Josette Frank. For those parents who are just beginning to explore children's books, a smaller, more compact list may be welcome. For this I suggest that handy little list entitled "Growing Up with Books," published by the R. R. Bowker Company (62 West Forty-fifth Street, New York). Over half a million copies have been distributed during the past year by booksellers, libraries, and schools.

There are many lists which you will want to consider in making recommendations to parents, such as those published by the Association for Childhood Education International, the Child Study Association of America, and the National Council of Teachers of English. All contain good recommendations, are inexpensive and easy to use.

In addition, many teachers are making a practice of encouraging children to prepare short lists of favorite books and recommended books, which can be taken home for parents to use.

IN CONCLUSION

With our horizons so vastly broadened by modern methods of communication, the opportunities for parents to stimulate children's reading interests seem almost endless. We know parents are concerned about their children's reading. We also know that children accept their book suggestions more readily than those of other adults.

How effective their suggestions will be will depend in part on the encouragement and specific help which they get from the school.

THE LIBRARIAN'S RESPONSIBILITY FOR DEVELOPING AND MAINTAINING READING INTERESTS

DORIS GATES

★

Once upon a time a visitor to my home commented on the number of books displayed on the bookshelves of my living-room. As collections go, it was not large, but he was plainly impressed that I should have even that many.

"It isn't often you see a wall full of books these days," he said.

I replied, hardly brilliantly, "What is a home without books in it?"

I assumed, of course, that he would agree that without books a home lacked something important. To my surprise, he fixed me with an amused eye and said, "You could be prejudiced." He knew my background of librarianship and knew, too, that I had even written some books. So I *could* be prejudiced.

I must admit that his response came as something of a shock to me because he was not an uncultured man. He was a college graduate, he loved music and made a living at photography. So it was a shock to learn that he considered a need for books as a mere quirk of character.

AMERICANS ARE NOT BOOK-READERS

Remembering this incident in my own experience, I was not so surprised as I might otherwise have been when I came across some interesting figures last year. They were the results of a Gallup poll,[1] showing that the American public has not acquired the book-reading habit to any very large degree. The poll showed

[1] *Los Angeles Times*, Part 1 (August 15, 1955), p. 14.

that 61 per cent of the people questioned had not read a book through in the preceding year. Seventeen per cent had read one book, but the poll did not reveal what that book was! Only one-fifth of those polled had visited a public library during the preceding year, though the public library was within a mile of each of their residences.

These are disquieting figures to anyone who believes in the value of books to quicken our sense of wonder, to intensify experience, to widen horizons, and in general to make life more meaningful. These figures make it clear that, despite the interest in books manifested by the wide sale of paperbacks and the increasing circulation of books in public libraries, there still remains a vast amount of work to be done by those missionaries of the book whom we call "librarians." That work is, simply stated, to try to develop the book-reading habit in the members of their communities. This they must do on every level of library work, in school and college libraries, as well as in public libraries. Habits are most easily and lastingly formed during childhood. So it is with the responsibility of the children's librarians that I would begin this discussion.

TYPES OF LIBRARY SERVICE TO CHILDREN

There are two types of library service for children: the school library and the children's room of the public library.

Each performs a special service, and a community is poor which cannot boast of both kinds. While their services may sometimes overlap, they need never be in competition, and it is axiomatic that, where a strong elementary and junior high school library program is functioning properly, the demand for books is carried over into the public library children's room. This is important because, if reading interest is to be maintained into adulthood, children must learn as they grow toward adulthood to use the public library.

What are the special functions of the public library children's room? To begin with, since children go there voluntarily, it is safe to assume that only the children who want to read have library cards. From that assumption we may go on to another: if children want to read, the chances are that they are good readers. So the children's-room collection of books should place emphasis on those titles that come under the heading of "literature." Often the school librarian does not feel justified in stocking those titles usually described in reviews as beautifully written, original, difficult, "will not appeal to the *average* child." Too often the school librarian must choose between those books that correlate with no specific curriculum subject matter and those that gear directly into the school program. I refer to such things as *The Children of Green Knowe* (Harcourt, 1955), *The Cat Who Went to Heaven* (Macmillan, 1943), *The Oregon Trail* (Binfords, 1949), and *Treasure Island* as Stevenson wrote it. I do not mean to imply that these titles do not belong in a school library. I merely cite them as examples of books which, by the quality of their writing, the originality of their subjects, and the demands they make on their readers, are placed in that bracket reserved for authentic lit-

erature, the kind of thing which every child may not want to read or may not be able to read. We bring to a book exactly what we have in us to give it, and many so-called "reluctant readers" simply are unable to absorb real literary fare.

It happens regrettably that the budgets of school libraries, as of all libraries, are limited. There may be some that can afford to buy all the leisure-reading material that they could possibly desire, with enough left over at the end of the school year for an extra set of the *Encyclopaedia Britannica*, but their number is not legion. By and large a school librarian must make a book serve as many readers as possible, and very often she must, in the interests of remedial reading, drop from her lists of new books and replacements the kind of thing which will only appeal to the exceptional reader. However, we ignore at our peril the literary needs of this exceptional reader; for, all other things being equal, it will be to him that the future will look for its leadership. It will be his imagination that will forge the brave new world we all await with what sometimes seems pathetic hope. On him the future depends, and the reading which will challenge his thinking and mold his dreams of the good and the true is as important as anything else that can happen to him in school or out. So it is one responsibility of the school librarian, if the school's collection is not adequate to meet this reader's needs, to see that he finds the public library and the special and continued reading guidance it can give. Even if the school collection is more than adequate, it is still important that the gifted reader know and use the public library so that he will be encouraged to use its resources after he has left school and college.

There is another difference between the services of the school library and children's room which I want to take a moment to discuss. While the school librarian is in every sense a teacher, the children's-room librarian is not a teacher, and should never think of herself as one. She is an introducer, a guide, a "good picker," as the children soon learn to call her, an awakener, and a story-teller. The time spent by the school librarian in preparing and giving lessons on the use of the library should be spent by the children's librarian in the preparation and the telling of stories. This is her special responsibility because by this means she is able to discover with children the delights of literature. Through story-telling, she can introduce new worlds of reading to them and lead them into their literary heritage. A children's room without a story hour is like a pudding without raisins, or a book without pictures. And, "What," said Alice, "is the use of a book without pictures?"

Probably the most obvious contrast between the work of the school and the children's librarian comes during the summer months when school closes, the school librarian goes off to Europe, and the children's librarian takes over all the children of the community. Gifted, run-of-the-mill, and reluctant readers (the latter because their teachers have dropped a hint to their parents)—all descend upon the children's room. But here is the children's librarian's big chance. Here is her opportunity to talk with the children in a leisurely way about their reading interests, to share with them her own enthusiasms. It isn't easy to do this during the after-school rush or on crowded Saturdays. But the long days of summer, with boys and girls coming in at all hours, offer time for book talk. For this reason I am saddened when I go into a library to find a harassed children's librarian listening with a dull ear to a book

report, when I witness children reading in a rush in order to win another set of spurs or to arrive at another planet via a rocket ship moved upward a notch on a poster full of names.

Much reading that children do is reading for a purpose, but the kind of reading which should be fostered by a children's room is the kind of reading that is its own reward. Are children never to learn about that kind? Are they never to savor books for their fun, taking time to reread a line in order to chuckle over it again? Are they never to be able to stop long enough to lift their eyes from the page and say, "That's the way I have felt sometimes. I wonder what this boy will do about it?" The responsibility of both school and children's librarians is to develop interest in reading by allowing children to relate books to their own lives, and by finding, through reading, solutions to their own life-problems. To offer rewards for the largest number of books read is to make a mockery of all that literature is and, in the end, will defeat the purpose for which the rewards were established. Competitive reading will not foster the book-reading habit. Too much even of a good thing can be bad. A child who, in order to stay at the top of a bulletin board, may read as many as fifty books during a summer, may well feel done with books for the rest of his life. Let children understand from the beginning that it is not the number of books you have read that determines how well read you are; it is the number of good books you remember.

THE RESPONSIBILITY OF THE
SCHOOL LIBRARIAN

Now what is the particular responsibility of the school librarian in this business of developing and maintaining reading interests? Does she spend all her time giving instructions in the use of the card catalogue, the dictionary, and the encyclopedia? Is she forever lining up assistants and training them to card books, stamp date slips, and shelve? Doesn't she have anything to do with books and readers? Not only does she have a grave responsibility for getting students and books together, but her special responsibility as a school librarian is to convince everyone on the faculty of the truth of what Robert Frost once wrote: "The whole reason for going to school is to get the impression fixed for life that there is a book side to everything."[2]

The teachers of art, of music, of reading, of science, of shop must learn, through the school librarian if they haven't learned before, that there are books to fit their subjects which their students will find valuable and which can implement the work of the classroom in the subjects. Caroline Dale Snedeker's *The Spartan* (Doubleday, 1912) and *The White Isle* (Doubleday, 1940) would be useful to a class in ancient history, as would Lucille Morrison's *The Lost Queen of Egypt* (Lippincott, 1937). The school librarian must read professional journals and new book lists always with an eye for that particular title that will fit some curriculum need. Not all teachers realize that books other than the textbook can assist the learning process, and, even when they are willing to go beyond the textbook, they are not always convinced that fiction can illuminate the subject. It is the school librarian's responsibility to convince them. I know of some "non-reading" boys whose faith in books was established when a clever librarian slipped some science fiction into a classroom collection of books on science.

In every way the school librarian takes full advantage of the fact that she knows

the children, that she has them from the time they enter school until they leave it. She can become well acquainted with them and use her knowledge of their outside interests to introduce books to them; for the school librarian, no less than the children's librarian, is a reading guide. Furthermore, when she is confronted with a reading problem, she can check immediately with that pupil's teacher or teachers. This group will find means of meeting the problem. As far as her budget will permit, she will add those adult books to her junior high collection which are suitable for readers beginning to reach out beyond the magical world of childhood. She will confer with her faculty as to what titles they would like to see on the library shelves and in every possible way elicit their interest in what she is doing.

The best way to develop reading interest among young people is to convince them of the importance of books. This, too, is the special responsibility of the school librarian. Somehow, she must get across to the young men and women who come into the library the fact that chance favors the well-informed mind and that the reading they do today may condition their future destiny. She should know about such experiments in education as the Bell Telephone Company's[3] where it was felt that books were mandatory to a man's success as a future executive in that company. Young people are impressed by such accounts, and a school librarian should be on the watch for them.

CONCLUDING STATEMENT

Despite the fact that America is not a book-reading public, there is evidence

---

[2] Robert Frost, "Poetry and School," *Atlantic Monthly*, CLXXXVII (June, 1951), 30.

[3] E. D. Baltzell, "Bell Telephone's Experiment in Education," *Harper's Magazine*, CCX (March, 1955), 73–77.

that thousands of people who are not book-lovers still feel an occasional need for the help of books in this "fugitive world." But the reading of an occasional book can do little, actually. It takes many books and much thinking about them to build those insights by means of which we chart our intellectual, social, and spiritual course through life. It has been rightly said that a man can be financially successful without books, he can learn to tyrannize over his fellows without books; but he cannot see God, he cannot live in a present charged with the past and pregnant with the future without a knowledge of the diary of our race. I think it is the high privilege and solemn responsibility of our librarians to make known to our children and young people the diary of our race, since they are the ones who will write the future on its pages.

CHAPTER XV

HOW THE LIBRARIAN FOSTERS READING INTEREST

✳

IN KINDERGARTEN THROUGH GRADE THREE

DONNA SECRIST

✳

IF WE are to foster a permanent interest in reading at this formative period in the child's life, the effort must be a co-operative undertaking with the parent, the teacher, and the librarian all working toward the same goal. The elementary-school library offers many opportunities for all three to work in close co-operation.

THE BEGINNING READER AND THE LIBRARY PROGRAM

Although the kindergarten in our school does not have a regularly scheduled library period, these children have many opportunities to use the facilities of the library. They make their grand debut to the library very near the end of the year, when they come to share "their" books with the librarian. Each child writes (that is, dictates and the teacher writes) and illustrates his own book. With great pride each pupil shows his book on airplanes, cowboys, or flowers. This may seem like just another sharing experience, but to the kindergarten child it is an important step in his introduction to the library.

During Grade I, learning to read simple materials independently is certainly a goal toward which all children strive. In helping to attain this end, the school library can play an important role. The teacher determines when the pupils are sufficiently skilled to start their library reading. This is a big event in the life of the first-grader, and it is important that his first venture with his own book be successful and satisfying. One first-grade teacher sends the following letter home with the first library book:

We are beginning library reading in our first grade. It is a very important event to your child.

We want the child to find success and enjoyment from his reading; therefore we ask you to tell him the new words as they occur. A readiness for sounding out words will come later.

After the book has been read will you please write a note to that effect, and sign your name. The note may be tucked in the pocket of the book. By doing this we know the child has read the book, and the note is used in school to stimulate reading other books.

We would appreciate it if the children can be helped to assume the responsibility for clean hands before reading. Then many other children can enjoy the books, too.

The parents are most responsive, and each book that the child returns contains a note to the teacher. These notes are most revealing and are often invaluable to the teacher and librarian. Some parents are so specific as to point out certain words with which the child had difficulty, while others quote the children as to the part of the story they liked best. Here are typical comments:

Berry has read these two books, *Buttons at the Zoo* and *Let's Go*, and has enjoyed them more than any other books he has had. They offered more of a challenge, and he learned many new words.

Jimmy has read both of these books fluently. *Jerry Goes Fishing* was the best book he ever did see!

Molly has read this book completely and has read some of the stories aloud to her younger sister and brother.

Kim has read *Up the Street and Down*. He really liked the story about old Mrs. Duck.

Tommy read both library books several times. He read them so fast we think he needs a larger book next time.

These notes clearly indicate to the librarian the child's interests and serve as an aid in reading guidance. Even at first-grade level, children are beginning to develop definite interests and to ask for a "funny book" or an "animal story."

One first-grade teacher believes that her pupils' ability grows by leaps and bounds when they start taking library books home to read. Often in reading groups she will hear a child comment, "Oh, I had that word in my library book!"

The child's first successful reading experiences must be nurtured and encouraged as he progresses. This is well stated in the following report:

The first encounters that a child has with books in the elementary school exert a strong influence on his future patterns. The child who finds reading a threat and a menace rarely in later years considers books a source of enjoyment or satisfaction.

Similarly, one who derives initial feelings of success and pleasure from his first forays into this extremely difficult new learning area is apt to return again and again to books for continued satisfactions. But even the most favorable initial impression must be fostered by repetitions.[1]

Thus it is important to help the child maintain both the skill and the enthusiasm that he has acquired for reading. The summer reading program is one means of perpetuating this interest and helps to serve as an important bridge between first- and second-grade reading, or in fact between any two grades. Here is an ideal opportunity for the school and the public library to co-operate in fostering a permanent interest in books. Again the parents are an invaluable link and are anxious to be made aware of this program. Teachers feel strongly that the summer reading program not only keeps the child's interest alive but also helps the child maintain reading skills which he has acquired during the year. There is an excellent carry-over to the beginning of the new school year, and children are eager to share their summer reading experiences. Often during the school year when a book is shown, they will comment, "Oh, I read that last summer at the public library!"

READING GUIDANCE

There are many ways in which the librarian can foster and encourage reading, but perhaps one of the most commonly used methods is that of individual reading guidance. The librarian comes to know each child in the elementary school but realizes that each year finds the child

[1] Jean D. Grambs, *The Development of Lifetime Reading Habits*, p. 1. New York: National Book Committee, Inc. (24 West Fortieth Street), [1954].

in a different environment. Through the genius of each succeeding teacher, new interests may be discovered and developed. Keeping abreast of the child's interests and needs is important, and the librarian finds there is no substitute for spending time with each pupil, talking with him and learning about his interests, his reading habits, and his hobbies.

Perhaps one of the ways in which the librarian can be of most service is to be an interested listener. Children are always eager to share their triumphs and discoveries with you. It is with tremendous pride that the first-grader says, "I sounded this word out all by myself!" The librarian who finds time to share the child's enthusiasm for a book which he is returning is all the richer for this experience. Encouraging the child at this early level to talk about his books is highly desirable. As he progresses in school, his ability to communicate to others what he has read becomes of even greater importance.

In guiding children's reading, the librarian must not overlook the fact that answering a question for a child sometimes kindles a real interest in reading. The child will return again and again when he finds books that meet his needs.

The librarian also hopes to foster an interest in books through telling stories and reading aloud. Providing these experiences for children can contribute immeasurably to the reading program, for in the early primary years the child's reading ability may not keep pace with his interests. When stories are told or read aloud to them, children grow in their appreciation of our traditional folklore and of our more recent imaginative tales. The spontaneous discussion that follows the story often reveals interesting aspects of the child's thinking. As the children

progress, they are able to read many of these stories for themselves, and by the third grade they will often exclaim, "Why, this is the same story we had last year in library!"

TECHNIQUES USED IN THE CLASSROOM

There are countless ways by which the teacher can stimulate and promote an interest in books. One first-grade teacher finds that a reading record kept in the room offers a wonderful incentive in maintaining a high level of interest in books completed at home. In one instance, *Katy No-Pocket* by Payne (Houghton, 1944) inspired the idea for the reading record. A large kangaroo was designed, with many pockets instead of one. A pocket was used for each child's reading record. For every book completed, a small kangaroo was placed in the child's pocket. Soon Katy's pockets were bulging with many little kangaroos!

Another teacher has a sharing time in the room. When the children return their books from home, each child may show a favorite picture and tell his favorite part of the story. Since most children are convincing salesmen, there are often long waiting lists for certain books.

In some classrooms, library helpers are chosen each week. These children come to the library with special requests for books and materials pertaining to current projects in the classroom. This is an excellent learning experience for the children, and it provides an opportunity to teach them some of the simple library skills in finding books. Indeed, it might be considered an early step in library research.

The teacher who fosters a child's natural curiosity and instils a desire to satisfy his curiosity through the use of the library points out one of the most important concepts in library service.

IN CONCLUSION

Not only does the school library support and enrich the curriculum, but it also strives to stimulate and foster independent, individualized reading. If during these early years the child's quest for knowledge and his enjoyment of books is fostered, then we shall have helped to further a lasting interest in the world of books.

* * *

IN GRADES FOUR THROUGH SIX

ALICE E. JOHNSON

*

A VITAL part of the school librarian's job is to bridge the gap between the library and the classroom,"[1] according to Katherine F. Barnes. This responsibility involves "understanding the necessity to teach children *what* to read as well as *how* to read, and being certain that children learn to *like* to read."[2]

CHILDREN'S INTERESTS

During the middle-grade years, many interests open up for children, and books will feed these interests. Their reading during these years is as varied as it will ever be, for they are sampling and experimenting. Children may read some things that we consider trash—series books, Westerns, mysteries, comics. But they will also choose books about the lives of real people and about heroes of legend and mythology; adventure in history and fiction; sports stories; science fiction; books giving information about atoms, dinosaurs, the constellations, and hamsters; stories about animals (horses and dogs especially); and some of the old and new classics.

The child of this age level has in most instances mastered the mechanics of reading, and he wants longer stories—maybe a hundred pages or more. Girls still like fairy tales and fantasy. They are beginning to be interested in love stories and will be satisfied with so-called "junior novels" and career stories with touches of romance. They will read boys' adventure stories, but boys seldom read girls' stories. Boys of this age want adventure and mystery, science and invention, exploration and discovery.

With all this variety of interests, one might think that selecting books for this age would be no problem. Many times, however, the middle-grader is loath to tell an adult about his preferences in reading. Frequently he will return books without having read them or will brush them off with the comment that the books are too young for him. The problem is to know which book to offer to a particular child and when to offer it.

BOOKS TO SATISFY THEIR INTERESTS

Our library is, in actuality, a materials center. We do not separate our records of Paul Bunyan and Pecos Bill, our filmstrips of the Louisiana Purchase and the Lewis and Clark Expedition, our colored films of the monarch butterfly and the life of the beaver, our transcriptions of the "March of Democracy" and "Blazing

[1] Katherine F. Barnes, "Liaison—Libraries and Learning," *I.L.A. Record*, IX (April, 1956), 73. (Springfield, Illinois: Illinois Library Association.)

[2] *Loc. cit.*

the Westward Trail." When we study the American Revolution, we laugh over Robert Lawson's *Mr. Revere and I* (Little, 1953) and the adventures of Scheherazade, Paul Revere's horse. We are thrilled with Esther Forbes's *Johnny Tremain* (Houghton, 1943), who took his place with the ragged patriots and learned through personal tragedy that "a man can stand up." We look at the film-strip of "Paul Revere and the Minute Men" and listen to French-born Apollos Revere instil in his young son Paul the love of freedom. And perhaps we will be grateful to Walt Disney for giving us on television the exciting drama for thousands of American children, who will then invade their libraries to read or reread the stories that describe in permanent form what they have caught but briefly. In my estimation, competition between the different media of communication is not necessary. They can unite to inform and entertain the young viewer, the young listener, and the young reader.

In the field of nature and science and technology, we can delight the slow, the average, and the gifted middle-grade child. Recently my students of children's literature took individual topics, such as birds, trees, insects, the earth, the stars, transportation, food and clothing, and built individual bibliographies showing us the grade and interest span of recent material on these subjects. In almost every instance they chose fourth or fifth grade for their problem and found books ranging from second-grade to seventh- or eighth-grade level in difficulty. This range would appeal to all the reading ages normally encountered in a single classroom.

When a second- or third-grade pupil has absorbed the homely details of Abraham Lincoln's boyhood through the pic-ture-text of Edgar and Ingri d'Aulaire or in the pages of Genevieve Foster's initial biography, by the middle grades he will progress with real pleasure and interest to Clara Ingram Judson's fine *Abraham Lincoln, Friend of the People* (Wilcox, 1950), which is enhanced by Kodachromes of the Chicago Historical Society Lincoln dioramas. It is but a step from these to Virginia S. Eifert's *Three Rivers South* (Dodd, 1953), an account of Lincoln's young manhood, and to her equally popu-lar *The Buffalo Trace* (Dodd, 1955), which follows the path that the grand-father of Abraham Lincoln and his family took as they followed the trail of Daniel Boone to the land of promise, opportuni-ty, and heartbreak.

In recent years we have had an in-crease in the number of books teaching intergroup and intercultural relations to children. One of the most successful writing teams has been Lorraine and Jer-rold Beim, who have given us stories like *Two Is a Team* (Harcourt, 1945), which shows how unimportant skin color can be between two children who are friends. Eleanor Estes in *The Hundred Dresses* (Harcourt, 1944), Marguerite de Angeli in *Bright April* (Doubleday, 1946), and Sydney Taylor in *All-of-a-Kind-Family* (Follett, 1951) have provided stories that children love because of the plots and characterizations. Almost unconsciously they absorb the moral that is to be found there.

The last two decades have provided us with wonderful stories of children of other lands and how they have adjusted to a life disrupted by war. Mabel Leigh Hunt's *Singing among Strangers* (Lippin-cott, 1954) will help American children make a place for the displaced person in our country and in our hearts. Our task of pointing up social and moral responsibility to our children has been made easy by the fine support given us by our contemporary authors.

THE LIBRARIAN IS THE BRIDGE

Frances Clarke Sayers says that "librarians are concerned with getting children's feet across the bridge of technical ability to read to the hills beyond where the great books await them."[3] This is true because we librarians know a great deal about the technical side of children's reading. In addition, when a child comes to the library, we find out his age and his grade and that helps to classify him. We are interested in children's intelligence levels and maintain a list of their reading interests. We study their vocabulary range. And we study the curriculum too.

If you can't take the whole field of children's literature for your own, perhaps you can select one subject or one author and make that your particular bridge to children. If you can read one chapter of Tom Sawyer and tell your young readers something about Mark Twain and his boyhood experiences, you have opened a fascinating world of river lore and life in a small midwestern town. It may begin a natural bridge to the adventures of Homer Price, Eddie Wilson, Henry Huggins, and the Moffats. Reading aloud to children from your favorite volumes may start them on the path to reading for themselves. It is important to remember that we must begin at each child's level in order to broaden and enrich his tastes if he is to develop a full appreciation of literature. It is sometimes a good idea to let pupils choose the story to be read. They may be more in-

clined to trust your judgment if you have shown readiness to use one of their choices.

The librarian also plays a unique role in the reading-guidance program of the school. If the teacher and the librarian keep a cumulative record of what the child has read, the librarian has tangible evidence to work from in guiding the child upward in his reading. Obviously, the librarian cannot supervise the reading of everyone, as he must operate within the limits of his time and staff. In general, he provides a well-rounded collection of materials and stimulates interest through book talks, displays, and informal discussions. It should be possible also for the librarian to work with smaller groups from year to year: stimulate the non-reader, encourage some to read in new channels, and raise the quality and standard for others. Such a program cannot be purely informal; it requires a planned program.

Being aware of the daily teaching program of the classroom, the librarian can feature and publicize related materials. As the child proceeds on his reference assignments, he will frequently be diverted and stimulated by what he sees in the leisure corner, on the bulletin board, or in the hobby display case. Because the librarian can meet the students as individuals, he has an excellent opportunity to know their activities and interests. Often club and group activities result from the sharing of interests which have been developed through library reading. Most libraries welcome the opportunity to display the work of various clubs and the hobbies of individual students. Prize-winning pictures from the camera club, or ceramics and metal-work from the art classes, will draw students to the library

[3] Frances Clarke Sayers, "The Hills Beyond," *NEA Journal*, XLIII (December, 1954), 548.

and lead them to new interests and hobbies.

To bring children and books together, we must know today's children and today's books. Of course we want pupils to read the classics: to know "my man Friday," to roam Sherwood Forest near Nottingham Town, to drink goat's milk high in the Alps, to act out plays in the March family's barn. Today's children do read the old favorites, but they read much more because they have much wider choices. They read *Blue Willow* by Doris Gates (Viking, 1940), *Caddie Woodlawn* by Carol Brink (Macmillan, 1935), *Rabbit Hill* by Robert Lawson (Viking, 1944), *Call It Courage* by Armstrong Sperry (Macmillan, 1943), *Corn Farm Boy* by Lois Lenski (Lippincott, 1954), *The Door in the Wall* by Marguerite de Angeli (Doubleday, 1949), *Justin Morgan Had a Horse* by Marguerite Henry (Rand McNally, 1954). They read many books because teachers and librarians have demonstrated to them that reading can be fun and because we have shared with them our pleasure in these great stories, both old and new.

⁴ Annis Duff, *"Longer Flight,"* pp. 222–25. New York: Viking Press, 1955.

CONCLUDING STATEMENT

In her stimulating volume *"Longer Flight,"* which describes the delights of reading, Annis Duff says:

A librarian has it in her power to help children to find stability and serenity in their relationships with other people and with people at large. It is within the librarian's power, too, to help them to find stability and serenity within themselves. This is done gradually, and perhaps imperceptibly, from the very first time a little child is introduced to a book he can laugh at, because innocent merriment is a real source of spiritual health. All the good books that children read for pure pleasure enlarge their whole selves. . . .

I like to think of children storing away good memories of beauty seen and felt and heard and known. It is a wonderful feeling to know that one has been able to add a little treasure to the store. How rich a librarian must feel in her giving! Think of it! Every single day she puts into the hands of children, little and big, beauties of every kind, from Leslie Brooke's droll and exquisite pigs, to the less tangible and greatly enduring beauties of wise and warm and truthful books like *The Wind in the Willows* and *Twenty Years a-Growing*. In accepting such gifts children do indeed accept a universe, a limitless sphere for their own growth.⁴

✳ ✳ ✳

IN GRADES SEVEN THROUGH NINE

BLANCHE JANECEK

✳

How a school librarian fosters reading interest among boys and girls may vary from school to school. Some techniques may be universal and probably can be used effectively in any school. On the other hand, some techniques can be effective only in a particular school because of the characteristics of the school population, library program, teachers, and curriculum. This discussion will deal with techniques of the latter class: techniques of fostering reading interest which I have found to be successful in my particular school, the Laboratory School of the University of Chicago.

Our library is the study center of the

school. The seventh- and eighth-grade students ("Pre-Freshmen" we call them since Grades VII and VIII are combined) are scheduled to the library for two periods a week. The same period of the other two days is spent in science class (our classes meet four times a week). All students, Freshmen through Seniors, are scheduled to the library for one period or more every day. The library is open to students for a half-hour before school, during lunch periods, and for two hours after classes are dismissed in the afternoon.

LOCATING MATERIALS

All students are exposed to the library on a scheduled basis for five years, Pre-Freshman through Senior years. Since the library is used for curricular research, for study, and for personal reading, one of the best ways for this librarian to foster reading interest is to make materials and services available and accessible. We have found that interest soars when a student can locate materials when he needs them or wants them. Making materials easily accessible necessitates the organization of materials so that students may use these resources independently. The students should be assured that the index to the book collection, the card catalogue, is up to date and that the other resources, magazines, and pamphlets are organized for effective use. Nothing is more discouraging for young adults than not to be able to locate materials independently. Interest can be deflated if, because of snags in library organization, even the librarian cannot help the student. I have found that *availability* and *accessibility* are key words in creating interest in reading among our young people. Because our students are intellectually capable, they bring to the library the air of expecting materials to

be ready for use, and they bring to the library the attitude that it is a right, not a privilege, to use the library. With these attitudes prevailing, organizational details must be provided to meet these demands.

MAKING NEW BOOKS AVAILABLE

Our students have a natural interest in reading and have a certain degree of sophistication. Consequently the librarian must utilize subtlety in the promotion program. I have found that our students enjoy examining new books. Since materials are being purchased and processed throughout the year, there is a display of new titles practically every week. Every week is "Book Week." No new titles are placed on the library shelves until they have been displayed for one week. Thus all students and teachers have an opportunity to examine them. A reserve card is attached to the front page of each book, and, if a boy or girl would like to be sure of reading it, he may sign his name. Our student reserve requests are very numerous. This is true in relation not only to new books but also to books in circulation. When a particular book is ready, the student is notified in the library. All library communications with students are carried on in the library. Books which are waiting for students are placed on a window ledge, arranged alphabetically by students' last names and with a note in each book of the date until which the book will be held, usually a week hence.

We have found that students themselves are good promoters of books. It is habitual with many to go over to this corner window ledge to see if there is a book for them, without waiting for their notification slips. Many students observe what their peers have selected and are stimulated to read the same books. I have also noted innumerable instances in which a book recommended by the librarian to one student makes the rounds of at least a dozen friends.

The librarian in our school is the only individual who knows every student over a period of five years. With a school population of four hundred, this is possible, but several aids other than the daily contact with the students assist her. At the beginning of the school year, every teacher receives from the Records Office a confidential report, giving personal data for each new and returning student. These include the number of years he has attended our school, birth date, intelligence quotient, scores on tests administered at the end of the preceding school year, or scores on placement tests. Our entire school faculty is divided into four "Little Faculty" groups on the basis of grade level. Close contact with home-room teachers through "Little Faculty" weekly meetings helps the librarian learn about each student, especially when individual students are discussed in relation to performance in the various areas and in relation to information received in parent conferences. The more thorough the knowledge that the librarian has of the patrons, the better the guidance and motivation that can be provided for them.

Many students have specific reading interests: stories about nurses, the various periods in American history, dogs, adventure. Our students are stimulated by books in the content areas—philosophy, the social sciences, all the natural and physical sciences, history, travel, biography, and the like. However, I have found that, in spite of a particular interest which a reader may have, he is interested mainly in reading a *good book*.

Sometimes the number of books on the shelves makes selection difficult for an individual. If time allows, I find it advantageous to accompany the student to the shelves and help select books he might enjoy. Of course I am assuming that the librarian has a thorough knowledge of the books in her collection and that she reads widely, since this is the basis on which she can establish good rapport and confidence. If time and other demands do not permit a leisurely examination and discussion of books on the shelves, I usually ask permission of the student to select several books for his consideration at my first free moment. With this opportunity at hand, I include different types of books, such as fiction, biography, and plays. The student feels free to take one, all, or none.

For the age group we are considering I have found that biography is an excellent bridge between books specifically written for adolescents and books written for adults. For those interested in adult books, a collection of at least twenty-five books is always available on two display racks for their consideration. The display provides an opportunity for the librarian to promote books which should be in the reading background of all our students but which might be missed by students themselves. No big sign identifies this collection. There is only a typewritten card in front of the book racks, which reads: "Here are some interesting adult books. Take one or as many as you like." Subtlety has been employed here. This collection does not stand out in the library as being special. If it appeared as special, our teen-agers might shy away from it. Some of our students are always ready for short adult books, and I always include one or two in my suggestions to the twelve- to fourteen-year-old group.

Such books as George Orwell's *Animal Farm* (Harcourt, 1946), Conrad Richter's *Light in the Forest* (Knopf, 1953), Ernest Hemingway's *The Old Man and the Sea* (Scribner, 1952), and Kathryn Forbes's *Mama's Bank Account* (Harcourt, 1943) are among thoese which can be suggested confidently.

CO-OPERATING WITH STUDENTS AND TEACHERS

Informing teachers and students of the library's new accessions is another important way to foster reading interest. Although the books have been displayed, periodic lists of these titles help further. Each teacher in the school receives a list, and any student who wishes may have a copy. These lists give a total picture of how the collection is growing.

Working with teachers in curricular areas is still another way of promoting interest. The more the library collection gives body and substance to the curriculum, the greater will be the excitement and enthusiasm when students find appropriate materials in the library in relation to curricular demands. The more a teacher knows about the library and resources, the greater will be its use. A librarian can do much to interest young people, but a teacher can do that and more too. How many times has a boy or girl come into the library excited because a book title was suggested in class and he could hardly wait to get it! And how many times has interest been created in an area heretofore unknown to a student just because a teacher had introduced it or had mentioned it in class! Relations between teachers and librarian must be cordial, informal, and co-operative, in order that the maximum use will be made of existing facilities.

Soliciting recommendations and suggestions for library materials is another important way to foster interest. Many of our students are better read in some content areas than is their librarian, and their suggestions are always welcome. We have noticed that, in general, if things are acceptable in the library, few comments are made. On the other hand, if the opposite is true, we hear about it. Last year it was necessary to curtail the magazine budget slightly, and we canceled *Sport, Mechanix Illustrated,* and *Furniture Forum.* When the students noticed that these magazine titles stopped coming, the librarian received petitions recommending their reinstatement. This was done, the first two being purchased at newsstands with our "fine money," and the last being obtained through subscription. If, among the 110 magazine titles, the loss of three provided such gaps and student interest was roused to the point of petitioning, these interests needed to be met by the librarian. These magazines will again be included in our annual magazine order.

Our students are magazine-readers as well as book-readers. Magazines are realistically important in the reading program of young people and of adults, too. Our students recognize that much of what is in magazines is not available in books and that both books and magazines must have vital places in any library collection. A monthly selection of ten outstanding magazine articles, selected by a council of librarians (Mayfair Agency, Englewood, New Jersey), is always displayed for interest or guidance. Our magazine collection is used heavily for curricular research and for personal investigation. For approximately sixty titles we have a ten-year collection available. Interest is increased when these young people can get material no matter how current is their subject choice. Seventh- and eighth-graders, sixth-graders, too, can use *Readers Guide to Periodical Literature* effectively if the library has the magazines.

Bulletin-board displays are also used to foster interest. These are prepared so that there will be correlation with a curricular area or school activity. Bulletin-board displays must be informative and attractive. They add another method for interesting library patrons.

CONCLUDING STATEMENT

These are some of the ways in which reading interest can be fostered in our school. Book talks, summer reading lists for individual students, book lists prepared with teachers for their students, book fairs, and other obvious methods utilized by all librarians have not been mentioned. Any techniques for interesting young people in reading that are appropriately related to the characteristics of the school population, teachers, curriculum, and librarian, should be used.

✳ ✳ ✳

IN GRADES TEN THROUGH FOURTEEN

MARY FRANCES McMANUS

✳

FOSTERING the reading interests of our busy young people is one of the most challenging, but rewarding, of the school and public librarians' tasks. To reach this group of young moderns in senior high school and junior college requires the acumen of a successful advertising man, the subtlety of an expert in psychology, the sense of humor of a TV star, the modernity of a disk jockey, the know-how of a teacher, the warmness of a friend, and the understanding and patience of a parent.

ROOM ATMOSPHERE

Public libraries have demonstrated their awareness of the adolescent readers by hiring librarians who devote their time to working with this group. Special rooms, alcoves, even an entire building— the Nathan Straus Branch of the New York Public Library—have been given over to the housing of book collections suited especially to the needs and interests of the teen-ager.

A new look in high-school libraries has been gradually appearing. Browsing corners and listening stations for the enjoyment of records are breaking the monotony of formalized rows of tables and chairs. Colorful draperies, new warm colors in paint, and lighter wood in furniture have made rooms more attractive and inviting so that students will like to come there for quiet study and leisure reading.

SELECTION OF MATERIALS

In addition to the general atmosphere of the library room itself, it is important to have a carefully selected book collection. The wide variety of interests and abilities of these students provides an almost frustrating challenge to the librarian trying to find the right books for all. Care must be taken so that the materials selected will meet the interests of the students, not those of the teachers or librarians.

A student committee to aid in the selection is a device that many librarians are using. In one Chicago school a committee from the student council is responsible for making suggestions for the fiction books which are to be selected for the annual book order. The librarian provides the committee with current book lists and reviews. Another plan is to have a committee from an English class compile a list of leisure-time books which they would like the library to purchase. Student library assistants also enjoy making suggestions. Through using such student groups, the librarian fosters an interest in reading by providing them with information about new books being published, an awareness that the library wishes to purchase books which they will enjoy, and an advance guard of advertisers who can promote the books with their friends.

A new source of books which will interest young people are the paper-bound books. Many school librarians have purchased these books, either as duplicates for books on their shelves, or as a means of attracting reluctant readers. It has not been surprising to find that a title of Dickens will circulate in the paperback edition, while its more sturdy brother will remain on the shelf. A display rack can make these books readily available for the boy or girl who is always in a hurry. Such a display also helps to make the library a more familiar place to the teen-ager. Once enticed into the room, he may find other things to his liking.

PUBLICIZING THE MATERIALS

Making books as attractive as possible is important in fostering their use. The use of plastic jackets to cover the publishers' dust jackets has sold many a book in school libraries. Covering drab books with a wallpaper jacket, then by the plastic jacket, has also helped in promoting the circulation of many of the standard and classic books.

Publicizing books around the school, as well as in the library, is an important means of fostering interest. A boy or girl is not likely to show interest in something about which he or she is not aware. While bulletin boards have always been an important means of publicity, they cannot do the job effectively if confined to the library proper. Therefore librarians have been using corridor boards and display cases and have been supplying classroom teachers with materials for their bulletin boards. It may just be a picture, a slogan, or a book jacket which will attract a student to the library. A traveling bulletin board can be set up in a corridor, moved to a study hall or a classroom, and then returned to the library. Special school events, such as the "prom," football season, and the music festival, are used as themes to promote a wider interest in books.

The school newspaper is another important source for news about books. A book-chatter column is often effective. Student reviews of their choices of popular titles will often insure a steady demand for the books reviewed. One school librarian, using information from the circulation files, worked with a reporter from the school newspaper on a "gossip" column about the students' selection of books. Such items as, "Is Carol Jones of Division 201 anticipating a date for the 'prom' in reading *Cues for You?*" or "Has Bill Jones of 302 reserved his place for a trip to the moon now that he has read *Rocket to the Moon?*" created quite a stir of interest in the library and its books.

"Book Week," of course, always provides an opportunity for wide publicizing of books and reading. The librarian usually is active in putting on special assemblies at this time. Student participation in preparing for such assemblies often furnishes a spark for a greater interest in reading by the participants. A musical about books, which was written and produced by the library student assistants in one of our Chicago high schools, created a warm and enthusiastic interest in the library and its wares.

Perhaps one of the most interesting things that school librarians are doing today is the gradual removal of many of the rules and regulations which tended to restrict rather than encourage wide reading. One library I know of has even abolished a specified loan period. Students return their books when they are finished. The personality of this librarian and her knowledge of her student body have made this a workable idea in her school. I cite it as an example of a trend in school libraries to adapt more and more to the needs of the specific school of which it is a part even though adaptation may mean wide deviation from what has been accepted as general practice. Interestingly enough, in many schools where the librarian has tried experimentation, it has been fellow-teachers and administrators who have been alarmed about the possible outcomes. I would not wish to give the impression that all rules and regulations about the use of library materials are being abandoned. However, a careful and considerate appraisal of these rules is being made, and many of these artificial obstacles in the way of the students' ready access to books are being withdrawn.

READING GUIDANCE

Creating a pleasant, inviting atmosphere to introduce students to books, carefully selecting the books themselves, and publicizing them to the students are all very important. But reading guidance by the librarian is the most effective means for fostering interest in reading. Everything that has been discussed so far would, of course, play a part in reading guidance. However, reading guidance is carried on specifically through group activities and through contact with individual students.

Group guidance is carried on in many ways. The librarian introduces students to many and varied books through book talks given in the individual classrooms. These book talks may be built around a discussion of books which develop a theme or may present a brief review of a new title. The librarian often brings along a book truck, on which there is a selection of books related to the topic of the talk, and circulates the books from the truck. Book talks by the librarian are not confined to the English classrooms but are given in the social-studies classrooms, the science classrooms, shop classes—in fact, in any department of the school.

On the other hand, one librarian felt that perhaps some potential readers were being lost because books were being too closely associated with class work. She began visiting the home rooms, where she could introduce books a little more informally. Reading for fun and as a leisure-time activity was stressed. Too often, in the stress placed on reading for class work, a boy or girl in senior high school or junior college loses his zest for what was once an absorbing hobby and habit. Since in many schools the librarian cannot visit all the home rooms as often as he would like, student representatives of the library or a home-room visiting committee from the student library staff may be sent to each home room. These students present new books to their fellow-students and bring news of library activities.

Teen-agers like to talk. To channel this activity into worth-while purposes, the school librarian often sponsors book forums or book clubs. Some have carried on a modified "Great Books" discussion group.

Another librarian sends a letter to each graduating Senior, in which she discusses the importance of reading even after he leaves school. She also reminds him that the public library can supply many books throughout his adult life which will help in his future occupation, keep him posted on current events, or fill his many hours of leisure time.

Probably the most satisfying of all activities are those in which the librarian makes personal contact with individual students. A certain rapport exists between the student and this special teacher, who requires nothing from him except an interest in books and reading. This lends itself to free and open discussion of the student's interests and ambitions. The student likes to discuss what he has read and enjoys being helped along to new horizons through the magic of books. To be effective, the librarian must know books and have a knowledge and understanding of the adolescent. Working closely with the school's guidance department, the librarian can, and should, help students develop reading habits which help them in solving some of their personal, social, and educational problems. Finding the right book for the right child at the right time is still the goal of the school librarian working with the young people of today. The informal guidance is carried on quietly, sincerely, and effectively each day.

WORKING WITH TEACHERS

Working on curriculum committees, at departmental meetings, and through informal contacts with fellow-teachers, the school librarian is constantly striving to foster interest in reading. He wants to know what the needs of the students are as seen by others. He is ever anxious to locate materials which will meet the curricular needs of teachers and students. Once the books arrive, he will endeavor to have them in the hands of the students as quickly as possible.

The school librarian also works closely with his library associate in the public library. He keeps the latter informed of the needs of the students in meeting library assignments. He publicizes public library programs and activities of interest to young people.

CONCLUDING COMMENT

To foster an interest in reading, the school librarian does all he can to create a warm, friendly room where the young people will like to come. He carefully selects materials which will meet the needs, the interests, and the abilities of the slow and the reluctant as well as the superior student soaring into adulthood. Working with groups of students, he guides and encourages the widest horizons of reading. Using the library and its materials as a compass, he plots the course for individual students who come for help. He co-operates and works closely with fellow-teachers and librarians. In short, all his efforts, his plans, his hopes, his dreams are directed toward fostering a deep and abiding interest in books and in reading.

CHAPTER XVI

JOHNNY WILL READ WHAT HE LIKES TO READ*

✳

CHARLES G. SPIEGLER

✳

OF ALL the indictments lodged against the public schools in recent years, the most stinging is the charge, "Johnny can't read." The bill of particulars is alarming. Johnny, we are told, hates reading. He sits for hours glued to a television set. He wallows in comics because pictures communicate more to him than words. He stumbles over simple sounds; he can't spell; he's illiterate. But, continues the indictment, the fault is not Johnny's. Modern teaching methods are to blame. We have discarded the good, old-fashioned alphabet and phonic approach to reading and have adopted instead the suspect "word-recognition" method. By stressing interest and readiness rather than drill, we have turned out a generation of reading cripples—confused, indifferent children who doggedly shy away from the printed word.

I deny the allegation. I deny it wholeheartedly. As one who has worked with young people for a quarter of a century, as present chairman of the English department in a New York City vocational high school, I maintain that Johnny *can* read, that he *does* read, that he is in fact reading *more* and *better* than ever. I maintain that the indictment, though it may have slivers of surface truth, is false at the core. Today's teaching methods, far from stifling Johnny's interest in books,

have stimulated it to an unprecedented high by adopting the one principle of all learning—by making reading *meaningful*, by making it *fun!*

Talk to publishers and librarians, and you'll learn that there are now 120,000 outlets for children's books, where there were but 800 a few years back. The largest book club in America is the Teen Age Book Club, with 850,000 members in 17,000 school clubs. According to a national survey, children borrow more than half of all the public library books circulated. Madison, Wisconsin, alone reports 426,215 books borrowed in one year.

Are there slow readers? Of course. There always have been slow readers—and nonreaders. Not every child is "book-minded." Tony Cipolla, who "never read a book," may be a whiz in shopwork. Fully 15 per cent of our children can't read, says the indictment. Statistics like this are misleading. Compulsory-education laws have filled our classrooms with the greatest cross-section of American youth ever assembled, thirty million strong—the dull along with the bright, the neurotic along with the wholesome, the interested along with the bored. In the past the laggards would have dropped out of school. Out of half a million children who began in New York City's ele-

* Courtesy *Parents' Magazine.*

mentary schools in 1900, only fourteen thousand survived until graduation. And not all of these went further. School was for bright children, not for the "dunce" who couldn't read. Him we sent to the corner until he despaired, quit in the fifth or sixth grade, and got lost. The "dunce" is no more; today he's a "slow learner." He stands in no corner, and we do our best to teach him. The former "drop-out" is now often a "poor reader" statistic.

By and large, today's youngster is reading. He is reading because he *likes* to. And the key to what he likes is *interest.* As Professor Arthur Gates put it to me recently, "The mechanics we teach are but the springs and spindles in a lock. Only interest will turn that lock and open the door to the world of fun, information, escape, and wonder that reading can be." Give Johnny a title, a book jacket, a theme that rings true. Talk to him colorfully about the world of books. Don't limit him to the confines of prescribed book lists and prescribed formulas for making book reports. Let the world and its infinite wonders be the subjects he may choose from. Let him read what he likes, appeal to his interests—and Johnny reads.

Come to my vocational school in lower New York to see what I mean. Here are nine hundred nonacademic students—all preparing to become butchers, bakers, and cooks—whose major cultural interests are boxing, the movies, baseball, and television. Their reading, you might think, would be confined to the movie magazines, comics, the sports page, the screaming headlines of the tabloid.

Yet sit in our book room, especially on a Friday afternoon at three. Listen to the dismissal gong, and watch the door thrown open a few seconds later as hordes of students descend on shelves appropri-

ately labeled "The Sea," "Sports," "Science Fiction," "Teen-Ager."

Come into my office. Look at some of the book reports on these books. "From start to finish," writes Tony Smathers of *Custer's Last Stand* (Random, 1951), "I was in suspense. I thought I was riding beside the hero, seeking adventure, and had found them all in a book." Sixteen-year-old Lila Schwartz enjoyed *Seventeenth Summer* (Dodd, 1942) because "this was *my* life I was reading about, my own boy friend, and the part where they sit and talk in the ice-cream parlor—that's us."

Yet only a year ago, when I first became chairman, many of these youngsters were not dreaming but *sleeping* over their books. I saw them in classes, heads on desks and eyes shut, while a teacher droned through *Idylls of the King* or drained old *Silas Marner* dry. Acceptable for the classroom a generation back, when the majority of students were college-bound, these were sleeping pills for vocation-bound youngsters. Book reports posed questions like, "Where was the climax?" "What was the denouement?" Few cared. Most weren't reading, and teachers had thrown in the sponge, "They *can't* read!" I believed they could —and would if only we gave them the books which could respond to their nature, attract their eye, help them dream!

When we inaugurated a three-day book fair, displaying two thousand books dressed in jolly jackets and written on hundreds of lively subjects I was sure youngsters liked, there was a shaking of heads among some members of the faculty. "I'll bet you won't sell a hundred books," one asserted smugly. "All these kids want is comics and girlie books. They won't buy anything decent!"

But they did. For three days, while

English classes were canceled, children browsed, read at random, bought or not as fancy struck them. And when the fair was over, we knew that these were the three days that shook our smug little world. Johnny, who would buy "only comics and girlie books," had dug into his weekly allowance and his after-school-odd-job savings to take home 1,123 good books. Granted, Bill Stern's *My Favorite Sports Stories* (MacDavis Features, 1946) and *The Real Story of Lucille Ball* (Ballantine) were best sellers, but not far behind were *The Burl Ives Song Book* (Ballantine), *Red Pony* (Viking, 1945), and books of science fiction. And higher than anyone dared predict were *The Cruel Sea* (Knopf, 1951), *Mutiny on the Bounty* (Little, 1932), and *Jane Eyre*. A terrific jam developed around the "Romance" table. *Huckleberry Finn*'s spectacular sale necessitated a rush call to the publisher (Pocket Books) for "fifty more."

Though no teachers were panting down the students' necks to "Read this!" they did guide student choice. Some, like the big, broad-shouldered lad who was about to buy *The Scarlet Letter* (Pocket Books), because he thought it was a football story, needed the guidance. Others passed by the proffered help, however, and bought many books with vocabulary somewhat beyond their level. It didn't matter. Interest, George Norvell, former New York State supervisor of English, has said, leaps over all reading barriers, including vocabulary.

Johnny wasn't sleeping through "Lit" class by now. We relegated *Idylls of the King* to a basement storeroom and gave the youngsters livelier fare. Booker T. Washington in his struggles for an education became a far more genuine superman to them than the comic-book man with wings.

By the end of the year, the majority of our nine hundred students were reading at least a book a month. Many were doing far better. Library circulation had gone from six hundred to fifteen hundred.

Neither "climax" nor "denouement" cluttered up book reports now. As make-believe salesmen, kid critics, Hollywood producers, television panelists, they reported in terms they knew. "I like," "I love," "I hate," "I get mad," it's "great," "exciting," "heartwarming"—indicated how books were felt. "I love that book because it suits my taste," wrote Johnny Gallardo about *Lives of a Bengal Lancer* (Viking, 1930). "I have a wild taste." For Stanley Cahn, a sixteen-year-old high-school Senior, the serious is his regular reading fare. He likes "books that disturb me . . . make me think" so much that he actually enjoyed *The Snake Pit* (Random, 1946) because it opened up the world of the subconscious to him.

Talk to teachers, librarians, and booksellers throughout the country, and what happened in one New York school proves to be part of a nationwide swing, among young people, to books.

Talk to children, as I have, when they're browsing in public library reading-rooms, and note how they tie their reading to their current hobbies, their expanding worlds. Visit the Riverside Branch of the New York Public Library, for example, one afternoon from 3 to 6 P.M.; by six o'clock, 213 books have left the shelves. There are 26 spaces now where the vividly written, well-illustrated lives of Ralph Bunche, Tom Jefferson, George Gershwin, Alexander Bell, Louis Braille, and Ben Franklin were standing under "Biography."

I check with Mrs. Garson, the librarian, after the youngsters have left. "Circulation has increased in the past five years," she tells me, "even though hundreds of our good readers during that period have moved to other communities." For the year July, 1950, through June, 1951, the number of books circulated was 27,373. In the year 1952–53 it was 33,000. In the year 1954–55 it rose to 44,316. We talk about television, and she shows me the reserve cards for *Robin Hood, Alice in Wonderland, Peter Pan*—all spoken for following television productions.

As a matter of fact, television, wisely used, is a book's best friend. A survey by Professor Paul Witty, of Northwestern University, points to a decrease in home reading only until the fascination and the novelty of the "TV toy" wears off; then a strong return to books. Where, on the other hand, parents establish their right to sit side by side with Johnny and watch while a Raymond Massey, a Helen Hayes, or a Burgess Meredith dramatizes Huck Finn or reads from Heywood Broun's "51st Dragon," television brings about such phenomena as six thousand written requests for a book list offered on one Ford Foundation show.

Beyond a doubt, Johnny reads if his interest is stirred, and, beyond a doubt too, Johnny can best be taught *reading* if interest is the keynote. "Teach him the sounds and the letters first," says one group. "Give him phonics from the start." We *did* just that in the old days, and Johnny often mastered the skill at the same time he lost the joy in using that skill. It made for a generation of good "train announcers" but not happy readers.[1]

Today Johnny learns to read the while he develops the *desire* to read. No modern, first-grade reading teacher insists

[1] Emmett A. Betts, "What about Phonics?" *Education*, LXXV (May, 1955), 557.

on teaching the alphabet until Johnny has first heard the lovely melody that words are. Once introduced to the beauty of the spoken word, Johnny must, to read, learn that the word has a face as well as a melody. And the first faces he learns how to recognize are those that have meaning to him—his own name, for example, pasted on top of his cubbyhole; the names of some classmates. If a boy has brought a frog to school and the children have played with and loved the frog, the word *frog* appearing in sentences on the blackboard is a word they will learn; similarly, *rain* on a rainy day, or *steam* if a radiator has begun to sizzle. Phonics—the analyzing of words by phonetic sounds—is an inevitable part of the learning process, not an end in itself.

Having faith that where there's life, there's interest, we catch the interest by the toe and never, never let it go. Even with the slowest readers, the skilful teacher makes interest the bridge. Frankie Smolen was branded by a teacher's note on his record: "Won't read . . . clinic case?" Nothing in his intelligence or reading scores indicated clinic treatment. Yet the record gave a clue to the one real love Frankie had. Hamsters! "What are your hobbies?" "Hamsters," he had written. "Your favorite recreation?" "Hamsters."

The hamster, not the clinic, was the bridge Frankie was to build from the non-reader island he had lived on to the land of books. It began with *Home Made Zoo* (McKay, 1952) and its delightful chapter on hamsters, so detailed it even told how to ease a hamster's toothache. His curiosity about animal books now whetted, Frankie came upon *Call of the Wild*, practically cornered the London market in his school library, and at last report was reading Irving Stone's *Sailor on Horse-*

back (Houghton, 1938), a biography of Jack London. For one upstate teacher the comic book becomes such a bridge. She allows a blood-and-thunder comic for the first book report, if Johnny will try *Three Musketeers* for his second; or *Tarzan* for a first, if he'll try Kipling's *Jungle Book* for a second. In her upper grades she allows the children to read the comic version first. Then as *detectives* they are asked to search for what the original had and the comic omitted. In short order the bridge is crossed, the comics discarded, and the depth and the beauty of the "real" take hold.

The road to reading is no royal road. It is as different for each American youngster as is the rainbow range of interests he develops at home, in school, in life. Yet most authorities agree that, whatever the path Johnny travels, if we but give him a fair start at home, if parents share with him the hundreds of fine books which the "Golden Age of Writing-for-Children" has produced, and bring him, thus delighted with pictures and words, into kindergarten and the first grade; if we there let him talk, draw, and see words (about the raindrops that drip on a windowpane, or the kitten that purrs in a basket, or the thousand and one experiences which his brand new world is daily revealing) until he is ready, nay aching, to read about these himself; if we can but keep alive this interest through the grades and high school by exposing him to books that absorb him, and to teachers and librarians who understand why; if we will but give him the sporting chance to read what he likes—Johnny reads.

CHAPTER XVII

ADMINISTRATIVE PROCEDURES IN DEVELOPING
READING INTERESTS

✱

HOW CAN ADMINISTRATORS AID THE STAFF IN DEVELOPING
OBJECTIVES RELATING TO READING INTERESTS?

C. H. PYGMAN

✱

SINCE administrators and supervisors are educational leaders, we might begin this discussion by asking ourselves this question, "Are the children who are depending on *us* learning to read effectively?" Certainly this question must have arisen frequently in our minds because of our responsibility for the education of children and especially because of the current criticism of the public schools. Since administrators and supervisors do not work directly with children, our contributions must be made through the classroom teacher. What kind of program can we set up to do this effectively?

The program can be built on the basis of our own hunches, which are unsatisfactory. It can be built on suggestions coming from the instructional staff, and this can be an adequate approach. But, sooner or later we shall probably ask, "Does it add up?" As we look back on our educational activities, do we see a logically organized design or a patchwork of institutes, workshops, and an endless series of faculty meetings with very little improvement being shown?

In part the answer is to be found in the co-operation of the people involved: the classroom teacher, the principal, the reading consultant, and the superintendent. These people must formulate an effective working team before the maximum benefits can be derived from the services of any one of them. Each has his own strengths and limitations.

If the superintendent becomes involved with purely administrative duties —budgeting, building problems, board meetings, and the like—he soon loses touch with the team. In his busy day he must find time to study curriculum, to meet with teachers, supervisors, and principals and be aware of the problems they face. His teammates must be made to feel that he is interested in learning situations as well as in the business operation of the school. He must assume responsibility for providing proper materials. He must exert every effort to provide for the proper pupil load. He must pave the way for principals, supervisors, and the reading consultant to attain the maximum in supervision.

Time must be spent in arriving at a common philosophy, to which all team members can subscribe. After this is done, necessary changes must be made to make it possible for teachers to follow this phi- losophy. Active participation by all mem- bers of the team is required to produce change. Too often no progress is made after the statement of philosophy is for- mulated; only lip service is given. We glibly state our beliefs and do not venture to look further to see if these beliefs are being implemented. Educators are in- clined to be long on talk and theory but short in the actual doing. Meetings may be held, lengthy bulletins may be writ- ten, bulky outlines of courses may be made up—to all of which we often point with pride—but none of them will be of value unless they affect the actual teaching.

THE KEY PERSON IS THE TEACHER

It is all too easy for administrators and supervisors to sit in a comfortable office —surrounded by books and papers, no- body to oppose an idea, nobody to argue a point—and write bulletins, courses of study, and directions. This is easy, too easy. What about the teacher who is struggling to weld forty-odd personalities into one working group? What about the difficulties with the child who won't be welded, or the one who can't be directed? And all the others in their varying de- grees of ability and background?

The key person in the school is the teacher, not the superintendent, not the board member, not the principal, not the reading consultant. In organizing any educational scheme, thought must be given to the teacher. How will he do this work? Has he the time, the material, the equipment, the place for the work that is necessary in the performance of the as- signed task? Too often, not enough thought is given to the actual perform- ance of the duties prescribed.

Teachers are usually willing workers and are usually well prepared for their profession. What they need is enlightened leadership in details of classroom per- formance. There must be someone whose duty it is to provide the right conditions for the teaching service. The leadership and the supervision should not stop at the classroom door. The real work, the functioning of the costly school systems of this country, goes on in the classroom between teacher and pupils. Consider the teacher first, and all the rest will follow.

WHAT KIND OF HELP DO TEACHERS EXPECT OF US?

Teachers expect help in improving their methods of instruction. Technical skill is essential to success in any profession. It is the one characteristic which distin- guishes the professional worker from the amateur. Poor teaching can be improved. Good teaching can be made better. But these results come only when the administrator shows concern for what goes on in the classroom. This means that administrators and supervisors must know curriculum—its content, its phi- losophy, and its methods.

Teachers need help in their efforts to know the pupil as an individual. In-serv- ice education for teachers must do more than emphasize improvement in the techniques of teaching. The how alone (methods to be employed) is not suffi- cient. In-service education must be con- cerned with the what and the why of the school program. The teacher must be helped to know the pupil's environment in terms of its economic, racial, and reli- gious complexities. Why does the pupil behave as he does? What is to be taught? Social insight on the part of the teacher is no less significant than acceptable teaching techniques. Without social com- petence of a high order, instruction will become stereotyped and lacking in vitality.

Teachers need help in evaluating their own work. They need help in seeing the relation of their particular work to the entire school curriculum. They need help in developing good conference techniques with parents. They need help in utilizing the community as a resource in teaching.

OBJECTIVES RELATED TO READING INTERESTS

In setting up objectives to promote reading interests, emphasis should be placed on developing and maintaining an active participation by all members of the staff. As each objective is determined, we should ask ourselves, "What are the requisites to achieve this goal?" We must remember that creating an interest in reading for all pupils is a gradual process, requiring time and continuous encouragement.

Some of the many objectives we may need to consider follow:

1. *Readiness.*—Teachers need to comprehend the meaning of readiness and what it involves, to understand that it is the development of a general mental and physical preparedness for reading. They need to know the activities and techniques required for this period, what activities may be carried out in the kindergarten and in the first grade, activities that will create an interest in reading. They need, also, to know the signs that will indicate when a child is ready to read.

2. *Attention to skills.*—What are the skills and abilities to be developed in learning to read? How are they to be taught? There must be an awareness that these skills are only a means to an end. Hence we must ask, "How can

they be taught in such a manner as to create and maintain an interest in reading?"

3. *Growth gradients.*—All people connected with the reading program must understand that, as children grow in any area of development, so do they grow in reading. Development in walking, for example, is a sequential process; each gradient of growth leads into the next, just as it does in reading. What are these steps? What comprise these levels? What satisfactions can the child gain to interest him in reading?

4. *Individual differences.*—We must do more than pay lip service to the concept of individual differences as they relate to the reading program. In reading, as with general growth, each child follows his own pace in moving along the reading-growth spiral. What does this mean? How will the teacher meet these needs? The problem cannot be solved by retreating to the traditional pattern of wholesale teaching. Nothing can more quickly deaden a child's interest in reading than to give him work at which he cannot achieve.

5. *Relation of reading to other language arts.*—Reading is related to writing, speaking, and listening. Reading is only one area of language. Reading lends to, and receives support from, each of the other areas.

6. *Needs of gifted children.*—More attention must be given to the reading needs of gifted children. The gifted child may not have reading problems, but he does have reading needs. What are these needs? How can they be met? What materials are necessary? How may libraries be utilized? What activities can be utilized to maintain interest?

7. *Development of skills.*—Attention must be given to the development of reading and study skills as they relate to each content area. What are the techniques to be used in reaching this objective? What are the skills needed—in map-reading, for example, in interpreting graphs, in getting meaning from the printed page in social studies?

8. *Culminating objectives.*—Certainly the culminating objective must be to see that growth in reading power is significant only insofar as it enables the child to enrich his experiences and to grow personally and socially. Reading has attained its highest purposes when the use of his power and skill in reading leads the child to new interests.

Reading must come alive for the child. It must be a medium through which he experiences the moods and emotions of the characters in the story; through which he creates vivid sensory images of sight, sound, movement, touch, and smell; through which he can formulate guiding principles that he uses in his own life. In this manner the child is not only taught to read, but also, through reading, taught to live.

After objectives such as these are set up by a staff, after they are carefully written down and distributed, the real work begins. Are we naïve enough to assume that, because they have been written down and are in the hands of every member of the team, they will be reached? Are we satisfied with the results?

CONCLUDING STATEMENT

In implementing objectives with teachers, we must realistically face the many limitations involved, such as class size, half-time sessions, mobile population, and inadequately trained teachers. Too often our objectives are reduced to the level of "hopes" or "wishful thinking."

The real danger is not so much the existence of these limitations as it is that they become the basis of rationalizing our lack of progress. In spite of limitations, we must keep before us clearly defined goals and the determination to work toward them under the most adverse circumstances.

✳ ✳ ✳

HOW CAN ADMINISTRATORS DETERMINE THE EXTENT OF CHILDREN'S PERSONAL READING AND THEIR INTERESTS?

MERLE M. KAUFFMAN

✳

PERSONAL reading, done spontaneously and without direction from others, is a response to interest. The interest in question may be merely a passing fancy, or it may be deep and abiding. However, ephemeral interest may turn into a more permanent one if the reading done in its pursuit proves to be challenging and informative. It is apparent, therefore, that examination of personal reading habits will help to identify interests and that a knowledge of needs and interests will in turn make it possible to provide materials which will encourage young people to read "on their own."

Children have many interests, which

are as varied and diverse as their physiological and psychological compositions dictate. Reading interests, therefore, comprise only one constellation in the total galaxy, and the procedures used to identify them will differ little from procedures used to identify desires, wants, and needs in general. It can be argued that so personal a concern will be difficult to isolate, and yet it must be admitted that a reading interest should be no more difficult to identify than any other attribute.

The responsibility of the particular administrative officer concerned with the search for reading interests will be to organize, co-ordinate, and direct the efforts of all in order to arrive at a usable conclusion. Such a study will, to some degree, involve all school personnel who come into contact with children. The procedures finally agreed upon must be adapted to a particular group of individuals, since the same practices are not necessarily valid for pupils from different age groups, pupils with different mental ages, pupils who are operating on different achievement levels, and so on.

It will be the purpose below to discuss briefly useful methods of surveying interests.

THE QUESTIONNAIRE

The questionnaire is a long-favored instrument for securing information of many kinds. It is the quickest and the easiest way to inventory a large group of individuals. Its use is limited to those who can understand the instrument well enough to make the appropriate mark in the proper place. Its validity is affected by the appropriateness of the items included for the individuals polled.

A number of inventories designed for particular purposes are available to the general public. The Ohio Interest Inventory (Ohio State Department of Education) is intended to discover special areas of interest. Children are to select their choices from a check list of 360 items, placed in groups of five. A second example, the Thorpe, Meyers, and Sea Inventory, "What I Like To Do" (Science Research Associates) is directed toward areas of interest that have particular value for school personnel. Among these are such areas as favorite school subjects, type of games preferred, and shop and household-arts interests. Both of these instruments are intended for use with children in the intermediate grades and beyond. A third instrument, the Kuder Preference Record (Science Research Associates), is intended to point out areas of vocational interest and has had general use in the junior and senior high schools for many years. For other published inventories, consult Buros,[1] where a very complete listing and evaluation of tests of many kinds currently on the market is provided.

Questionnaires of the type mentioned above usually employ direct, undisguised items. Valid results, therefore, depend upon proper rapport between teacher and pupil. There is always the inclination to check items that will make a good impression or to express defiance through the opposite procedure, and dull children mark items without understanding their significance. Also, it may not be possible to find a ready-made inventory that provides the particular information desired.

If it is felt that an original inventory will best serve the purpose at hand, certain principles should be kept in mind. First, the purpose of the study should be defined so that the inventory will contain

[1] Oscar Krisen Buros, *The Fourth Mental Measurements Yearbook*. Highland Park, New Jersey: Gryphon Press, 1953.

all needed items. In some instances the inclusion of a number of nonpertinent items might help insure good responses on all. Second, all items must be within the limit of understanding of the respondents. Vocabulary, spelling, sentence structure, paragraphs, and so on, must be at the proper level so that those completing the inventory can do so accurately. Primary-grade scales can be devised with pictures, and responses can be marked following teacher presentation of each item. Third, items will preferably be of the open-ended or completion type, in order not to inhibit responses. Check lists can be satisfactory for some purposes but wholly inadequate for others. Fourth, eliminate any items that are not absolutely clear as to meaning. Ambiguity will invalidate any inventory. Fifth, set up the items and the total questionnaire so that summaries can be developed quickly and accurately. This can best be done while the instrument is being constructed. Sixth, assure respondents that confidential information will be treated as such—and make provisions for such treatment. Establishing rapport is almost impossible under any other circumstance. Finally, arrange for a trial run of the inventory. This will possibly bring out any imperfections before extensive usage. It will also enable the staff to set up tabulating procedures so that final summaries can be developed quickly.

A questionnaire should not be carelessly administered. The inventory should be thoroughly discussed with the respondents, and every effort made to secure their co-operation in giving honest replies. Show children how the outcomes of the study will be of help to them. Emphasize that the results do not affect their class scores and that there will be no time

limit. If some of the items are personal in nature, assure them that replies will be treated in confidence and ask that they not write their name anywhere on the inventory. If group data are not sufficient, the papers can be coded either by number or symbol, and a copy of the class roll then keyed so that individuals can later be identified for purposes of the study. Betrayal of confidence secured in this manner is unthinkable and must not be tolerated.

Summarizing the data from a large number of inventories can be a tremendous task unless some mechanical means is used. A check list readily lends itself to the employment of mechanical equipment for scoring. A flexible system is needed when open-ended, or free-choice, items are used. In such an inventory, responses will vary greatly in nature, quality, and quantity. They can readily be tabulated, however, by setting up categories for each item.

OBSERVATION

Personal reading, a response to interest, can be observed. To make a complete record and analysis of all a child reads, however, requires the co-operation of many persons.

Within the classroom the teacher is most favorably situated for this purpose. At the secondary-school level this would include both home-room and study-hall teachers. The chart, in many forms, upon which children record the books read is a familiar sight in the primary grades. At other levels, teachers have devised many schemes—from gold stars to book reports —for keeping a similar account. Direct observation of free reading within the room is commonly done.

Noting selections made in the library

is also a fruitful activity. One method is to collect data from the library cards themselves. The cards can be sorted, classified, and data recorded by school, class, and individual pupil. The school librarian, teacher, clerk, or any other qualified person can make this tabulation. Books should be identified by categories so that a particular title will be known as "Animal Story," "Biography," "Historical Novel," and so on. Since the Dewey decimal number will not suffice, a code number should be placed upon each card by the librarian. Another method to discover interest is to note the books taken from the shelves by children. Some will longingly examine books that they cannot read and finally return them to the shelves. While they may not check out such books, their choices will point both to interest and to need.

Reading done outside of school is not so easily observed, but it is of great importance. Parents can be of assistance here, if they will. Invitations to children to bring their favorite reading material to the classroom for a free-reading period or for sharing with others can be helpful. Teachers are sometimes surprised at items which appear when such an invitation is given.

A satisfactory method of keeping reading records will provide for the inclusion of all personal reading that can be observed by all who will participate in the study. Such data should be summarized and analyzed.

FREE DISCUSSION

Some teachers are so skilful at establishing an informal, friendly atmosphere that free discussion can be very enlightening. In such a situation, discussion of favorite books and magazines will have real value. The press of required reading frequently is so great that very little time is left for personal reading. This is especially true of the slower child, who may have no opportunity at all to follow his bent in school. Informal, friendly discussion may provide the clues to interest which may, in turn, lead to personal reading. Even secondary-school students can be frank and honest when they don't have to write "for the record." Such discussion is a recognized technique for general guidance purposes. It can well be used to explore needs and interests.

THE INDIVIDUAL CASE STUDY

Many kinds of data are assembled in the pupil's cumulative folder. Clues to interest should be found there if the record is at all comprehensive. Analysis of such data can be done for individual pupils and later tabulated for the group if that is desired. The single case study, carefully and completely developed, will also help the teacher to gain insight into problems and needs of other individuals within the group. For example, the reading interests of a certain twelve-year-old boy might well be similar to those of other boys his age. Also, the development of the case history will familiarize the teacher with techniques and procedures which can be utilized in studying others.

THE CONTROLLED STUDY

An investigation, conducted under controlled conditions, to determine preferences of children could be expected to produce reliable information. Such a study could conceivably provide clues to latent interests, as well as more apparent desires. This type of study would be out of the question for most public schools, however, since it is difficult to set up and control and is costly in terms of time, money, and personnel. This does not deny the need for such studies by agencies that can carry them to conclusion.

SUMMARY

Personal reading is a response to interest. Knowledge of children's interests, therefore, will make it possible to guide and motivate personal reading.

Identification of interests is not an easy task, but they can be discovered as reliably as any other trait. The most generally used approach is the questionnaire or inventory, but observation, discussion, and case study are also useful procedures.

✻ ✻ ✻

HOW CAN ADMINISTRATORS IDENTIFY AND PROVIDE MATERIALS ESSENTIAL FOR DEVELOPING READING INTERESTS?

R U T H   M A R Y   W E E K S

✻

THE value of reading is primarily the enlargement of life and the development of judgment. An individual man lives but briefly—longer than the beasts, but not long enough to secure continuity of progress without cataclysm were it not for the immortality bestowed on man through literature.

How can one secure this immortality? By reading the master-books of all time, in which experience outlasts the centuries. There we see, as in a great apocalypse, the causes and consequences of individual, class, and national behavior. There we learn what experiences yield the greatest good and how they can be obtained at the cheapest cost. In an age of slow movement, devoted to the elaboration and perfection of settled ideals, humanity can exist in the present. But in a time like ours, when we are struggling "between two worlds, one dead, the other powerless to be born," it is imperative that not just the intelligentsia, but the mass of men as well, look backward and forward through the ages, seeing by what sound, gradual processes man bridged the gap of progress without cataclysm, and why certain ages and certain peoples paid so high a price for change. This is the great use of history. This is the more priceless value of that richer knowledge of life and human nature gained through the world's great books.

SELECTING BOOKS FOR STUDENTS

As we survey the books of the past for what our young should read, how can we select, from the great treasury of human experience, the things that will be most suitable, profitable, and interesting? We make no mistakes in choosing first the most durable and widely read books. Such are the epics of nations which have most fertilized the minds of men. There we see refined, by the catalyst of time, the great human virtues and errors that have saved or wrecked peoples and individuals. There we see the problems on which the destiny of man has turned. Such are the Hindu epics, the treasury of Semitic legend preserved in the Old Testament, Greek mythology and the works of Homer, the tales of Arthur—all noble documents of times when men faced destiny in nature, family, or nation. When we turn to the literature of our own race and nation, we choose again those peak books which searchlight the ageless problems of humanity.

Shall we read, then, only that tested in the crucible of time? No. We must take the risk of contemporary reading to show our students how worthy modern writers also seek for the critical problems of our age and bring to bear on them the light of reason. But the tried and true must still balance the contemporary.

If the reading course is built around theme-centered units (a sound and excellent idea now somewhat overdone), the course should be drawn from every age and clime so that the basic human problems, stripped of their local and temporal trappings, can be seen looming above life like Annapurna and Everest above the high Himalayas. For instance, in a unit on family life, Hergesheimer's "The Token," Ibsen's *A Doll's House*, the Hindu *Ramayana*, Hector's farewell to his wife from the *Iliad*, the Chinese *Lute Song*, Euripides' *Alcestis*, Shakespeare's *Macbeth*, Morrison's "That Brute Simmons," de Maupassant's "Happiness," Bennett's *Milestones*, Shakespeare's *Romeo and Juliet* and *King Lear*, W. A. White's "Mary White," Tarkington's "Penrod's Busy Day," Wharton's *Ethan Frome*, Dorothy Canfield Fisher's "Heyday of the Blood," and Carroll's *As the Earth Turns* can all contribute to an understanding of the success or failure of family relations. That these things were as true three thousand years ago as they are now is an impressive fact not wasted on the younger generation, and it is borne into their minds by the literature of the older world with ten times the force of a mere general statement. My students remember Shakespeare's sonnet stressing the intellectual element in wedded love when reading Mrs. Browning's "How Do I Love Thee?" They suggest that Torvald Helmar had apparently not read Solomon's description of the ancient Hebrew wife and mother. And they think Anna Karenina could have profited by the tale of Guinevere. Even a queen, they see, cannot win that game.

A special variety of reading which is overwhelmingly significant in our era is the scientific. To show our students what science is, how scientists think and work, and how society utilizes their findings, we read *Microbe Hunters* by de Kruif (Harcourt, 1927). Students then prepare three-by-five-inch cards on each of three scientists dealt with in this volume, stating concisely:

What unknown is sought? What is the precise method of search employed?
What hypothesis is formed? How does the scientist test it?
What fact, theory, or law is discovered?
What are the practical, intellectual, or spiritual values of the discovery?

If any religious objections should arise, *Hunger Fighters* (Harcourt, 1928) will do nearly as well, although it is not so overwhelmingly interesting to students. This brief study will enable students not only to read in other scientific fields but to appreciate the slow and patient sureness of progress.

Yes, when looking for something to interest students in reading, look to the great, live issues as dealt with by the masters and read by one-half the human race.

PROVIDING FOR A WIDE RANGE OF ABILITIES

What provisions can be made in courses based on such materials for students of varying abilities? In my school,

English courses are set up for A, B, and C students. Materials for Sections A and B are roughly comparable, the difference appearing in the speed, depth, and difficulty of the work done with each book. The C sections study the same topical units but use literature adapted to their thinking and reading skill. Our best method of selecting readings for these weaker students is still trial and error. Sometimes C sections read cut or simplified versions of famous books in order that they may not feel handicapped by not knowing the books. But these books must not be cheapened ones. If we think that with a slower pace a C section can read an original, and it is worth the time, we take it. C classes in the hands of a competent and sympathetic teacher enjoy their work and blossom as they never can at the ruthless pace and on the difficult level suitable for better students.

But still we must remember in all our teaching that it is not essential that students understand completely everything they read. There must be something left for a rereading. We live in a world that is full of mystery—and it is the mystery that makes us love to live.

PROVIDING THE MATERIALS

Who selects materials? Not, I think, administrators or supervisors, not department heads, but committees of superior teachers from all a city's schools working in concert. In my case, while I am a department head, I am also a full-time, five-class teacher. In this latter capacity I have served on several local curriculum committees, organized by an official curriculum director. He has several assistants, who schedule committee meetings and gather from the library or buy materials asked for by the committee. The committee of representative classroom teachers practically always has the final word on the content and organization of the course.

This, in my opinion, is the best procedure. Competent teachers are better judges of the workability of a program than are administrators or supervisors, more conversant with materials and more inventive of methods and devices which will interest and develop students. They are also less prone to use the changing jargon of educational theory, which often either substitutes for thought or baffles the teaching personnel.

How can we provide students with the varied and numerous readings that are needed? It is obvious that the individual students cannot buy them. It is also plain that free textbooks from the state or books drawn from public libraries cannot suffice. At Paseo High School and other public high schools in Kansas City, the English department charges a semester book fee of seventy-five cents for Juniors and Seniors, and fifty cents for Sophomores and Freshmen. With this income we have built up an English-department library covering all our literary needs. Class sets of each work to be read are placed by a paid "book crew" of students in each teacher's room before the beginning of the semester, enough sets being supplied so that, with planned rotation of units between classes in the room, students can complete all units in the course.

Books are stamped and numbered and charged out to each student as a unit comes up. Damage and loss are more than of yore, but less than we had feared and less than in the public libraries. Pride can be developed in these department libraries, and students see with satisfaction the greater interest, variety, and volume of what they read in comparison with their friends in schools where anthologies are used. We purchase not only single titles but anthologies of certain literary types, which contain many selections we read in one or another unit. This gives students a chance to read for their amusement items in books not studied in any unit, and a surprising number do so read.

CONCLUDING STATEMENT

Administrators should stimulate the members of their staff to work co-operatively in identifying materials essential to develop reading interests.

The essential materials should be provided in part by school libraries, but other means, such as charging a nominal book fee, have proved to be effective as a source of supply.

* * *

HOW CAN SCHOOLS SET UP AND EFFECT THE USE OF RADIO AND TELEVISION TO PROMOTE READING INTERESTS?

ELIZABETH E. MARSHALL

*

BEFORE one can intelligently discuss the how of effectively using radio and television to promote reading interests, one must know something of the why which makes them ideal for educational purposes. One answer to the why lies in the attributes of these teaching aids. Radio and television are immediate, universal in their appeal, widely accepted and enjoyed by young and old alike. Students find radio-listening and television-viewing highly pleasurable experiences, which, carried over into classroom use, bring a welcome change of voice and face and pace, making for improved learning.

Because of their versatility, radio and television can be potent teaching tools, for they offer a wealth of fine, free program fare related to a wide variety of language-arts abilities. Herein lies their affinity for reading interests; radio and television belong to reading's own language-arts-in-action family.

RADIO AND TELEVISION DEVELOP SKILLS
BASIC TO READING

Like reading, radio and television are concerned with interpretation and word perception, with perception of relationships and recognizing of emotional reactions. Radio and television help listeners to form, and to react to, sensory images and thus develop the ability to form images of sight, sound, smell, taste, touch, and movement. Like reading, radio and television transform the listening-viewing experience into something vivid, meaningful, and personal. There is definite carry-over value to reading in this kindred image-forming ability which results from consistent radio and television experience.

Related skills of keen listening and attentive viewing make reading all the more desirable and purposeful because of their interrelationships within the communications-family membership. Most broadcasts contribute to the listener's vocabulary development. In television, seeing and hearing are combined to strengthen the subject presentation; often the visuals used involve various kinds of reading activity.

Similarly, educational broadcasts are prime interest-arousers and motivate a great deal of worth-while research and integration of what is read in content-subject areas carried on largely through reading. Good listeners also become involved with broadcast content. They agree or argue. Radio and television help build this personal background so that the student is encouraged to develop thinking skill—another skill basic to full interpretation in reading.

SCHOOL ORGANIZATION ESSENTIAL TO EFFECTIVE UTILIZATION

We must organize our schools for the administration and use of educational radio and television currently available. This responsibility may be centered in a teacher radio-television chairman (usually one per school) whose duty it is to locate, secure, and channel, to his colleagues, pertinent information about radio and television materials, equipment, and services. Some schools prefer dividing this responsibility among members of a committee. Student helpers, trained in routing, operating, maintaining, and storing equipment, render invaluable service as teachers' assistants.

Good school organization includes the library, recognizing the vital role played by the teacher-librarian in servicing and supplementing the in-school and out-of-school listening program.

Local parent-teachers' associations usually appoint full-time radio-television chairmen to serve these interests in home, school, and community. The chairmen

are well trained to serve the school's needs, whatever they may be.

EDUCATIONAL RADIO-TELEVISION PROGRAM RESOURCES

If your board of education owns its own radio and television station, then you are fortunate in having both worth-while educational programs, and a division of radio and television to co-ordinate the radio-television information within your school system and community. In Chicago we have Station WBEZ, owned by the Chicago Board of Education and operated by the Division of Radio and Television of the Chicago public schools.

Station WBEZ now broadcasts more than one hundred programs weekly, serving all grades and major subject areas. The schedules of WBEZ and the teachers' guides that it issues illustrate the wealth of reading-literature programs available to the schools.

The reading-literature series over WBEZ are built purposely to motivate good reading. For this purpose they rely on dynamic presentation, devices of good showmanship, and special techniques. Dramatic scenes whet the students' reading appetite and spur them to read the complete book versions on which the broadcast adaptations are based, as well as other stories similar to the ones broadcast.

Programs within the series are planned, written, produced, and co-ordinated so as to increase the listener's reading pleasure, his reading comprehension, and his desire to do more reading. The following excerpts from WBEZ handbooks illustrate common reading-interest purposes and emphases:

Bag of Tales.—New and old stories to delight young listeners and nourish a taste for good literature.

Book Box.—Stories to encourage upper-elementary students to use our libraries and to read better books.

Book Magic.—Dramatized scenes from young people's classics designed to promote good reading.

Book Parade.—Stimulating reviews of interesting books to encourage teen-agers to read.

Battle of Books.—Book-quiz programs developing good reading habits and building appreciation for good literature.

That these objectives are achieved is ascertained through a program of continuing evaluation and is reflected in comments from teachers and students:

Bag of Tales.—We made up our own reading lessons afterward. This series has increased notably the children's vocabulary.—GRADE II, HAMMOND SCHOOL.

Battle of Books.—This series aids us in our library instruction.—GRADE VII, LAWSON SCHOOL.

Messages and Men.—These programs sparked post-library research in social studies, relating the story with the wonderful works of the monks in the Dark Ages.—GRADE VIII, GAGE PARK SCHOOL.

News Programs.—The news program is the framework that lends itself easily to reading, reference, and composition work on real, live materials and issues. Tangible materials are outlined on the board for post-broadcast follow-up.—GRADE VI, BEIDLER SCHOOL.

Science Reporter.—These broadcasts give students experience in tracking down science interests through research, reading, conversing, and discussing.—GRADE VII, FARREN SCHOOL.

Jeffersonian Heritage.—We recorded this series for permanent use because of Claude Rains's superb portrayal of Thomas Jefferson—a rendition of the English language in all its beauty, spoken as it should be spoken. —DEPARTMENT OF ENGLISH, LAKE VIEW HIGH SCHOOL.

Included in the foregoing evaluations you will note several broadcast series other than those primarily intended to promote literature-reading interests. Such programs also contribute greatly to the furtherance of reading interests. One has but to refer to their respective teachers' guides to note the many suggestions for activities and utilization which underline the importance of reading to the interpretation and understanding of these subjects. The news handbooks point out that regular listening to news is basic to integrating ideas from a variety of sources and to summarizing and organizing ideas (again, skills which are highly essential to reading). General activities spark many kinds of reading activity: posting on the bulletin board notices, posters, pictures, and clippings related to the broadcast; reading classmates' reports, outlines, and compositions growing out of broadcast listening; sharing with fellow-students books and other reading materials which supplement the content of the programs heard together; arranging with the school librarian to reserve special "radio-television bookshelves" in the library for materials supplementing specific series.

COMMERCIAL STATIONS AND READING-INTEREST PROGRAMS

We cannot afford to overlook the rich reading-literature offerings of the commercial stations and networks. Among these are the programs of "WLS-Schooltime" and programs produced by the Division of Radio and Television of the Chicago public schools over WGN-TV. NBC's "Playhouse," "Kraft Theater," "Hallmark Hall of Fame," "Carnival of Books"; Dumont-TV's "Author Meets the Critic"; ABC's "U.S. Steel Hour";

the "Ford Theater" of CBS; WMAQ's "Literary Portraits," "Americana," and "World of Nordine" are all worthy of note as conducive to literature appreciation, particularly at the high-school and college levels. Many of the networks prepare teachers' guides for use with their series and special-events programs.

I have reserved for special mention Dr. Frank Baxter's superior teaching in "Shakespeare on TV"—a college-level telecourse whose series outcomes, according to research, include the listeners' greater association with educational, library, and literature activities. Dr. Baxter's telecourse is outstanding because it combines his own personal talent as a teacher with appealing subject matter, professional production, good promotion, convenient hour of presentation, and smooth administration.

MORE WAYS OF PROMOTING READING VIA RADIO AND TELEVISION

Many educational organizations and publications regularly release carefully screened recommendations to assist teachers and parents in their selection of suitable radio and television fare for in-school and out-of-school use.

Radio-television workshops and other groups offer numerous opportunities for reading and related-to-reading activities. Developmental reading values are especially evident in production, student announcing, narrating, and acting; in reading and writing continuity, script copy, and spot announcements; and in other broadcast-presentation techniques. All these apply students' over-all reading ability in real communications situations and serve constantly as incentives for doing one's best and working for improved reading performance.

TEACHER TRAINING IN USE OF RADIO AND TELEVISION

Too few teachers know what is available on radio and television; too few know the purposes for which various broadcast series are designed or the listener levels to which they are beamed; and far too few know how to use the programs and how to incorporate them within the classroom program to meet immediate teaching needs. Through our administrative services and supervision, we must help our teachers to gain this knowledge and understanding. We must see that they are provided with adequate consultant services, supervision, special conferences, demonstrations, inspirational institutes, and clinics to give them the training they need in these areas.

Administrators and supervisors themselves must be thoroughly informed so that they in turn can relay and share this knowledge with those under their direction. Send for sample radio-television program bulletins, listings, and schedules of other school systems. Study the scripts and teachers' guides to learn what others are doing and, from their example, what you might be doing within your own schools. Such materials serve as one kind of in-service training, for they have been prepared by teacher experts for other teachers' use; they are utilization-centered, based on study courses and units of learning as prescribed in the curriculum for specific grade levels. Moreover, they are controlled by continuous evaluation from teachers and students who use them regularly.

Radio and television in the classroom give pupils all the advantages of contact with many new teachers without having to give up their own teacher. It is the classroom teacher who is all-important in the use of these new teaching tools, for the success or failure of the broadcast program is determined in the classroom and dependent upon the teacher. The finest program on the air can be a dismal failure under the guidance of a poor teacher; a mediocre program becomes a fine listening experience under the guidance of an able teacher who knows how to use the broadcast to inspire and enhance the learning program.

These lively arts, radio and television, can serve as a "lure" for good reading as they do for so many other educational interests. Let them help you to promote the reading interests of your students by providing the incentive, the wanting to know and to learn and to read more. Reading is our product; we are its sponsors; radio and television can be our most effective "sales" media. If we are to develop a permanent interest in reading, then we must continue to "sell" it through smooth administration, adequate supervision, and continuous promotion to prove constantly the many worth-while values and rich rewards that good reading can bring to everyday living.

✳ ✳ ✳

HOW TO DEVELOP STAFF COMPETENCE IN PROMOTING MAXIMAL READING INTEREST THROUGH BASAL INSTRUCTION

ELIZABETH GRAF

✳

ONE of the greatest challenges to the administrative and supervisory staff of any school system is to promote maximal interest on the part of students in reading—reading for information; reading for fun; reading for recreation; reading to become acquainted with the vast amount of written materials that supply knowledge of the culture of the past, describe the wonders of the present, and indicate the promise of the future. Without the ability to read and the incentive to do independent reading, the student is denied much of the richness of the world's accumulated knowledge.

The teacher in the classroom has a wide responsibility to instil desirable attitudes and appreciations while giving children adequate and efficient command of reading skills. But teachers need help. They need to become acquainted with the best thinking of experts in the field of reading. They need to have an intimate knowledge of children. They need to be supplied with the best and the most appropriate materials. They need to be given inspiration and encouragement to forge ahead. They need to be reminded to give enthusiastic approval and praise to each child as he works to improve and use his reading skills. Administrators and supervisors, as they work with teachers, can provide leadership, inspiration, information, and encouragement through in-service activities.

The foundation for promoting and maintaining maximal reading interest can be laid through the intelligent use of a basic reading program. Adopt the best possible basic program, and help teachers to use that program, suiting the materials and methods to the interests, needs, and abilities of boys and girls. However, the crux of the success of the entire program is staff competence. Without a staff competent to carry out the program, maximal reading interest is not possible for most children.

As supervisors and teachers work together, three phases of in-service activities stand out as essential: teachers must help with all phases of the planning of the reading curriculum; teachers need help in identifying needs of children; and teachers need help in using the program effectively.

TEACHERS MUST HELP WITH PLANNING

For real professional growth, teachers must be a part of the reading-program planning at every step of the way: evaluating the program, determining the best program for the future, recommending policies and procedures. These activities were successfully accomplished by one school system through the Reading Overview Committee. Teachers from kindergarten through Grade XII were represented. Principals and supervisors became working members of the group. After good rapport had been established, members confessed that few teachers were well acquainted with the entire reading program. Four subgroups were formed: kindergarten-primary, intermediate, junior high school, and senior high school. Each group reported on the materials, methods, and achievements of that particular division of the school. These reports constituted a revelation to most teachers, who developed a sympathetic understanding of the work of other grade levels.

The second phase of the work came as the group delved into research to determine what other school systems were doing and to become acquainted with the opinions of experts in the reading field. Gradually members began to formulate an improved program for the school system. Members of the Overview Committee went back to their own buildings and shared information. They returned to the committee with the results of the thinking of their fellow-workers. Promising practices were experimented with in the classrooms. Even before the program was recorded, the new ideas were being accepted and used. When an interim report was released, the teaching staff was not surprised, because they had been a part of the reading program from its inception.

From the Overview Committee came recommendations for a total program in reading—for kindergarten through Grade XII—a program providing for continuity within the grade and between grades. An excellent basal reading program was adopted, with materials provided for children of all grades and all reading-achievement levels. Teachers had a real opportunity to begin instruction where each child was able to read and continue growth from that point. General acceptance of the Overview Committee's report and subsequent use of the recommendations in the classroom called for the continuance of the committee, whose membership changed periodically. Continued evaluation, constant study, application of promising practices to local situations provided growth, raised sights and ideals.

HELPING TEACHERS IDENTIFY READING NEEDS OF CHILDREN

Before teachers can know what materials are required, they must know each child's achievement in reading. Permanent, maximal interest in reading will only be promoted when a child is led to read materials near his independent reading level on a subject of interest to him. At the beginning of the school year, when teachers need help in becoming acquainted with children and their abilities, compiled data from a testing program will supply much needed information. A good plan would provide for the annual administration of a standardized reading test to each child. For a large school system, administrators and supervisors can analyze test data for each grade on a city-wide basis. Then teachers can be guided to make similar analyses for members of their own classes. If testing is regularly administered, comparative data are available, showing each child's achievement, his relative ability to achieve, his progress during a year and from one year to another.

Thus the range of reading levels within the class will be evident in a very objective fashion. Teachers will see the achievement of superior students, the average readers, and the slow learners. As teachers observe, the desirability of differentiating instruction will be evident. This procedure seems so logical and so practical that many administrators and supervisors fail to realize that all teachers do not accept it. Many teachers secretly adhere to the old idea that every child in a classroom should achieve at the same grade level. If this type of thinking prevails, only a few children in the room will develop maximal interest in reading. Certainly, if a child is to develop a permanent interest in reading, he must succeed in, and constantly grow through, the basal program. But each child can only grow when instruction begins where he can achieve.

Administrators and supervisors must constantly assure teachers that a wide range of reading abilities is acceptable, that each child should not and cannot read on the grade level. By the same token, many children, because of their intelligence, can be expected to achieve far above the average child's attainment.

To make instruction practical and effective, test data for each child need to be studied to determine the proper distribution of books. Various levels of basic readers should be supplied. A wide and varied supply of supplementary books is needed to stimulate children to read independently. Here interest inventories will be helpful in identifying books which are proper for individual pupils. The basal program has a wide appeal. It leads the child into stories about the past, about faraway places, about physical science, natural science, and biography.

To the child who has been inspired through the unit theme to read further, a well-chosen classroom library will prove to be a constant source of wonder, of attraction, of fascination. Here again the administrators and supervisors can help. Lists of available books can be provided. Perhaps the source of additional titles is the city library or purchases made by the parent-teachers' association. Committees of teachers can make valuable suggestions. Once the materials have been obtained at the central office, a well-organized and a simplified plan for ordering, distributing, and sharing books is a necessity.

HELPING TEACHERS USE THE PROGRAM EFFECTIVELY

Administrators and supervisors can aid teachers through various types of in-service activities. These may be classified as those which are concerned with individual teachers in the classrooms and those in which groups of teachers meet and discuss common problems and common needs. Supervisors can help early in the fall, as the teacher meets a new group and faces the necessity of rapidly becoming acquainted with the needs of every boy and girl in the room.

A study of the range in reading achievement reveals that groups of children going into the fifth year will need basic readers at the fifth-grade, the fourth-grade, and possibly at the third-grade, level. A few children will need special help. Supplementary materials based upon the interest inventories of the boys and girls must be supplied on at least three, and perhaps more, levels of ability. One class will need many such books to appeal to superior readers; a second class will need many books at the grade level; and still another class will need many books for the slow readers.

Grouping for instruction will be necessary, with the teacher selecting those children in the room who have common problems and common needs and placing them in the same group. The grouping will be flexible as individual pupils are ready to join other groups. Most teachers need help in scheduling. When the teacher works with one group, the biggest problem is frequently to supply the best type of seatwork for other members of the class. Children will also appreciate time for reading in their own area of interest. The arrangement of furniture has its effect on promoting interest. A quiet corner for reading is always more inviting to the child who has a few minutes to do what he would like. The place for active teaching should be as far removed from this area as possible.

Administrators and supervisors can arrange to have groups of teachers who have common problems and similar needs meet together. In one school system, no more than ten teachers were invited to a demonstration held in a nearby school. The classroom teacher had been scheduled to teach a reading lesson demonstrating certain techniques that had been clearly identified as those in which these particular teachers needed help. The visiting teachers actually saw the teacher at work with children. The schedule which the children followed, the work habits, the placement of materials —all these were incidental to the main purpose, but you may be sure that teachers went back to their classrooms and applied what they had observed.

After the children had been dismissed, the teachers discussed the lesson. Questions were answered, procedures discussed, solutions of problems suggested. Such demonstrations are sources of inspiration and practical help. Meetings of this kind produce better results if the supervisor has planned with the teacher who is demonstrating and has alerted the visiting teachers to the techniques that they will see in use.

Many other effective ways of stimulating groups of teachers have been used. Exhibits of materials showing reading charts, children's book reports and reviews, dramatizations, book jackets, book lists, professional libraries—all these give teachers opportunities to learn, to refine their own teaching techniques, and to stimulate creativity.

These are some practical and successful ways in which administrators and supervisors have worked with teachers to develop skills for learning to read more efficiently and for promoting permanent, maximal interest in reading. As we know how to read, we become better readers by reading widely. Children, as well as adults, will read if books in which they are interested and which are within their reading ability level are placed within their reach. Remember, enthusiasm begets enthusiasm. When the teacher is enthusiastic, the pupils will also be enthusiastic.

Administrators and supervisors need to encourage teachers to become well acquainted with individual children—to know how well they read, to know their particular interests, to know books well enough so that the right book can be made available to the right child. Test data and interest inventories are important and contribute to our understanding. Administrators and supervisors should remember to bring teachers into co-operative planning; to help teachers identify needs of children; to help teachers use the program effectively; to give teachers encouragement and appreciation for work well done; to give teachers outlets for creativity; to know what is going on in the classroom; to care what happens to the teacher and to the child; to show enthusiasm themselves so that teachers will be enthusiastic and impart enthusiasm to their pupils.

When each child is able to read as well as his ability permits, when he is surrounded with books that he can read independently on the interest which is closest to his heart, then we shall develop and maintain a maximal interest in reading because reading satisfies a basic need in his life; it is pleasurable, exciting, and rewarding.

✳   ✳   ✳

HOW TO AID THE STAFF IN EXPANDING READING INTERESTS IN AND THROUGH THE CONTENT AREAS

BEN A. SYLLA

✳

ADMINISTRATION and supervision are not ends in any enterprise. They are but the means for facilitating effectiveness and efficiency in the attainment of the objectives of the enterprise, be it education or any other.

As educationists, we are committed to the development of the growth potential of children and youth—their physical, mental, social, emotional, and spiritual potential—through the process of education in school. We are here concerned with their development through significant learning experiences afforded by the content areas of the school program and, more specifically, through the experience of wide reading as related to, and stemming from, the content of most school subjects.

The prime responsibility of administration and supervision is to help teachers in their work with children. All teachers need help. Some need much more help than others, but even the master-teacher needs, wants, and is entitled to more effective aid than most administrators and supervisors are able to provide. Theirs is a great challenge and unique opportunity for creative effort.

UNDERSTANDING AND ACCEPTANCE BY THE STAFF

To aid teachers in expanding the reading interests of children and youth in and through the content areas, administrators and supervisors must lead all members of the staff to understand and accept the thesis that, while instruction in basic reading skills is primarily the responsibility of the teacher of reading, the extension and expansion of reading skills is the responsibility of all teachers who prescribe materials to be read by pupils.

To obtain such acceptance may take time, skill, and patience, particularly with the teacher who finds it difficult to give up the notion that he is supposed to teach the subject and not reading. I would suggest that the approach be made through the technique of having the content teachers collaborate in formulating the objectives for their respective subjects. Undoubtedly they will include and accept goals similar to the following as listed by Gray and Liek:

1. To extend and organize experience in each subject.
2. To promote desirable interests, attitudes, and appreciations.
3. To cultivate correct habits of thinking and interpretation while reading.
4. To extend and enrich the meaning vocabulary in each subject.
5. To develop and refine the reading abilities peculiar to given fields.[1]

Most teachers will concede that the foregoing goals are beyond the province of basic instruction in reading. Acceptance of these aims by the content teachers implies that they recognize (a) that their responsibility "for guidance in reading begins with, and is determined by, the use which they make of reading in attaining worth-while goals in their respective areas"[2] and (b) that they have three important obligations relative to the reading of their pupils, namely:

1. To provide for the full use of such competence in reading as pupils already have.
2. To give instruction in those phases of reading that are peculiar to the given content area, because each subject has its own vocabulary, concepts, and content, its own body of relationships, its pattern of thinking, and its special contributions to the solution of important problems.
3. To give specific help in basic reading skills when they assign reading materials that are above the reading ability of the pupil.

PROVIDING THE KNOW-HOW

Understanding and acceptance of the responsibility by the staff constitute but the first step. However willing and eager teachers may be, they need much help as they strive to expand the reading interests of pupils in the content areas. Administrators and supervisors must be ready to aid the teachers by:

1. Pinpointing the specific purposes of wide reading at different grade levels as new motives for reading develop.
2. Identifying the specific skills required for wide reading and suggesting appropriate techniques for developing such skills.
3. Suggesting techniques for launching a pupil on a program of wide reading.
4. Making clear that wholesome growth depends not so much upon the quantity of reading as it does upon the quality of content read, the quality of reading performance, and the definite-

[1] William S. Gray and Edna B. Liek, *Teacher's Guidebook for the Elson Basic Readers*, Book Four, pp. 6–9. Chicago: Scott, Foresman & Co., 1932.

[2] William S. Gray, *Improving Reading in Content Fields*, p. 3. Supplementary Educational Monographs, No. 62. Chicago: University of Chicago Press, 1947.

ness and validity of the reader's purpose. Merely to read is not sufficient. Critical reading is a requisite for the development of the understandings, values, and attitudes that are essential for competent citizenship.

5. Stressing the fundamental fact that the pupil's interest in the subject must be aroused before he can be led to read related materials of his own volition. Without interest, learning is limited to the mere acquisition of bare and unrelated facts and information.

6. Urging that some class time be reserved for brief reports and discussion of voluntary related reading found stimulating and worth while by members of the group.

ORGANIZING THE PROGRAM

Administrators and supervisors are responsible for setting up conditions which are conducive to effective learning and teaching. One of these conditions is reasonable class size. A teacher who is obliged to carry an excessive pupil load cannot be expected to know the needs, interests, and abilities of each pupil well enough to give him the kind of guidance in his reading that he is entitled to receive. In these days, when enrolments are rapidly rising and the proportionate supplies of teachers, classrooms, and funds are falling, the problem is formidable indeed. Where reasonable class size cannot be maintained, at least two alternatives should be seriously considered:

1. *Assignment of personnel help to the teacher.*—There is much that a teacher does in the classroom that does not involve professional skills, such as record-keeping, preparing reports, distributing supplies, collecting money, operating projectors and record-players, playing the piano, etc. These tasks can be reasonably well done under the supervision of the teacher by a responsible mature person without professional training in education.

2. *Ability grouping.*—In a school with enrolment large enough to have more than one classroom per grade, ability grouping may be instituted for the express purpose of assigning a relatively large number of pupils of advanced ability to one teacher and a somewhat smaller number of average ability to another teacher, thus to keep the number of the slow learners within reasonable limits for the third teacher.

Neither help for the teacher nor ability grouping should be construed as an acceptable substitute for reasonable class size. At best, these can merely serve to ease the burden of the teaching staff.

In some respects the departmental pattern of organization of the school program, particularly at the early secondary level, hinders effective guidance in reading. Because of their special developmental characteristics and extraordinary personal problems, early adolescents need more, not less, guidance than they did as preadolescents. For most of them, the abrupt change from the elementary school, where they depend largely on one teacher for guidance in the several learning areas, to the secondary school, with a fully departmentalized pattern of organization, makes satisfactory adjustment difficult. Many of them become bewildered, confused, and discouraged. Their teachers are not able really to offer much help in the adjustment process until they learn to know, reasonably well, each pupil as an individual. But this takes several weeks when a teacher meets five different class groups, each for but one class period daily.

Administrators and supervisors should take steps to modify the fully departmentalized program so as to make the transition from the elementary to the secondary school more gradual for the early adolescent. This can be done by organizing the school program so that each teacher can keep a group for two or three class periods (not necessarily consecutive) for instruction in two or three subject combinations, such as mathematics and science, social studies and literature.

To guide pupils effectively in reading related to content areas, teachers must know the level at which each pupil can read with relative ease. This requires an annual program of testing and making the results promptly available to the staff. Administrators and supervisors are responsible for initiating the testing program and leading the staff to due consideration of the results in planning and directing the reading of each pupil insofar as it relates to each content area.

Because a high score on a reading test does not necessarily mean competence in all the skills and abilities essential to good reading for all purposes, teachers must be encouraged to look for, and take into account, other factors involved, such as the pupil's intellectual potential, his emotional and social adjustment, and his experiential background.

Interest inventories are available for obtaining data about a pupil's play activities, preferences, hobbies, and vocational interests. Such data on each pupil should be made readily available to all teachers early in the school term.

SELECTING AND PROVIDING THE MATERIALS

It is the primary responsibility of the administrative and supervisory staff to convince the board of education of the need of adequate funds for a wide range of appropriate reading materials and to give the content teachers, as well as the school librarian, the opportunity to share in the process of screening and selecting such materials. Teacher participation in selection serves to develop a collection of materials better adapted to the diverse needs and interests of pupils and a staff the better informed about the materials available. Staff participation in the process of selection of materials does not just happen; it needs positive encouragement by those whose responsibility it is to help and guide the staff.

Some of the larger school systems maintain a materials center, where teachers and school librarians are given the opportunity to examine promising new materials with the view to possible purchase.

For some years past, the smaller school districts in the suburban areas of Chicago have jointly prevailed upon the publishers of school and library materials to exhibit their new publications annually for the convenience of teachers in the south, west, and north portions of the county. Teachers have been released to visit these exhibits on school time.

It is more important to have the right kind of materials at the right time than too many. A school may be oversupplied with books, illustrative materials, and teaching gadgets and yet be meagerly equipped for a good learning program. Right materials depend more on careful selection and effective use than on quantity. Buying a single title in quantity may preclude the purchase of variety; if varied materials are available, class discussion will offer the opportunity for an exchange of information and interpretation, with evaluation of ideas. Those who plan and execute the reading program should assist in deciding how the available funds shall be used. Administrators and supervisors are responsible for bringing together the materials, the users, and the goals and then for guiding the evaluation and selection of materials.

A central library in a school is the most effective means for insuring easy access to a large collection of materials, without which a vigorous and creative educational program is scarcely possible. Such a library must be adequately staffed so that pupils and teachers can get the kind of help they need from a library. There should be time for the library staff and the teachers to plan and work effectively together. This is especially important for planning the extended reading program in the content areas.

All pupils should be regularly scheduled in the central library part of the time for instruction in what a library is for and how it is used, for browsing, and for self-directed reading. There is a place for the classroom library, not as a substitute for, but rather as an extension of, the central library, which should be used to supply the classrooms with a wide variety of reading materials as needed from time to time.

In those schools where space for a central library is not available, the local public library, if there is one, may be able and willing to stock some appropriate materials (at the request of, and in co-operation with, school officials) for the use of pupils and teachers. Though less conveniently located and equipped for serving the school, the public library can meet the need to a limited extent.

IN CONCLUSION

Content subjects are critically important, not as ends, but rather as the media for pupil growth and development. The better content teachers are not content to confine their efforts to the mere merchandising of factual information. They strive to help their pupils develop sound concepts, the ability to think critically, abiding interests, and wholesome attitudes. This they do in good part by guiding the pupils to the wide reading of worth-while related materials.

Guiding children and youth to wide reading is not easy. It requires extraordinary skill, a strong conviction of its educational value, and contagious enthusiasm. In brief, it requires the master-teacher.

But master-teachers are not born; they are developed. To develop more of them is the challenge and the opportunity of administration and supervision. This too requires extraordinary skill, strong conviction, and contagious enthusiasm.

THE RESPONSIBILITY OF THE SCHOOL IN PROVIDING FOR THE EXTENSION OF CHILDREN'S READING INTERESTS THROUGH THE LIBRARY

MARY HELEN MAHAR

✳

IN ORDER for the school to carry out its responsibilities for the extension of children's reading interests through the library, administrators need to work cooperatively with teachers and librarians to establish an environment where wide reading takes place easily and naturally. The philosophy and the curriculum of the school, the programing, and the library must be conducive to the identification of children's reading interests and to their encouragement in the classroom, in the library, and in out-of-school activities. The very nature of reading requires a great deal of informality of approach, and the development of reading interests is often a highly individual matter in the student's life. Nevertheless, a vital reading program for all children is based essentially on the educational philosophy of the school and on a complete and mutual understanding of its execution by the whole faculty. The unplanned, haphazard curriculum, the textbook-centered school, the library with inadequate funds or with restrictions on its use—all are serious obstacles to the development of reading interests.

THE SCHOOL PHILOSOPHY AND ENVIRONMENT

Administrators and supervisors must develop, with their faculties, a stated school philosophy, in which many and varied library books and other reading materials are the accepted tools of teaching. They must plan together, in the subject fields and other areas of the school program, how to provide a wide selection of books for all the children. A master-teacher in social studies may teach the meaning of democracy through the reading of biographies and fiction which can translate the philosophy of democracy into real and human terms (and may at the same time interest the students in reading this kind of literature). But unless the whole social-studies department is committed to this method, only a fraction of the children in the school benefit by the reading experience. This kind of planning requires frequent meetings of librarians and teachers. It requires a knowledge of the tools of book selection and reading guidance on the part of the teachers as well as the librarians. It requires that librarians and teachers find out about children's books by reading them. It also necessitates the development of all kinds of bibliographies in the school—lists on special subjects, on specific reading interests, and in some instructional subjects—comprehensive and continually revised lists of the available books in the library. These activities in relation to a school's reading program can take place only in a school where the administrator is deeply interested in the program of reading and gives incentive and opportunity for teachers and librarians to meet and work together.

The school has the responsibility, in making schedules for faculty and students, to allow them time for the library and to enable the librarians to go with books to the classroom. At the junior high school level there is a tendency to schedule the same classes to the library every week at the same periods for library instruction. "Library instruction" usually includes the teaching of the use of the card catalogue and reference books and the location of materials, with no opportunity for reading and often with no relation to the subject of instruction in the classroom at the time. Instruction in the use of the library is important, but this approach easily stifles reading interests and excludes a large part of the school's population from using the books in the library. Both classes and individual students need to have continual access to the library, but the scheduling of classes should take place at the times when the classes need the resources of the library, and not every Tuesday in the second period. Flexibility of program and accessibility of books are essential to the development of reading and reading interests.

In the creation of a school philosophy and environment conducive to reading, the third point—the library—is, of course, the fundamental consideration of the administrator in planning a reading program. It is placed third, not because it is of least importance in this picture, but because the library functions best in the development of reading when the whole school curriculum is pointed toward its use. The school has the responsibility to establish and maintain a library and library service which can meet the demands of a developed reading plan. It must employ librarians who can initiate and build, co-operatively with teachers, a pervasive reading program, and it must furnish the appropriation necessary for a rich, varied, and continually refreshed collection of books and other materials in both elementary and secondary schools. There must be sufficient staff, not only to administer the library, but to work at all times with individual students, teachers, and classes in guiding the reading.

When these conditions exist in a school, the development and extension of reading interests of children are made possible. Children in school respond to an atmosphere sympathetic to reading and, in such an environment, will provide librarians and teachers with insights into their feeling for books and will seek encouragement and guidance. I remember a shy, seventh-grade girl who returned a story by Laura Ingalls Wilder and confided to me that it made her "feel all funny inside." I remember also a brilliant, twelfth-grade girl who asked me to make a list of classics in world literature, which she could read in her leisure time. Both of these girls revealed a sensitivity to books and a love of reading which could be encouraged by guidance and by providing in the school environment the books and opportunity to read freely and happily. With these children (and there are many of them), we must beware of the overly clinical approach, must only help them to find their way into maturing and permanent reading interests.

In all our schools, however, there are children who read reluctantly or not at all. With these children, librarians need to work more directly than is the usual practice in schools. When there is a special reading class or remedial-reading program, a portion of the library's budget should be used for special books and other printed materials for these groups, and the reading teacher and the librarian should work closely together in the selection of these materials. Many school librarians have training in reading problems and can use effectively the method of helping children to read on the basis of interest. It is sound educational practice for librarians to work with individual slow readers by the conference method, to build reading interests by suggesting books which can lead gradually to broader interests and a genuine liking for books related to these interests. The librarian at times can be more successful with this case method than the remedial teacher.

HELPING THE AVERAGE PUPILS

In assisting classes of boys and girls to select books close to their abilities and interests, librarians and teachers need to confer, not only on the general requirement of the reading of the class, but on the personalities, hobbies, and special characteristics of the children themselves. They should communicate their knowledge to each other, and both need to use the resources of the guidance department in order to understand better the children whose reading they are attempting to direct.

For example, within the science classes in the later elementary and early junior high school years, there are boys and girls who have incipient, developing, or even mature interests in various phases of science. Animals, nature, the sea, astronomy—all are subjects of varying degrees of interest to younger adolescents. If the teachers allow a flexible approach to the study of these subjects and build on the special interests of each individual child, and if the children are guided to the books in these fields, reading interests will be cultivated, and learning will take place. There exists a growing and extensive body of science literature written especially for children of this age, and many of these books are attractive, readable, and reliable in content. There are well-written biographies of scientists and books of fiction in the field which will not only increase understanding and enjoyment of a scientific subject but also show its relationship to all aspects of life. When these groups of children come to the library, the librarian should be able to provide a wide enough range of subjects, titles, and types of books to satisfy the interests of the members of the groups.

HELPING THE GIFTED

We are turning our attention in schools at this time, and rightly so, to the needs of gifted children. Books and libraries are important for all children of all ages, but they have a special place in the education of exceptional boys and girls. It is particularly essential to remember the needs of these children in the elementary grades. Imaginative young children need to be provided in elementary-school libraries with poetry, fairy tales, folk literature, modern and beautifully illustrated stories in profusion, and for no other age of children are so many fine books available. These elementary-school libraries need full-time librarians, who can select the books and provide them every day and all day for the children of the school—in the classroom, in the library, in story hours—in order to nurture the creative interests of small children. In addition to maintaining an attractive and well-stocked library, the elementary school has the responsibility for leading children to the public library as an additional source of enjoyable and useful books.

The reading of gifted children needs our special consideration at the secondary-school level. We have done a good deal of talking about acceleration and advanced standing and the adjustment of gifted boys and girls of high-school age, but we have not as yet, except in isolated instances, offered them a more provocative curriculum. In very few schools are they reading to satisfy their great intellectual curiosity or finding their way in life through books. We know that the secondary schools of Europe have always pushed their gifted children to the limit of their ability, and even to the limit of their physical strength. In the grammar schools of the United Kingdom, for example, it is not unusual for boys and girls to be studying several languages, several sciences, mathematics, English, and history, all at the same time, and to be reading the adult literature of these fields.

Here and there in the United States, administrators, librarians, and teachers have recognized the needs of able students and have helped them to pursue individual reading to satisfy their needs. But there is need to build a more substantial curriculum for these children and to relate their mature interests to significant reading. These exceptional children have a great range of reading interests, and the limited collections of many secondary-school libraries do not contain the books which these children need. Secondary-school libraries should provide adult, philosophic, scientific, and creative literature, both classical and modern, and the course offerings, in the eleventh and twelfth grades especially, should lead to these books.

CONCLUDING COMMENT

In addition to, and parallel with, our planning of reading for the boys and girls of our schools, and relating the materials of our curriculums to the interests of children, the school must provide elementary- and secondary-school libraries, in which all the children have time to browse, select, and read on their own initiative. Guidance of reading must lead the student to an independent approach to books and a desire to read continually on a higher level as his own personality and interests develop. Given the incentive, confidence, and opportunity to use the school library and the public library during his school years, and to exercise his own judgment in the choice of books, he will build habits of reading which will sustain him through life. He will grow in the power to educate himself, and the light which will shine in him will be diffused to the world in which he lives.

CHAPTER XVIII

NOTEWORTHY BOOKS PUBLISHED SINCE THE 1955
READING CONFERENCE

✳

BOOKS FOR ELEMENTARY-SCHOOL PUPILS

MARY K. EAKIN

✳

TODAY the adult who is concerned with developing permanent interests in reading among children in the elementary grades finds a rich and varied selection of books with which to work. There is scarcely a subject found in current magazines and newspapers or shown on television or the movie screen that does not have at least one counterpart in a good book for children. Frequently books in the subject fields can be found in a wide range of difficulty levels, so that the child in the primary grades who has a budding interest in interplanetary travel or in prehistoric animals can find his interest furthered in a book that is as suitable for his use as are the more detailed, technical treatments published for the upper-grade student or the adult. The trend in writing nonfiction books for children is toward a straightforward, factual presentation, which combines accuracy of information with clarity of presentation to produce books with a wide span of interest and appeal.

In the field of fiction the outlook is equally favorable. For the more literal-minded child there are stories of modern children in realistic, modern settings, who solve problems that are similar to the reader's own. For the imaginative child there is a wealth of fanciful tales, most of them following the pattern that is of current appeal and combining fantasy and realism into a story with just enough truth to it to leave the child with the pleasurable feeling that, fantasy though it may be, it just might have happened.

There are excellent biographies and historical fiction to help the child understand his past and to open new vistas of interest to him as he gains an understanding of what the past has meant in shaping his life of today.

Other countries and other cultures that the child may meet for the first time in current magazines and news reports are made more understandable through fiction, biography, and nonfiction accounts that give sympathetic, accurate pictures of the people of those countries and cultures. These people thus become for the child real human beings and not just strange-sounding names on maps or in picture captions.

The following list represents only a few of the many good books that are available for increasing a child's understanding of the world in which he lives

214

and to open for him the wide range of possible interests that can be satisfied in part or wholly through reading.

BOOKS FOR PRIMARY GRADES

ANDERSON, J. *Hippolyte—Crab King.* Harcourt. (Story of a small boy in Trinidad.)

BEHN, H. *The Wizard in the Well.* Harcourt. (Poetry.)

BEIM, J. *Country School.* Morrow.

BROMHALL, W. *The Princess and the Woodcutter's Daughter.* Knopf.

DE REGNIERS, B. S. *What Can You do with a Shoe?* Harper. (Nonsense.)

DU BOIS, W. P. *Lion.* Viking.

EICHENBERG, F. *Dancing in the Moon.* Harcourt. (Nonsense counting-book.)

FATIO, L. *The Happy Lion in Africa.* Whittlesey.

FRASCONI, A. *See and Say.* Harcourt. (Familiar words and phrases in four languages.)

GOUDEY, A. *Here Come the Lions!* Scribner.

HARRIS, L. D. *Slim Green.* Little. (Life-story of a grass snake.)

HAYS, W. P. *The Story of Valentine.* Coward-McCann.

JOHNSON, C. *Harold and the Purple Crayon.* Harper.

JOHNSTON, J. *Sugarplum.* Knopf. (Adventures of a small doll.)

KAY, H. *One Mitten Lewis.* Lothrop.

McCLUNG, R. M. *Major, the Story of a Black Bear.* Morrow.

MACGREGOR, E. *Theodore Turtle.* Whittlesey. (Fantasy.)

MERRILL, J. *The Tree House of Jimmy Domino.* Oxford.

MILHOUS, K. *With Bells On.* Scribner. (A Mennonite Christmas of Colonial days.)

PODENDORF, I. *The True Book of Weeds and Wild Flowers.* Children's Press.

RAPAPORT, S. F. *A Whittle Too Much.* Putnam. (Story of the Gaspé.)

RUKEYSER, M. *Come Back, Paul.* Harper.

WILL. *Chaga.* Harcourt. (Fanciful tale of a baby elephant.)

ZION, E. *Really Spring.* Harper.

ZION, E. *The Summer Snowman.* Harper.

ZOLOTOW, C. S. *One Step, Two. . . .* Lothrop. (A small girl and her mother go for a walk.)

BOOKS FOR MIDDLE GRADES

ADLER, I. *Tools in Your Life.* Day.

BAKER, A. (editor). *The Talking Tree.* Lippincott. (Folk tales.)

BAKER, N. B. *Amerigo Vespucci.* Knopf.

BENARY-ISBERT, M. *The Wicked Enchantment.* Harcourt. (Modern fanciful tale.)

BLEEKER, S. *The Chippewa Indians.* Morrow.

BOSTON, L. M. *The Children of Green Knowe.* Harcourt. (Modern fanciful tale.)

BROCK, E. L. *Plug-Horse Derby.* Knopf.

BROWN, P. *The Silver Nutmeg.* Harper. (Modern fanciful tale.)

BUTTERS, D. G. *Papa Dolphin's Table.* Knopf. (Humor.)

BUTTERWORTH, O. *The Enormous Egg.* Little. (Humorous tale of a modern dinosaur.)

CROWLEY, M. *Tor and Azor.* Oxford. (Friendship between a Norwegian boy and a boy from Maine.)

DARLING, L. *Seals and Walruses.* Morrow.

DE JONG, M. *The Little Cow and the Turtle.* Harper. (Humorous fantasy.)

DOWNER, M. *David and the Sea Gulls.* Lothrop. (Excellent photographs.)

GAUL, A. *The Pond Book.* Coward-McCann.

HAMILTON, E. *The First Book of Caves.* Watts.

HAYWOOD, C. *Eddie and His Big Deals.* Morrow. (Humor.)

HOFSINDE, R. *Indian Sign Language.* Morrow.

HYDE, M. O. *Atoms Today and Tomorrow.* Whittlesey.

IRVING, R. *Hurricanes and Twisters.* Knopf.

KIRKUS, V. *The First Book of Gardening.* Watts.

LENSKI, L. *San Francisco Boy.* Lippincott. (Modern Chinese-American boy.)

LEWELLEN, J. B. *Helicopters: How They Work.* Crowell.

LINDQUIST, J. D. *The Golden Name Day.* Harper. (Scandinavians in the United States.)

MIRSKY, R. P. *Seven Grandmothers.* Follett. (Story of South Africa.)

MORRISON, L. (compiler). *A Diller, a Dollar.* Crowell. (School-inspired rhymes and chants.)

PELS, G. *The Care of Water Pets.* Crowell.

RAPAPORT, S. F. *Reindeer Rescue.* Putnam. (Eskimos in Alaska.)

RIEDMAN, S. R. *Let's Take a Trip to a Sky-scraper.* Abelard-Schuman.

SELSAM, M. E. *The Plants We Eat.* Morrow.

SELSAM, M. E. *See through the Sea.* Harper.

SORENSEN, V. E. *Plain Girl.* Harcourt. (The Amish in Pennsylvania.)

STEELE, W. O. *Davy Crockett's Earthquake.* Harcourt.

SWAIN, S. N. *Insects in Their World.* Garden City Books.

SYME, R. *Henry Hudson.* Morrow.

TOR, R. *Getting To Know Puerto Rico.* Coward-McCann.

TUNIS, E. *Wheels.* World Publishing Co. (History of travel.)

VOIGHT, V. F. *Lions in the Barn.* Holiday. (A circus in winter quarters.)

WORCESTER, D. *Lone Hunter's Gray Pony.* Oxford. (Plains Indians of early days.)

BOOKS FOR UPPER GRADES

BENDICK, J. *Electronics for Young People.* Whittlesey.

BLOCH, M. H. *Tony of the Ghost Towns.* Coward-McCann. (Gold-mining country of Colorado.)

CITIZENSHIP EDUCATION PROJECT. *When Men Are Free.* Houghton.

CLARK, D. *Boomer.* Viking. (Australian kangaroo.)

CLARK, L. F. *Explorers' Digest.* Houghton. (True accounts of famous explorations.)

COLVER, A. *Yankee Doodle Painter.* Knopf. (Story of the painting of the "Spirit of '76.")

COY, H. *Doctors and What They Do.* Watts.

DORIAN, E. M. *Trails West and Men Who Made Them.* Whittlesey.

GOLDMAN, I. *First Men.* Abelard-Schuman.

HALL-QUEST, O. W. *Wyatt Earp: Marshal of the Old West.* Ariel.

HIGHTOWER, F. C. *Mrs. Wappinger's Secret.* Houghton. (Treasure-seeking on an island.)

HOGARTH, G. A. *The Funny Guy.* Harcourt. (The trials of a child who is different.)

HYDE, M. O. *Where Speed Is King.* Whittlesey. (Sports that involve speed.)

JUDSON, C. I. *The Mighty Soo.* Follett.

KJELGAARD, J. A. *Lion Hound.* Holiday. (Lion-hunting in Arizona.)

KNIGHT, R. A. Y. *First the Lightning.* Doubleday. (Story of post-war Italy.)

KUHN, F. *Commodore Perry and the Opening of Japan.* Random.

LA CROIX, R. DE. *Mysteries of the North Pole.* Day.

LAMBERT, E. *Our Language.* Lothrop.

LATHAM, J. L. *Carry On, Mr. Bowditch.* Houghton. (Newbery award for 1956.)

LAUBER, P. *Battle against the Sea.* Coward-McCann. (Holland's struggle against the North Sea.)

MANTON, J. *The Story of Albert Schweitzer.* Abelard-Schuman.

MARSHALL, C. *The Unwilling Heart.* Longmans. (Novel of a young girl whose father is jailed for embezzlement.)

MEANS, F. C. *Knock at the Door, Emmy.* Houghton. (Migrant workers.)

MUSGRAVE, F. *Marged.* Ariel. (Welsh in the United States.)

NORTON, A. *Star Guard.* Harcourt. (Science fiction.)

PARKER, E. M. (compiler). *100 Poems about People.* Crowell.

PATON, A. *The Land and People of South Africa.* Lippincott.

POOLE, L. *Diving for Science.* Whittlesey.

SHIPPEN, K. B. *Miracle in Motion.* Harper. (Development of machines in America.)

SIMPSON, D. *Island in the Bay.* Lippincott. (A young boy's struggle for independence.)

STOLZ, M. S. *The Day and the Way We Met.* Harper. (Light romance.)

TURNGREN, E. *Listen, My Heart.* Longmans.

BOOKS FOR HIGH-SCHOOL AND JUNIOR-COLLEGE STUDENTS

BARBARA D. WIDEM

✱

BOOKS which will appeal to young people and satisfy their reading interests are necessarily as varied in content and style as the interests and personalities of young people themselves. This year's selection of noteworthy books for use in high school and junior college represents a wide range of reading difficulty and subject matter. Several of the titles are available in paper-bound editions, suited to the convenience and pocketbook of the young reader. Illustrations are plentiful, type is readable, and the books are well designed to attract and hold the reader's interest.

The majority of the titles are adult publications chosen for their excellence, clarity of presentation, and mature consideration of timely and timeless topics. Several titles of high quality which were written specifically for the adolescent reader are included.

Sports enthusiasts will find their interests treated in books of baseball biography, golf instruction, underwater exploration, adventure tales of hunting, reminiscences of an automobile racer, and two new books by the heroes of Mount Everest. Men and women outside the sports field are represented by brief sketches, biographical fiction, and full-length biographies.

Many aspects of science are presented in fact and fiction about the universe, the history of mathematics, biology and world health, sex in nature, and poems of science and mathematics. The science

fiction reader as well as the student of literature will find exciting analysis and a tantalizing reading list in the slim volume *Inquiry into Science Fiction.*

Thoughtful and readable works of literature are particularly outstanding this year, including two new contributions to modern drama and several choice books of poetry. The arts are further represented by books on free brush designing, American music, the ballad, television drama, and the photographic collection, *Family of Man,* compiled by Steichen. Humor takes many forms: essays, short stories, personal narrative, romance, and Wibberly's brief fantasy, *McGillicuddy McGotham.*

Interest in archeology and anthropology continues to be met by sound scholarship and entertaining presentation. Serious nonfiction also includes discussions of world peace, censorship, the role of the President, and Ketchum's two pictorial treatments *What Is Communism?* and *What Is Democracy?* Historical fiction and documentary narrative present backgrounds of early Christianity, the French Middle Ages, the nineteenth-century English theater, and several works about World War II. Many young adults will be vitally interested in Pasley's study of the twenty-one American G.I.'s who chose to remain in Communist China.

From this wide range of subjects and treatments, the teacher and librarian will find it an increasingly easy task to select materials to guide the young person in

217

developing current interests and in acquiring new ones.

ADAMS, S. H. *Grandfather Stories*. Random.

ANOUILH, J. *The Lark*. Oxford. (Drama of the life of Joan of Arc.)

ARKELL, R. *The Miracle of Merriford*. Viking. (Humorous romance.)

ARMSTRONG, R. *Cold Hazard*. Houghton. (Sea adventure.)

ATTWOOD, W. *Still the Most Exciting Country*. Knopf. (A reporter's view of America.)

AVERY, I. *The Five Fathers of Pepi*. Bobbs-Merrill. (A story of an Italian orphan.)

BACHARACH, B. *Right Dress*. Barnes. (Clothing for men.)

BALDWIN, H. W. *Sea Fights and Shipwrecks*. Garden City Books.

BANNISTER, R. *The Four Minute Mile*. Dodd. (Life of a track star.)

BEACH, E. L. *Run Silent, Run Deep*. Holt. (World War II novel.)

BENARY-ISBERT, M. *Castle on the Border*. Harcourt. (Novel of postwar Germany.)

BENCHLEY, N. *Robert Benchley*. McGraw.

BISHOP, E. *Poems: North and South*. Houghton.

BISHOP, J. A. *The Day Lincoln Was Shot*. Harper.

BJORN, T. F. *Papa's Wife*. Rinehart. (Laplanders in the United States.)

BLANSHARD, P. *The Right To Read*. Beacon. (A look at modern censorship.)

BOWLES, C. *The New Dimensions of Peace*. Harper.

BRIDGEMAN, W. B., and HAZARD, J. *The Lonely Sky*. Holt. (World War II.)

BROCKWAY, W. (editor). *High Moment*. Simon & Schuster. (True stories of great men.)

BROOKS, V. W. *Helen Keller: Sketch for a Portrait*. Dutton.

BROWN, C. *My Left Foot*. Simon & Schuster. (Heroic mastery over physical handicap.)

BURROWS, M. *The Dead Sea Scrolls*. Viking.

CARLSON, R. L. *The Edge of the Sea*. Houghton.

CERAM, C. W. *The Secret of the Hittites*. Knopf. (Ancient civilization.)

CHASE, G. *America's Music*. McGraw.

CHASE, M. E. *Life and Language in the Old Testament*. Norton.

CHUBB, M. A. *Nefertiti Lived Here*. Crowell.

CLIFFORD, J. L. *Young Sam Johnson*. McGraw.

DAICHES, D. *Two Worlds*. Harcourt. (A Jewish-Scottish childhood.)

DANE, C. *The Flower Girls*. Norton. (Novel of the English theater.)

DAVENPORT, B. *Inquiry into Science Fiction*. Longmans.

DENIS, M. *Leopard in My Lap*. Messner. (Adventure.)

DE VOTO, B. A. *The Easy Chair*. Houghton. (Essays.)

DE WOHL, L. *The Spear*. Lippincott. (Novel of Rome and early Christianity.)

DUGGAN, A. L. *Julius Caesar*. Knopf.

DUNSCOMB, C. *The Bond and the Free*. Houghton. (Novel of Rome and early Christianity.)

DURRELL, G. M. *Three Tickets to Adventure*. Viking. (A naturalist in British Guiana.)

EDEL, M. M. *The Story of Our Ancestors*. Little.

EGBERT, E. L. F., and BARNET, R. *Free Brush Designing*. Lothrop.

EICHELBERGER, C. M. *UN: The First Ten Years*. Harper.

ENGLE, P., and CARRIER, W. P. (editors). *Reading Modern Poetry*. Scott, Foresman.

ERDMAN, L. G. *The Far Journey*. Dodd. (Frontier romance.)

FARALLA, D. *A Circle of Trees*. Lippincott. (Prairie romance.)

FAULKNER, W. *The Big Woods*. Random. (Hunting stories.)

FINCHER, E. B. *The President of the United States*. Abelard-Schuman.

FORD, D. *Start Golf Young*. Sterling.

FORESTER, C. S. *Good Shepherd*. Little. (World War II novel.)

FOSTER, G. S. *When and Where in Italy*. Rand McNally.

FUNK, C. E. *Heavens to Betsy!* Harper. (Origins of curious sayings.)

GARCIA LORCA, F. *Selected Poems*. New Directions.

GODDEN, R. *An Episode of Sparrows*. Viking. (Novel set in postwar England.)

GRANT, M. P. *Biology and World Health*. Abelard-Schuman.

GUNTHER, J. *Inside Africa*. Harper.

GWYTHER, J. M. *Captain Cook and the South Pacific*. Houghton.

HEINLEIN, R. A. *Tunnel in the Sky*. Scribner. (Science fiction.)

HILLARY, E. *High Adventure*. Dutton. (Conquest of Everest.)

HOGBEN, L. T. *The Wonderful World of Mathematics*. Garden City Books.

HOOD, M. V. *Outdoor Hazards*. Macmillan. (Nature lore and safety.)

HOUOT, G., and WILLM, P. H. *2000 Fathoms Down*. Dutton.

HOWARTH, D. A. *We Die Alone*. Macmillan. (World War II.)

HOWE, M. *The Prince and I*. Day. (An American in Morocco.)

HOYLE, F. *Frontiers of Astronomy*. Harper.

JOHNSON, T. H. *Emily Dickinson*. Harvard.

KEARNS, W. H., and BRITTON, B. L. *The Silent Continent*. Harper.

KEENE, D. (editor). *Anthology of Japanese Literature*. Grove.

KEENE, D. *Japanese Literature*. Grove. (Also available in paper-bound edition.)

KETCHUM, R. M. (editor). *What Is Communism?* Dutton.

KETCHUM, R. M. (editor). *What Is Democracy?* Dutton.

KINKEAD, E. *Spider, Egg, and Microcosm*. Knopf.

KRUTCH, J. W. *The Voice of the Desert*. Sloane.

LAMB, H. *New Found World*. Doubleday. (Discovery of North America.)

LANGDON-DAVIES, J. *Seeds of Life*. Devin-Adair. (Study of sex in nature.)

LAWRENCE, J., and LEE, R. E. *Inherit the Wind*. Random. (Drama based on the Scopes trial.)

LEACH, M. (editor). *The Ballad Book*. Harper.

LEY, W. *Salamanders and Other Wonders*. Viking.

LORD, W. *A Night To Remember*. Holt. (The "Titanic" disaster.)

MALTHE-BRUUN, K. *Heroic Heart*. Random (Letters of World War II.)

MARKANDAYA, K. *Nectar in a Sieve*. Day. (Novel of modern India.)

MAYS, W. H. *Born To Play Ball*. Putnam. (The story of Willie Mays.)

MORISON, S. E. *Christopher Columbus, Mariner*. Little.

OLDENBOURG, Z. *Cornerstone*. Pantheon. (Novel of France during the Middle Ages.)

O'NEAL, C. *The Very Young Mrs. Poe*. Crown. (Novel of the poet and his wife.)

PAK, C. Y., and CARROLL, J. *Korean Boy*. Lothrop. (Wartime Korea.)

PASLEY, V. S. *21 Stayed*. Farrar. (American G.I.'s who remained in Communist China.)

PAUL, C. *Minding Our Own Business*. Random. (A newspaper couple's own story.)

PETRY, A. L. *Harriet Tubman, Conductor on the Underground Railroad*. Crowell.

PIERSALL, J. A., and HIRSHBERG, A. *Fear Strikes Out*. Little. (Jim Piersall's recovery from mental illness.)

PLOTZ, H. R. (compiler). *Imagination's Other Place*. Crowell. (Poems of science.)

REID, C. *From Zero to Infinity*. Crowell. (Meaning and history of numbers.)

ROOSEVELT, T. *Hunting and Exploring Adventures*. Dial.

ROSE, R. *Six Television Plays*. Simon & Schuster.

SANDERSON, I. T. *Living Mammals of the World*. Garden City Books.

SANDOZ, M. *Miss Morissa*. McGraw. (Novel of a pioneer woman doctor.)

SHAW, W. W. *Gentlemen, Start Your Engines*. Coward-McCann. (Biography of an automobile racer.)

SHOR, J. B. *After You, Marco Polo*. McGraw. (Honeymoon trip from Venice to Peiping.)

SINCLAIR, J. *The Changelings*. McGraw. (Novel of youth and urban life.)

STEICHEN, E. (compiler). *Family of Man*. Simon & Schuster. (Photographs of people.)

STOLZ, M. S. *Rosemary*. Harper. (Novel of adolescence.)

TENZING, N. *Tiger of the Snows*. Putnam.

THOMAS, L. J. (editor). *Great True Adventures*. Hawthorne. (Selections from true accounts.)

THURBER, J. *Thurber's Dogs*. Simon & Schuster. (Humor.)

VANDERKOGEL, A., and LARDNER, R. *Underwater Sport*. Holt.

VARBLE, R. M. *Pepys' Boy*. Doubleday. (Fictional hero of Pepys' London.)

WELTY, E. *Bride of the Innisfallen*. Harcourt. (Short stories.)

WEST, J. *Love, Death, and the Ladies' Drill Team*. Harcourt. (Short stories.)

WIBBERLY, L. *McGillicuddy McGotham*. Little. (Humorous fantasy.)

WOODWARD, E. C., and ROBERTS, E. B. *The Pink Rose*. Lothrop. (Light romance.)

INDEX